CONTAINING CHILDHOOD

Children's Literature Association Series

CONTAINING CHILDHOOD

Space and Identity in Children's Literature

Edited by Danielle Russell

University Press of Mississippi / Jackson

The University Press of Mississippi is the scholarly publishing agency of
the Mississippi Institutions of Higher Learning: Alcorn State University,
Delta State University, Jackson State University, Mississippi State University,
Mississippi University for Women, Mississippi Valley State University,
University of Mississippi, and University of Southern Mississippi.

www.upress.state.ms.us

The University Press of Mississippi is a member
of the Association of University Presses.

Copyright © 2022 by University Press of Mississippi
All rights reserved

First printing 2022

∞

Library of Congress Cataloging-in-Publication Data

Names: Russell, Danielle, 1967– editor.
Title: Containing childhood : space and identity in children's literature /
edited by Danielle Russell.
Other titles: Children's Literature Association series.
Description: Jackson : University Press of Mississippi, 2022. |
Series: Children's Literature Association series |
Includes bibliographical references and index.
Identifiers: LCCN 2022027208 (print) | LCCN 2022027209 (ebook) |
ISBN 9781496841179 (hardback) | ISBN 9781496841186 (trade paperback) |
ISBN 9781496841193 (epub) | ISBN 9781496841209 (epub) |
ISBN 9781496841216 (pdf) | ISBN 9781496841223 (pdf)
Subjects: LCSH: Children's literature—Psychological aspects. | Children's
literature—History and criticism. | Space in literature. | Identity (Psychology) in
literature. | LCGFT: Essays. | Literary criticism.
Classification: LCC PN1009.5.P78 C66 2022 (print) | LCC PN1009.5.P78 (ebook) |
DDC 809/.89282—dc23/eng/20220910
LC record available at https://lccn.loc.gov/2022027208
LC ebook record available at https://lccn.loc.gov/2022027209

British Library Cataloging-in-Publication Data available

This collection is dedicated to Sally Backo, whose memory is irrevocably woven into the shared spaces of our past and carried with love and gratitude into the indeterminate spaces of my future.

CONTENTS

Introduction. Contested Territory: The Spatialization of 3
   Children's Literature

Section One. Negotiating Boundaries: Liminality, Adolescence, and Spatial Agency

Chapter One. The Open Gates of Eden: Uncontainable 29
   Adolescence in Philip Pullman's *His Dark Materials*
   Kathleen Kellett

Chapter Two. Empowering Girls: The Liminal Spaces 48
   of Schools in Nineteenth-Century Transatlantic
   Literature for Girls
   Sonya Sawyer Fritz and Miranda A. Green-Barteet

Chapter Three. "There's No Place like Home": 69
   Dystopian Depictions of Home in *The Giver*
   Quartet and the *Unwind* Dystology
   Danielle Russell

Section Two. (Re)Active Engagement: Childhood Forays into the Production of Space

Chapter Four: Taking It to the Streets: Production of Space in 97
   Louise Fitzhugh's *Harriet the Spy*
   Richardine Woodall

Chapter Five. Race and Space in Daniel José Older's 115
   Shadowshaper
   Cristina Rivera and Andrew Trevarrow

Chapter Six. The Wide, Starlit Sky: Childhood Space and 135
    Changing Identity in the Work of Laura Ingalls Wilder
    Joyce McPherson

Section Three. Transformative Acts: Creating Resistant Spaces in Institutionalized Places

Chapter Seven. Proud to Be a Rugby Boy? The Shifting 155
    Relation between School Space and Student Bodies in
    Tom Brown's Schooldays and *The Loom of Youth*
    Anah-Jayne Samuelson

Chapter Eight. "An Elaborate Cover": Staging Identities at 176
    School and Abroad in Robin Stevens's Murder Mysteries
    Rebecca Mills and Andrew McInnes

Chapter Nine. Space, Identity, and Voice: 200
    Angie Thomas's *The Hate U Give*
    Wendy Rountree

Conclusion as Inclusion. 219
Contributors 223
Index 227

CONTAINING CHILDHOOD

CONTESTED TERRITORY

The Spatialization of Children's Literature

> The mythical landscapes of childhood constitute a kind of parallel universe, one that bears a similarity to physical geography but has the virtue of being invulnerable to both temporal and spatial changes that are constantly transforming the real world. The mythical landscapes of childhood reassure adults that things are what they wish them to be. It is a geography to live *in*. It does not exist on maps but is present in literature, in art and photography, and is alive in popular culture. (John Gillis, 317)

Adult constructions of the "mythical landscapes of childhood" are seemingly benign in Gillis's view. They "reassure adults that things are what they wish them to be." Where does that leave the child? This book is a collection of essays exploring the relationship between space and identity in children's literature. The authors address such questions as: What is the nature of that relationship? What happens to the spaces associated with childhood over time? How do children conceptualize and/or claim their own spaces? Can the same space fulfill adult goals *and* the needs of children? The mythical landscapes of children's literature are not necessarily "invulnerable to both temporal and spatial changes that are constantly transforming the real world." Space is multifaceted in the essays—emotional, imaginative, physical, political, psychological, social—and dynamic—clearly affecting the children within the various texts under discussion but also (potentially) affecting the children reading of those experiences.

Home. School. Nature. The spaces identified with childhood are both descriptive and prescriptive. They reflect/reveal adult expectations of where we (read: adults) expect to "find" children, of where children "belong." Certainly, the trio of spaces is important in children's lives and children's literature but not in a simplistic or straightforward way. In their depictions of setting, many authors deliberately complicate these spaces *and* expand those accessed by their child characters. Mobility—movement between and within a variety of spaces—is often a key factor in the development of child characters. It reflects real-world experiences. The spaces we occupy physically and imaginatively are influential in terms of identity formation, particularly in childhood. D. W. Meinig offers the astute observation that "any landscape is composed not only of what lies before our eyes but what lies within our heads" (34)—the landscapes of childhood largely lie in our adult heads. There is no such thing as detached observation; individual and collective associations and expectations merge in our assessments of geography. Space is never neutral. It carries social, cultural, and political histories; it imposes—or attempts to—behavioral expectations. Setting is not superfluous in literature, a fact which takes on a heightened significance in children's literature. The mythical landscapes Gillis identifies have real-world repercussions.

The title of this volume uses the all-encompassing category of children's literature. Titles are (generally) a kind of roadmap, part of the process of (pro)claiming territory. We, however, would like to issue a disclaimer: no single collection can provide an all-encompassing statement about space and children's literature. Is that an invitation to stop reading? No! It is an invitation into a shared space. This book is part of a larger "conversation" about this rich and diverse terrain. Each foray into this territory complicates—in thoughtful and thought-provoking ways—the notion of a simple, easily recognizable (and understandable) landscape of childhood. Peter Hunt's point that "space and place can be read in many different and productive ways" is at the heart of this project (24). Our goal is to expand the critical landscape, to venture into new and familiar settings with fresh perspectives.

The field of children's literature is itself a hybrid territory, drawing upon other scholarly areas—philosophy, history, and race, class, and gender studies spring to mind—"cross-fertilization" is a hallmark of the field. This book continues that tradition: the texts discussed include popular and lesser-known works of fiction from North America and Great Britain. The common bond between the chapters is an analysis of textual spaces in children's literature without reducing the issues to any single theory or perspective. Reading the individual pieces provides insight into specific treatments of space in specific periods of time; contextualizing those pieces within the larger narrative of the book affords a greater appreciation of the diverse spatial patterns found in children's literature.

The "Containing" in the title of the book signals the complexity of space in children's literature. Sites of containment that come to mind include home and school, with nature, at least theoretically, serving as a space of escape.

The structures, with their codes of conduct and social norms, are seemingly restrictive, static spaces: containment as detainment, in contrast to the unstructured expanse of the natural environment. Liberty is located outside in this paradigm. This model, however, raises a question: Can the same location fulfill multiple, and even conflicting, functions? On one level containing suggests controlling, restraining, preventing or limiting, but it also implies an opening for a subversive response to that external action. Containing also raises the possibility of accommodation, inclusion, protective but not necessarily prescriptive space—a cake contains sugar, a jar accommodates a certain amount of spice. As the essays in this book make clear, the spaces that contain childhood can, and do, include children's perceptions and productions of space. Adult control is not absolute.

CHILDREN'S LITERATURE AS CULTURAL SPACE

Books occupy many spaces—physically in libraries, bookstores, homes, e-readers, etc., and imaginatively in the (transitory and transformative) memories of readers. Kimberley Reynolds identifies children's literature itself as a dynamic, complex space, arguing that it

> provides a curious and paradoxical cultural space: . . . simultaneously highly regulated and overlooked, orthodox and radical, didactic and subversive. It is a space ostensibly for children— . . . children encounter ideas, images and vocabularies that help them think and ask questions about the world—but children's literature has also provided a space in which writers, illustrators, printers and publishers have . . . experimented with voices, formats and media, played with conventions, and contested thinking abut cultural norms (including those surrounding childhood) and how societies should be organised. (3)

For a "simple" genre—ostensibly targeted at beginning and developing readers—children's literature serves a variety of functions for a variety of users. It is a complex and shifting cultural space that is further complicated by the openings for resistance built into any practice of reading. Real-world child readers do not necessarily "behave" as expected. Recognizing this probability, the authors in this volume focus on the child characters and implied child readers. It is not a case of "dodging" the issue of what children take away from a given book but an acknowledgment of, and respect for, the space a child creates within any text. Reading is not a passive activity. Once a writer sends a book out into the world, he or she runs the risk of reader manipulation—not quite cultural appropriation but certainly a personalization of the material.

Reading a book opens a personal space. It is, generally, a solitary act. Peter Hunt, in *Space and Place in Children's Literature, 1789 to the Present*, posits that the book is in fact an act of negotiating space: "a children's book is a negotiation of the space between the adult writer and the child reader, a complex negotiation of an inevitable, and often radical, imbalance of power" (23). While experience and the authority of authorship are on the adult writer's "side," the child reader is not necessarily disempowered. Hunt's interpretation privileges the adult, but negotiating holds the possibility of mutual exchange—a more equitable interaction. Philip Pullman's concept of the borderland supports this idea of reading as an act of personal negotiation:

> The land along the border is the space that opens up between the private mind of the reader and the book they're reading. It'll be different for every individual, because while parts of the borderland belong to the book, other parts belong only to that particular reader—to us: our own memories, the associations we have with this or that particular word or landscape, the aspects that resonate with our own individual temperament; so whereas many readers might be reading the same book, no two of them will read it in exactly the same way. However, we can talk about our experience of it, and compare our part of the borderland with other people's. (216)

Pullman highlights the individualized act of reading. To read is a personal, private act; to share a reading experience with someone else is to move between borderlands. It is an excursion into an unknown space and an invitation for another reader to enter your imaginative territory.

Many critics share Pullman's emphasis on the adaptability of children's literature, arguing that there is a *need* to open space for the child reader to intervene in the story. Tove Jansson insists "there is a plethora of very fine children's books that mainly portray the writers' disappointments, phobias and depressions, tales of punishment, injustice and loneliness. But *one* thing he always owes his readers is a happy ending, some kind of happy ending. Or a way left open for the child to spin the tale further" (quoted in Weinreich, 118). Interesting psychological assessment aside, the idea that space for the child reader to enter the process of creating the narrative is necessary deserves attention. Jansson assumes that the child's intervention will take a positive direction—the happy non-ending, a kind of antidote to the narrative provided by the jaded/damaged adult author! It is a paradoxical call for openness while shutting down the direction it can take.

The openness to interpretation, combined with a desire to "protect" children—whether by maintaining their innocence or guarding them from further corruption—has made children's literature a frequent target of censorship. As Lois Lowry observes, it is in fact a disservice to the child reader:

> pretending that there are no choices to be made—reading only books, for example, which are cheery and safe and nice—is a prescription for disaster for the young! Submitting to censorship is to enter [a] seductive world . . . where there are no bad words and no bad deeds. But it is also the world where choice has been taken away and reality distorted. And that is the most dangerous world of all. (quoted in Apseloff, 484)

Censorship creates an artificial world, which leaves the child reader ill prepared for the real world. Lowry asserts that the books children read are instructive—not necessarily overt didacticism but clearly a type of preparation for participation in social and political life.

The necessity for a "safe" space to confront real-world fears is a key argument against the censorship of children's literature. It is bolstered by the insistence that avoidance of serious issues is simply not possible: the effects of violence, racism, and injustice are experienced daily by children. Kimberley Reynolds contends that "the need for books that both acknowledge and help to manage topical fears has increased in the new millennium following major international terrorist attacks" (151). Reynolds identifies a particular set of global events as triggering the need for more-nuanced children's literature. In a more general sense, children do not occupy a space divorced from real-world events; their literature should not evade that fact. The responses to these factors, notes Reynolds, are varied: "While many writers find it most appropriate to write about horrifying events in cathartic and reassuring ways, some require readers to grapple with the social and political complexities which have given rise to them and the consequences of failing to address such problems" (151). Both scenarios—cathartic reassurance and the vicarious "experience"—afford the reader a safe space for an imaginative engagement with the world outside the book. The space of children's literature is open enough to accommodate multiple approaches to a variety of topics.

To say that children's literature is an open space, however, would be disingenuous. The terms "childhood" and "children" are neither straightforward nor concise; they seem neutral but are often racialized and gendered.

Historically, children's literature in Great Britain and North America has targeted, and reflected, a white, middle-class, Christian audience. While some space has opened for diversity—in authors, characters, and readers—mainstream children's literature still targets, and reflects, a predominantly white, middle-class audience. It can appear to be a closed space to child readers who do not see themselves reflected in the narratives. Expanding the material available to children is imperative, but it is not simply a case of numbers. The new texts need to reflect the complex relationships between individuals and space in order to avoid reinforcing the mythical but deeply entrenched image of childhood and children's literature as all inclusive.

SPATIAL EFFECTS OF THE CONCEPT OF INNOCENCE

The mythical landscapes Gillis identifies at the opening of this chapter have clear associations with the conceptual spaces of innocence. Never changing, reassuring "adults that things are what they wish them to be," innocence and mythical landscape represent spaces that are impossible for children to occupy. Yi-Fu Tuan, in "Rootedness versus Sense of Place," proposes that adults always conceptualize childhood space to serve their own emotional and psychological agendas. Childhood is linked with ideas of stability and rootedness—a space free of the burdens of adulthood. Terms like "innocent" and "peaceful" create an idealized (sanitized) past. Building on his work, Karen Fog Olwig and Eva Gulløv argue that "places for children . . . are defined by adult moral values about a cherished past and a desirable future, clothed in common-sense notions about children's best interests" (3). Concepts of childhood provide a useful container for adult desires; reassurance comes from the relocation—at least theoretically—to a safe space. Gillis labels this self-indulgent practice "islanding": "the islanding of children must be considered a creation of adults, a response to their own needs rather than to those of children. Islanding children is a way that adults have developed to cherish their angels and exorcise their demons" (317). It is an agenda-driven process. Islanding occurs on both physical and imaginative levels, according to Gillis: "Adults have not only islanded children physically but have also constructed mythical landscapes that sustain childhood . . . in its idealized forms, even when it is no longer sustainable in the real world" (317). It is not necessary for the imaginative space to be anchored in recognizable, physically accessible space.

Complete separation of children and adults is neither practical nor practicable, but many adults remain invested in the idea. It is akin to Gaston

Bachelard's influential theory of "felicitous space," which focuses on "the human value of the sorts of space that may be grasped, that may be defended against adverse forces, the spaces we love" (xxxi)—what we might expect from children's literature. But, unlike with Bachelard's conscious void—he refuses to address what he labels "hostile space"—many authors for children incorporate that difficult terrain in their narratives. Bachelard insists that the "space of hatred and combat can only be studied in the context of impassioned subject matter and apocalyptic images" (xxxii). The conflicting needs/agendas of adults and children often take a spatial form. This space can be hostile or combative, but the "combat" can, and does, take a subtler form. Children's literature is a powerful vehicle for creating and sustaining the mythical landscapes imposed on childhood. It is an equally powerful vehicle for critiquing and deconstructing the mythical landscapes imposed on childhood.

The concept of childhood in need of protection, with its roots in the seventeenth and eighteenth centuries—the Romantic model of childhood as innocent, imaginative, and in harmony with nature—continues to resonate in Western cultures in the twenty-first century. It has real-world effects on the physical spaces associated with children. Geographers Edward H. Cornell and Kenneth A. Hull document a trend in the designed environments of cities and suburbs that provide "for ease of travel, elimination or isolation of hazards" (39). Clearly all the inhabitants experience this planned space, but, equally clearly, it imposes a particular kind of childhood—one that privileges safety over self-sufficiency. M. Vittoria Giuliani and Antonella Rissotto explore this trend, referring to the "growth in the idea that a good parent is one who gives greater importance to the protection, rather than to the independence, of his/her child" (77). "Good" parents provide sheltering spaces, escorting their children through other spaces. Containment versus movement, protection versus independence—conflicting generational demands have spatial effects. One effect, perhaps, is the increased importance of the space of reading. Mark Blades, Beverly Plester, and Christopher Spencer point out:

> We experience the world around us in two ways. By direct experience of living in, travelling through or manipulating our environment.... But we also learn about the world through secondary sources—for example from spatial representations like maps, from written descriptions, such as guide books, and from visual images like films. These are particularly important sources of knowledge for environments that we have not had the opportunity to experience directly. (43)

I would add we experience the world (or, rather, worlds) vicariously through literature. In this context, children's literature functions as a type of guidebook for the child reader. The popular phrase "to get lost in a book" speaks to the allure of reading—a kind of transcendence of self. Blades, Plester, and Spencer hold out the possibility that one can also get found in a book—a kind of self-discovery. It affords a safe space for exploration.

NATURALIZED CHILDHOOD AS "OTHERING"

Uncorrupted nature, nature in its pristine state, is a symbolic representation of the purity of the innocent child. It serves as a protective space; a buffer against the influences of the world of experience. Linked to the association of children/childhood with innocence is a concomitant association with nature. Stories about rural childhoods are fairly commonplace in children's literature, and in many cases the natural setting takes on a heightened significance. Sarah L. Holloway and Gill Valentine offer a succinct assessment of the process:

> In these stories of and about childhood, children's presence in the country is naturalised: children are portrayed playing outdoors, with companions, beyond the surveillance of adults, blessed through their proximity to and interaction with nature. These are "angelic" children whose innocence is reproduced through their closeness with and to nature. In the context of the rural idyll, Apollonian conceptions of childhood merge with idealised understandings of the rural, to produce a new subtheme in rural discourse, the rural childhood idyll. (17)

Nature is the space of freedom removed from adult control. It is also a means of elevating the child's status to "angelic" (but not quite angel). By necessity, then, it can be only a temporary experience of space. Holloway and Valentine are in fact discussing stories from adults about their "remembered" childhoods and their hopes for their children upon moving to the country. Such stories are heavily influenced by nostalgia (a yearning for an idealized past) and fear of the harmful effects of urban life (a yearning for an escape from a less-than-ideal present); (re)locating childhood in the spaces of nature is a protective gesture that is not inherently detrimental to children.

Associations with nature may, however, be more insidious when used as a means of excluding individuals from access to other spaces. Feminist scholars have given a great deal of attention to the practice of identifying a group with nature. Historically, women have been associated with nature in contrast to the association of men with culture. The paradigm privileges one group at the expense of the other. Gillian Rose acknowledges that feminists "have discussed the distinction between Nature and Culture at some length, because they see it as one of those oppositions which are heavily gendered and power-ridden" (68). The same distinction, based upon age, also deserves discussion. Linking children/childhood with nature is problematic: growth/experience requires a movement away from nature. As Sidney I. Dobrin observes, "if children are understood to be inexperienced—and simultaneously innocent—their greenness has also been understood to provide a connection to nature that is lost as one loses innocence and gains experience. Loss of youth and innocence distances one from nature and environment, a trope profoundly evident throughout children's literature" (15). A childhood immersed in nature is idealized but transitory. Infused with an element of sadness, it is a temporary stay in a "separate" sphere.

One of the effects of associating children with nature/the natural world is a resultant "othering" of childhood spatially. The spaces connected with children tend to exclude adults. Gill Valentine contends the "'othering' of children is being (re)produced and articulated through space" (597). Children occupy a particular but shifting spatial status in relation to adults. The link to nature can grant children an elevated status—they are "angelic"—but adult control of their access to space "demotes" them. Terri Doughty and Dawn Thompson note that "the idea that children should know their place has its roots in a traditional Western hierarchy that places children subordinate to, and some might argue subject to colonization by, adults" (1). Physical distinctions are often part of the process of (or perhaps the impulse for) the "othering" of children. The editors of *Space and Place* suggest that "perhaps the most pervasive situation in which children find themselves is that of physical smallness and children's literature is, correspondingly, often preoccupied with questions of size and stature" (Cecire et al. 3). They continue, "The child's place in the world is frequently as the smaller, usually weaker Other to the adult norm" (3). It is an odd process. As Stuart C. Aitken points out, "of all people that can be constituted as *other* in that they are different from ourselves, children are perhaps the most perplexing because they are also, in large part, constituted by what we are and what we do" (30). Adults are part of the othering of children, but they are also a key part of the development of children. And, it is worth noting, that status as other (based upon age), is temporary: children are expected to become adults.

CONSTRUCTING CHILDHOOD: SPACE AND IDENTITY

In chapter 5 of Lewis Carroll's *Alice's Adventures in Wonderland*, the caterpillar poses what is seemingly a straightforward question: "Who are you?" Alice's struggle to identify herself is exacerbated by her bizarre experiences in Wonderland: she is unsure because she has been several "whos" (albeit in a dreamscape). It is of course a heightened version of the struggle to achieve identity with which children must grapple. Children occupy multiple spaces and employ multiple identities daily. There is a logical assumption that identity is being formed in childhood—whether Locke's blank slate or the Romantic elevation of the child as pure or the traditional Christian child born in sin—and, historically, this emphasis on development has intensified the importance of what a child reads. The fear may be corruption or the desire for correction but there is a shared belief in the power of a book to, if not shape, at least affect, character—different approach, similar impulse. It is a belief that still influences the production of (on all levels) and the (public and private) dissemination of children's literature.

Two (broad) theoretical approaches dominate discussions about the nature of identity: the essentialist and the constructionist arguments. Briefly, essentialists contend that an inner essence exists that is expressible through language; constructionists insist that the subject is shaped by systems of language, culture, and ideology. Oddly enough, both "camps" approach identity as particularly malleable in childhood—it is a developmental stage, not an end unto itself. Nor is it a static state once achieved; there is a growing consensus that identity is pluralistic. Stuart Hall, for example, theorizes that multiple, sometimes contradictory, identities constitute the self. He asserts that such identities depend on difference/the other:

> identities are constructed through, not outside, difference. This entails the radically disturbing recognition that it is only through the relation to the Other, the relation to what it is not, to precisely what it lacks, to what has been called its *constitutive outside* that the "positive" meaning of any term—and thus its "identity"—can be constructed. (4–5)

Hall's assertion provides an insight into the relationship of the (concept of) the adult and the (concept of) the child. Adults lack what children possess—innocence; children lack what adults possess—experience. Identity is always contingent. In Hall's context, it is contingent on those who are different from us. While that contention may be open to debate, it is more difficult to discount the assertion that our identities are contingent on the spaces we occupy. Children quickly learn that the "character" they display in the playground with peers is not as acceptable in the front row of a church, synagogue, mosque, or temple. Maureen Whitebrook refers to identity as expressing "something of one's self . . . for public consumption" (6). In this context identity is always fragmentary, adaptable, and, above all, strategic. She insists on the recognition that "that expression may need to be modified by the reaction of others" (6). In a similar vein, Zygmunt Bauman, insists that "identity," despite being a noun, "behaves like a verb" (19). Identity is not just in process; it is in processes. The notion of identity as performance resonates in the children's literature under discussion in this book. It would be disingenuous to say that children are oblivious to the expectations of their audiences. Space affects the performance of identity. Identity is fluid, not fixed.

The fluidity of identity is most recognizable when considering teenagers. Adolescence itself is frequently referred to as a type of liminal status. Terri Doughty clarifies the link between adolescence and liminality: "The connection between liminality and young adulthood is often based upon the notion that both are transient stages on the way to a more fixed stage: in cultural anthropology the liminal phase marks the process of transition between the pre-liminal and post-liminal self, and adolescence marks the process of transition from child to adult" (156). Adolescence and liminality share a process of forming, of becoming; they are both "incomplete" identities. The postliminal self, in cultural anthropology, is the fixed identity that awaits after the initiation rite. For adolescents, there may be ceremonial rites of passage—getting a driver's license, a bar mitzvah/bat mitzvah, a quinceañera, or a confirmation—but these do not, in themselves, lead to a postadolescent self. "In a globalized world," Doughty concludes, "adolescents must constantly renegotiate their sense of their self as they encounter transforming/transformative cultures and hybridizations. Moreover, identity formation is not a linear process with a finished goal" (157). External influences on identity are continually changing in adolescence. Alison Waller concurs, identifying adolescence as "a less stable and more fluid concept defined by its 'in-between-ness,' its transitory position between childhood and adulthood, and its dependence on fleeting popular culture" (6). Adolescents occupy a (temporary) conceptual, social, and chronological space that differs from that of the two groups that "frame" them. Fluidity is not limited to adolescence; Waller acknowledges that "some contemporary theory would suggest that identity is fluid, plural or fragmented at all stages of life"—a condition not limited to adolescence but certainly heightened in that stage of life (1). Of interest to this project is the spatial effect of this "in-between-ness"; a question arises: does adolescence physically occupy a liminal space or transform mainstream geography into liminal space?

Identity is, to some degree, a choice: a choice about what to include and what to exclude. In the case of children, the choice is not always theirs to make; adults attempt to impose specific identities on them. Adult constructions of childhood space function in a similar way. Identity and space are intimately connected—a specific site can affect an individual's worldview as much as an individual can affect the physical landscape. Geography has at least two aspects: what the eye can see, and the mind imagine (whether from firsthand or other experience—including reading). "Landscape and identity reinforce one another," Naomi Wood insists (253). Hun Beynon and Ray Hudson share this perspective: "Place is identity," they succinctly state (177). Recognition that identity is formed in (and through) specific spaces is important in explorations of all identity formation, but it is particularly necessary when considering children and identity formation.

Books for children are one such space of (potential) identity formation. The influence may be felt through characterization, themes, or settings; or it may not be felt at all. Space for resistance or indifference exists in any reading process. While conceding this point, the essays in this collection consider the *potential* influence of space on the reading experience. The listing technique used above seemingly implies that characterization, themes, and settings are separate and distinct. They are actually interconnected and, I would argue, interdependent. "A particular text's investment in places may not be immediately obvious; nonetheless, texts, as well as their characters, derive their identities from and through the places contained within them," Ruth Feingold contends (131). Despite the tendency of some readers to dismiss the "background," the setting of a story is a crucial aspect of any book. The prominence of the setting in literature in general is clear. "As a literary form," Stephen Daniels and Simon Rycroft observe, "the novel is inherently geographical [...] made up of locations and settings, arenas and boundaries, perspectives and horizons" (460). Jane Suzanne Carroll's assessment reinforces this idea; she points out that "landscape shapes literature both contextually and textually" (1). Setting shapes a book in overt and covert ways.

HOME SWEET HOME: HOUSING CHILDHOOD

The socially sanctioned spaces of childhood are typically nature, home, and school. In the twentieth and twenty-first centuries, childhood itself has been undergoing a process of intensified domestication—children are increasingly situated within the home, argue Sarah L. Holloway and Gill Valentine. "Childhood, for many in the North at least, has been increasingly domesticated over the course of the past two centuries" (15). It is not just a matter of "spending increasing amounts of time in the home"; it is "also ideological, in that there is a sense in which this is where children should spend their time" (15). It is an ideology that is firmly grounded in children's literature. The home has long been deemed an "appropriate" space for children in the books targeting them. Perry Nodelman and Mavis Reimer discuss the didactic depictions of the home that try "to persuade young readers that despite its boredom, home, representative of adult values, is a better place to be than the dangerous world outside'" (200). The secure but dull home is privileged over the erratic but enticing larger world in many books for children. The importance of a home in childhood is clearly a frequent theme in children's literature; so too is the difficulty of achieving that home. In addition to being a physical space, emotional and psychological experiences are built into the concept of the home.

Hayden points out the duality of the home: it is both "the physical space and the nurturing that takes place there" (63). Home is both a building *and* an experience. Mavis Reimer proposes, "Because home normally is the site of the satisfaction of the most basic human needs for shelter and food, the depiction of stable and safe housing in narratives for children can be read as the adult promise, or hope, that the world is a place in which children can not only survive, but also thrive" (xiii). The implication is that the depiction of unstable and dangerous housing is some kind of betrayal on the part of adults. Increasingly, children's literature acknowledges the absence of the kind of housing Reimer describes. It is not a case of rejecting the importance of the home but a recognition that, in many cases, child characters must seek out and/or create such homes for themselves. They are not passive recipients of all the home entails; they are active participants in its creation.

It also fulfills a political purpose. bell hooks, writing about the importance of the home in the African American community, argues it has a "radical political dimension": "one's homeplace was the site where one could resist. Black women resisted by making homes where all black people could strive to be subjects, not objects, where we could be affirmed in our minds and hearts" (42). While by no means an equivalent condition, childhood is also politicized, and children are vulnerable to the power structures that disenfranchise them. They too need safe spaces in which to thrive. Elizabeth Goodenough asserts

> the lure of secret spaces finds its first fulfillment in the local, somewhere within or just outside the safe matrix of home. Locating a place

under the bed, the bed-covers, or the dining-room table is the primal discovery of self-ish space, a site detached from the ongoing, intimate relation with siblings, parents, or other adults.... This site endures in memory as a receptacle of the growing imagination, which needs to feel protected as it expands with safe boundaries. (3)

A rather unabashed romantic take on it, but Goodenough raises an important idea: there is a basic human need for individualized space that begins in childhood.

Institutionalized space is an equally dominant influence in childhood. The school can be construed as an extension of the home. In theory, they share expectations about behavior, values, and (basic) life goals. School settings, particularly boarding schools, have a long history in children's literature. Sheila Ray proposes, "The world of school is a microcosm of the larger world, in which minor events and concerns loom large and older children, at least have power, responsibilities and an importance they do not have in the world of outside. Despite the rules and regulations, children enjoy a certain kind of freedom" (467). Oddly enough, the institutionalized space affords freedom; largely because the child characters are removed from the control of their parents. It should be noted, however, that the classroom and other spaces carefully supervised by adults do not offer freedom. The "unofficial" spaces found in school settings hold out that possibility, as does the generic space of the story. "Through reading an entertaining story," Ray suggests, "children can 'test the water,' learn how people may react in specific situations and see what lies ahead" (467). The space of the school story, in this context, functions as an informal classroom—a type of freedom in a phase of life that is frequently circumscribed by adult interventions.

PLACING CHILDREN VERSUS CHILDREN'S PLACES

Adults determine where children belong—or so the theory goes. However, anthropologists, Karen Fog Olwig and Eva Gulløv caution: "It is important ... not to equate institutions intended as places for children with children's places. Places constructed for children do constitute important frameworks of life for children. They do not, however, determine children's lives, nor do they preclude the existence of other kinds of places that may be of central importance to children" (7). The places children occupy—whether real or fictional—are not limited to socially sanctioned spaces. In identifying the tendency of children to appropriate spaces not designated for them, Marta

Gutman and Ning de Conick-Smith draw on Herb Childress's concept of "'the inter-spaces of adult society,' meaning structures and objects not necessarily made for children but which children, teenagers, and young adults have claimed and made an integral part of youth culture" (3). Redefining specific spaces is a strategic maneuver on the part of children. It is an attempt to redress a power imbalance. Stuart C. Aitken identifies the contrasting spatial experiences of children: "On the one hand are the institutional environments which mold the will of children and on the other, are the special places (often unrecognizable to our adult senses) which are molded by the will of children" (x–xi). Children, he suggests, are not mere consumers of space. They are more than capable of manipulating their environments.

The impulse to reduce space to recognizable, manageable spaces is widely recognized. "As psychologists and anthropologists have ... been discovering, people instinctively mark out zones or territories that they use and react to in many ways," Carolyn Emrick Massad observes (9). The human tendency to mark off space is deeply rooted and well documented. Adults clearly do this *to* children, but it raises the question of whether children do it too. Owain Jones focuses on "otherable space" to determine "to what extent the dominant, striated fabrics of adults' geographies are, or can be, rendered flexible or porous enough for children to form their own geographies within them" (30). Can children manipulate malleable space to their own ends? The answer will determine whether they are mere consumers of space—passive recipients of adult demarcated space—or producers of specific spaces. Jones insists that "this question is vital because the opportunity for children to create their own geographies ... to spatialize their lives according to their own rather than adult agendas, at least to some extent, is seen as vital to their self-expression and their 'development'" (30). If adults are concerned with the healthy development of children, then there must be a recognition that an ability to function within a spatialized world is crucial to their identities.

"Healthy childhood development" and city/street spaces are seemingly contradictory; idealized childhood is located in nature, not the unnatural. Jenny Bavidge notes, "Children are largely excluded from accounts of the city, either literary or theoretical, and when they are present their roles are strongly circumscribed, especially given the powerful cultural association of childhood with the rural and natural" (323). The city is conceptualized as detrimental to the innocent or inexperienced individual. Fraught with danger, prone to corruption, filled with indifferent, if not predatory, adults, the city is thought by many to be no place for a child alone. Perception can create its own kind of "reality"; if adults determine that the child is vulnerable to external forces, then the city is an undesirable space. The perceptions and experiences of children, however, may be decidedly different. Jane Suzanne Carroll examines the contrast in terms of the identity of the child within each space: "Whereas the home is usually the centre of fixed identifications in children's literature; the street is often a space of provisional, rootless and unformed identifications. In the street, the security of the domestic space is regularly subverted" (97). One adult fear of the city/street is its potential to challenge the authority of the parent/guardian. The loss of control experienced by the adults contrasts with the increasing self-control claimed by the child characters. Gill Valentine discusses the "problem" of public space in the real world. She highlights the two extremes of the concept of the child in the city: "contemporary parents perceive their own children to be innocent and vulnerable (angels) whilst simultaneously representing other people's children as out of control in public space and a threat to the moral order of society (devils)" (581–82). Valentine insists that "underlying parents' anxieties about 'dangerous children' is an assumption that the streets belong to adults" (582). The tendency to shield children from public space—to place restrictions on spatial activities—is posited as protection but is very much self-serving. It fulfills adult needs, perhaps at the expense of those of the child.

The city is also a place of potential. It can permit a child the room required to explore a more personal space. The city/street, Hugh Matthews theorizes, "is presented as a liminal space, a place of separation and a domain of transition" (102). In the case of adolescents, it can be a space of empowerment, rather than automatic victimization. The author proposes that "occupancy of the street, particularly with the exodus of adults after dark, enables young people to take on the fluid identity of the hybrid, persons who are not quite adult but no longer child. In this sense, the street represents a place on the margin . . . a location in which young people can establish their independence, display their ambivalence and set out their public identity" (102). The city/street is not the romanticized space that Elizabeth Goodenough writes of, and yet "this site [also] endures in memory as a receptacle of the growing imagination, which needs to feel protected as it expands with safe boundaries" (3).

Transgressing boundaries is a crucial element of childhood. It is a means of renegotiating inequitable relationships to space. "By exploring fantastical mobilities that can never be replicated in the real world," Lesley Murray and Sonia Overall argue, "fiction also allows children to imagine a level of mobility and agency that is beyond the experience of adults" (583). The process grants the child reader a power "not available to adults or subject to their constraints: a form of imagined mobility and agency without limits," conclude Murray and Overall (583). The ability to navigate boundaries is a crucial skill, particularly for child readers. As Jones asserts, "boundaries are critical in the structuring of children's lives. These can come in both physical and symbolic forms and often are constructions combining both to varying degrees" (40). They are also imposed by adults for adult purposes. "A border," caution Jessica Elbert Decker and Dylan Winchock, "is more than just a physical limit: it is also the limit of ideas. It is the line we draw with words, through definition, sketching out the edges of a concept, as well as the edges of the categories we use to contain the world around us" (1). The conceptual and physical borders of childhood are meant to contain it. Borders, however, are vulnerable to transgression. Decker and Winchock point out that "the permeability of these Borderland spaces opens up possibilities for reimagining our categories and creating new paradigms that recognize difference and resist hierarchical structures of identity" (12). Borders are spaces of potential. Strategic responses (on the part of child characters and/or authors) tap into that potential; such responses can range from accommodation, to innovation, to covert undermining or overt rejection.

ESTABLISHING OUR TERRITORY

There is a strong tendency toward binaries in discussions of space—public/private, exterior/interior, adult/child, safe/dangerous—and in discussions of childhood/children's literature. Do the texts under discussion challenge these simplistic divisions? Absolutely! Some complicate rather than refute the categories, others subvert the divisions (rebel within), others obliterate/expose the artificiality, and some focus on sheltering spaces—accepting the importance of the home but with a more expansive definition. The environments are replete with variety, contrasting and conflicting spaces, spaces that challenge the very core of identity. The essayists in this study address a broad range of texts; the spaces and places under consideration are diverse and complex: physical, cultural, social, psychological.

Several of the authors discussed in this study appropriate real-world settings—iconic ones like New York, the Orient Express, mundane ones like home and school; other authors establish new landscapes in the space of fantasy. Despite these neat categories, the essays that follow make clear that borders are porous, they blur; marginality/liminality is a concern in several of the chapters. It becomes very clear that the developmental stages of childhood take spatial forms. Adolescence in particular is constructed as a space between—chronologically between childhood and adulthood; it is a vibrant, kinetic space. Child characters are revealed to be manipulators of, perhaps even producers of, space.

The first section, "Negotiating Boundaries: Liminality, Adolescence, and Spatial Agency," focuses on subversive uses of the margin. Kathleen Kellett, in "The Open Gates of Eden: Uncontainable Adolescence in Philip Pullman's *His Dark Materials*," explores adolescent opposition to enclosed spaces in Philip Pullman's *His Dark Materials*. There are two types of borders in *His Dark Materials*: the natural and the cultural. At first, Lyra and Will break both with abandon, but they come to realize that while natural boundaries exist for a reason, cultural boundaries often conflict with nature. Kellett argues that Lyra and Will slip from one ostensibly impermeable space to the next, breaking boundaries and (re)integrating disparate aspects of existence.

The importance of malleable spaces in personal development is also central to chapter 2, by Sonya Sawyer Fritz and Miranda A. Green-Barteet, "Empowering Girls: The Liminal Spaces of Schools in Nineteenth-Century Transatlantic Literature for Girls." It analyzes school spaces in nineteenth-century transatlantic literature as liminal space that provides a crucial site of autonomy for young women across racial and national divides. In the US, Harriet Wilson's *Our Nig* (1859) and Elizabeth Stuart Phelps's *The Story of Avis* (1877) portray schools as liminal sites where young women can escape the confines of home and develop an empowered sense of subjectivity. In England popular girls' school stories such as Agnes Loudon's "The Moss Rose" (1850) and L. T. Meade's *Betty, a Schoolgirl* (1894) privilege the private, less-regulated spaces of the school as crucial to girls' identity work, reflecting how girls could define and perform scholarship, friendship, and defiance, even as school aimed to train them to adhere to broader cultural norms. While these fictional girls do receive traditional educations, Fritz and Green-Barteet conclude, they also use school spaces to test the boundaries that limit girls to the domestic sphere. School is represented as a potentially liberating interstitial space for young women and girls despite its ostensible nature as a disciplined and regimented environment intended to acculturate students.

Performing identities and challenging gender expectations is a shared concern in chapter 3, where liminality takes a perverse turn. Danielle Russell's "'There's No Place like Home': Dystopian Depictions of Home in *The Giver* Quartet and the *Unwind* Dystology," explores the concept and experience of home in two dystopian series. The real homes of the male protagonists are fraught with danger and are thus sites of imposed vulnerability, and yet the young men cling to the positive concepts associated with the idea of home as a key aspect of their survival "strategies." The movement toward self-definition and personal security occurs in a hostile world, which heightens the need to achieve an alternative home. While paths of escape, spaces which permit freedom of movement and self-reliance, have received a great deal of attention in recent analysis of children's literature, home—literal or longed for—remains a crucial setting. Creating some type of home is crucial to physical and psychological survival; these texts demand readers look beyond the traditional definition of what constitutes a home. Home can function as a creative, social, and/or political outlet, but it can also be an oppressive, isolating site of disenfranchisement. To fulfill a potentially nurturing and life-affirming function, the home must be approached as a process rather than a structure.

The second section, "(Re)Active Engagement: Childhood Forays into the Production of Space," considers the child character as producer of space. Richardine Woodall, in chapter 4, "Taking It to the Streets: Production of Space in Louise Fitzhugh's *Harriet the Spy*," focuses on Louise Fitzhugh's *Harriet the Spy*, in which the heroine breaches repeatedly the divide between the home and the streets. The streets become spaces of becoming in which Harriet works out her existence; in these spaces she is actively and creatively engaged in the production of space. Fitzhugh penetrates beneath the surface of the urban landscape and takes the reader into the substratum of society in which the spaces of childhood are subversive and transgressive, and in which children are engaged in practices that change lives and change societies. In these spaces, Woodall argues, children are architects, urban planners, and creators of social spaces.

In chapter 5, Cristina Rivera and Andrew Trevarrow's "Race and Space in Daniel José Older's *Shadowshaper*" expands the discussion of child characters as producers of space. *Shadowshaper* (2015) follows Sierra Santiago, an Afro–Puerto Rican teenager living in Brooklyn. To protest the neighborhood's gentrification, its community leader, Sierra's *abuelo*, tasks her with painting a giant mural on the infamous Tower, a grotesque and unfinished concrete building amidst their familiar brownstones. In the process she discovers *shadowshaping*, an ancestral spiritual magic unique to her Afro-Latinx community. She learns that she can infuse her art with the spirits of her ancestors, who pass through her into the murals and bring them to life temporarily. She realizes that, as the old, decaying murals fade into nothing, so too do the memories and spirits of her community. She must urgently protect and restore the spaces of her neighborhood. To achieve this goal, she must navigate its physical and cultural spaces, both familiar and unfamiliar, as she learns more about her supernatural powers and, unbeknownst to Sierra, her pivotal role as the community's next spiritual leader.

Joyce McPherson in chapter 6, "The Wide, Starlit Sky: Childhood Space and Changing Identity in the Work of Laura Ingalls Wilder," enters a decidedly different landscape but has a shared interest in spatial mobility. Wilder expands the American literary landscape—placing the family on the frontier becomes an imaginative means of reopening the frontier. Julie Roy Jeffrey "warns against describing women as passive victims of men's choices rather than as active participants in the process of emigration" and insists on the recognition that, in many cases, women were willing to go (36). As McPherson's essay makes clear, while children had no real choice in journeying, that is not equivalent to being a victim. Earlier works tended to privilege home as a child's proper sphere, and journeys away from home concluded with a return to that space. In addition, the focus tended to be on events rather than the child's interior perspective, so that space was consistently outward rather than inward. McPherson argues that Wilder transformed the conventional space for children from a defined building or place to the wide-open world and the journey of exploration. Wilder turns the focus to the internal space by employing a close third-person perspective to relate the impressions and thoughts of her child protagonist. This interiority not only changes the focus of the narrative but draws the child reader into the story's world.

The final section, "Transformative Acts: Creating Resistant Spaces in Institutionalized Places" examines how child characters adapt mainstream spaces for their own agendas. Chapter 7, Anah-Jayne Samuelson's "Proud to Be a Rugby Boy? The Shifting Relation between School Space and Student Bodies in *Tom Brown's Schooldays* and *The Loom of Youth*," considers how the depiction of schools as material, physical and architectural spaces implicates adult power over child/youth-student bodies over time in the school-story genre. Initially the school functions as a miniature world molding students into responsible future adult citizens. In these stories the school space is largely idealized. After the First World War, however, the school environment is frequently depicted as attempting to crush students into conformity by inhibiting their personal development and repressing those who fall outside dominant societal standards. Rather than reestablishing cultural norms (the traditional outcome of school stories), these stories blatantly challenge them in depicting students that rebel against the system. The two trends demonstrate a shift in the genre to containing two streams: one idealized with loyal students, and the other negative with rebellious students.

Chapter 8, Rebecca Mills and Andrew McInnes's "'An Elaborate Cover': Staging Identities at School and Abroad in Robin Stevens's Murder Mysteries," shares an interest in the school setting's effect on identity. This essay argues that Robin Stevens's 'Murder Most Unladylike' series neatly reverses conventional ideas of child's play: her teenage heroines, Daisy Wells and Hazel Wong, pretend to be normal schoolgirls while taking their work as amateur sleuths deadly seriously. Both of these roles—detective and schoolgirl—are conceptualized spatially, mapped onto the conventional coordinates of boarding-school stories and detective fiction: the school itself, a country house, a famous train, and the sports field. Golden Age detective fiction and interwar boarding-school stories both map spaces where individual, communal, and national identities and relationships are examined via tensions between transgression and belonging. By taking a critical approach that looks beyond detective fiction and boarding-school stories as formulas, Mills and McInnes demonstrate that Stevens brings the subtexts of queerness and anxieties about otherness and belonging inherent in both genres to the foreground. The pairing of Hazel and Daisy allows Stevens to enthusiastically exploit and negotiate spaces and notions of home, school, and travel—and by extension England and the "Orient"—and show how the identities of her adolescent heroines are formed and performed in these spaces.

The final chapter, Wendy Rountree's "Space, Identity, and Voice: Angie Thomas's *The Hate U Give*," draws upon Robert Stepto's concept of ritual ground to explore the controversial novel. Stepto defines ritual grounds as "those specifically Afro-American spatial configurations within the structural topography that are, in varying ways, elaborate responses to social structure *in this world*. . . . They serve as a spatial expression of the tensions and contradictions besetting any reactionary social structure, aggressive or latent, subsumed by a dominant social structure" (68). For African Americans, their communities/homes can be "ritual grounds," "black spaces" where they are generally separated from surrounding "white spaces." Rountree uses this idea of ritual ground, combined with W. E. B. Du Bois's double consciousness concept, to analyze Angie Thomas's *The Hate U Give* (2017). The sixteen-year-old protagonist, Starr Carter, simultaneously finds comfort and kinship/friendship within two particular ritual grounds in the book—Garden Heights, her urban neighborhood, and Williamson Prep, the private, predominantly white school she attends—*and* experiences psychological anxiety in both because she feels she does not completely belong/"fit" in either. Her internal struggles within these spaces challenge the young protagonist to claim both spaces as her own, while growing emotionally, socially, and psychologically through the process, which leads her to finding her political voice.

Works Cited

Aitken, Stuart C. *Putting Children in Their Place*. Washington, DC: Association of American Geographers, 1994.

Apseloff, M. F. "Lois Lowry: Facing the Censors." *Paradoxa* 2 (1996): 480–85.

Bachelard, Gaston. *The Poetics of Space*. 1958. Trans. Maria Jolas. Boston: Beacon Press, 1969.

Bauman, Zygmunt. "From Pilgrim to Tourist—or a Short History of Identity." Ed. Paul du Gay and Stuart Hall. *Questions of Cultural Identity*. Washington: Sage Publications, 1996. 18–36.

Bavidge, Jenny. "Stories in Space: The Geographies of Children's Literature." *Children's Geographies* 4 (2006): 319–30.

Beynon, Hun, and Ray Hudson. "Place and Space in Contemporary Europe: Some Lessons and Reflections.'" *Antipodes* 25.3 (1993): 177–90.

Blades, Mark, and Christopher Spencer, eds. *Children and Their Environments: Learning, Using and Designing Spaces*. Cambridge: Cambridge UP, 2006.

Blades, Mark, Beverly Plester, and Christopher Spencer. "Children's Understanding of Environmental Representations: Aerial Photographs and Model Towns." Ed. Mark Blades and Christopher Spencer. *Children and Their Environments*. Cambridge: Cambridge UP, 2006. 42–56.

Carroll, Jane Suzanne. *Landscape in Children's Literature*. London and New York: Routledge, 2011.

Cecire, Maria Sachiko, Hannah Field, Kavita Mudan Finn, and Malini Roy, eds. "Introduction: Spaces of Power, Places of Play." *Space and Place in Children's Literature, 1789 to the Present*. Surrey: Ashgate, 2015. 1–19.

Cornell, Edward H., and Kenneth A. Hull. "The Problem of Lost Children." Ed. Mark Blades and Christopher Spencer. *Children and Their Environments*. Cambridge: Cambridge UP, 2006. 26–41.

Elbert Decker, Jessica Elbert, and Dylan Winchock. "Introduction: Borderlands and Liminality across Philosophy and Literature." Ed. Decker and Winchock. *Borderlands and Liminal Subjects: Transgressing the Limits in Philosophy and Literature*. New York: Palgrave Macmillan, 2017. pp. 1–18.

Daniels, Stephen, and Simon Rycroft. "Mapping the Modern City: Alan Sillitoe's Nottingham Novels." *Transactions of the Institute of British Geographies* 18.4 (1993): 460–80.

Dobrin, Sidney I. "Through Green Eyes: Complex Visual Culture and Post-literacy." Ed. Amy Cutler Mackenzie, Philip G. Payne, and Alan Reid. *Experiencing Environment and Place through Children's Literature*. New York and London: Routledge, 2011. 13–26.

Doughty, Terri. "Dreaming into Being: Liminal Spaces in Charles De Lint's Young Adult Mythic Fiction." Ed. Terri Doughty and Dawn Thompson. *Knowing Their Place? Identity and Space in Children's Literature*. Newcastle upon Tyne: Cambridge Scholars, 2011. 155–69.

Doughty, Terri, and Dawn Thompson, eds. "Introduction: Identity, Place, and Space in Children's and Young Adult Literature." *Knowing Their Place? Identity and Space in Children's Literature*. Newcastle upon Tyne: Cambridge Scholars Publishing, 2011. 1–5.

Feingold, Ruth. "Mapping the Interior: Place, Self, and Nation in the *Dreamhunter Duet*." Ed. Maria Sachiko Cecire, Hannah Field, Kavita Mudan Finn, and Malini Roy. *Space and Place in Children's Literature, 1789 to the Present*. Surrey: Ashgate, 2015. 129–46.

Gillis, John R. "Epilogue: The Islanding of Children—Reshaping the Mythical Landscapes of Childhood." Ed. Marta Gutman and Ning de Coninck-Smith. *Designing Modern*

Childhoods: History, Space, and the Material Culture of Children. New Brunswick and London: Rutgers UP, 2008. 316–30.

Giuliani, M. Vittoria, and Antonella Rissotto. "Learning Neighbourhood Environments: The Loss of Experience in a Modern World." *Children and Their Environments*. Ed. Mark Blades and Christopher Spencer. Cambridge: Cambridge UP, 2006. 75–90.

Goodenough, Elizabeth, ed. *Secret Spaces of Childhood*. Ann Arbor: U of Michigan P, 2006.

Gutman, Marta, and Ning de Coninck-Smith. "Introduction: Good to Think with History, Space and Modern Childhoods." *Designing Modern Childhoods: History, Space, and the Material Culture of Children*. New Brunswick and London: Rutgers UP, 2008. 1–19.

Hall, Stuart. "Introduction: Who Needs 'Identity'?" *Questions of Cultural Identity*. Ed. Paul du Gay and Stuart Hall. Washington, DC: Sage Publications, 1996. 1–17.

Hayden, Dolores. *Redesigning the American Dream: The Future of Housing, Work, and Family Life*. New York: W. W. Norton, 1986.

Holloway, Sarah L., and Gill Valentine, eds. *Children's Geographies: Playing, Living, Learning*. New York and London: Routledge, 2000.

hooks, bell. "Homeplace: A Site of Resistance." *Yearning: Race, Gender, and Cultural Politics*. Toronto: Between the Lines, 1992. 41–49.

Hunt, Peter. "Unstable Metaphors: Symbolic Spaces and Specific Places." Ed. Maria Sachiko Cecire, Hannah Field, Kavita Mudan Finn, and Malini Roy. *Space and Place in Children's Literature, 1789 to the Present*. Surrey: Ashgate, 2015. 23–37.

Jeffrey, Julie Roy. *Frontier Women: The Trans-Mississippi West, 1840–1880*. New York: Hill and Wang, 1979.

Jones, Owain. "Melting Geography: Purity, Disorder, Childhood and Space." *Children's Geographies: Playing, Living, Learning*. Ed. Sarah L. and Gill Valentine Holloway. New York and London: Routledge, 2000. 29–47.

Massad, Carolyn Emrick. "Time and Space in Space and Time." *Children in Time and Space*. Ed. Kaorou Yamamota. Arizona State UP, 1979.

Matthews, Hugh. "The Street as a Liminal Space: The Barbed Spaces of Childhood." Ed. Pia Christensen and Margaret O'Brien. *Children in the City: Home, Neighborhood and Community*. London: Routledge, 2002. 101–17.

Meinig, D. W., ed. *The Interpretation of Ordinary Landscapes: Geographical Essays*. Oxford: Oxford UP, 1979.

Murray, Lesley, and Sonia Overall. "Moving around Children's Fiction: Agentic and Impossible Mobilities." *Mobilities* 12 (2017): 572–84.

Nodelman, Perry, and Mavis Reimer. *The Pleasures of Children's Literature*. New York: Longman, 1992.

Olwig, Karen Fog, and Eva Gulløv, eds. "Towards an Anthropology of Children and Place." *Children's Places: Cross-Cultural Perspectives*. London and New York: Routledge, 2003. 1–19.

Pullman, Philip. "Epilogue: Inside, Outside, Elsewhere." Ed. Maria Sachiko Cecire, Hannah Field, Kavita Mudan Finn, and Malini Roy. *Space and Place in Children's Literature, 1789 to the Present*. Surrey: Ashgate, 2015. 215–39.

Ray, Sheila. "School Stories." Ed. Peter Hunt. *International Companion Encyclopedia of Children's Literature*. Vol. I. 2nd ed. London and New York: Routledge, 2004.

Reimer, Mavis, ed. *Home Words: Discourses of Children's Literature in Canada*. Waterloo, ON: Wilfrid Laurier UP, 2008.

Reynolds, Kimberley. *Radical Children's Literature: Future Visions and Aesthetic Transformations in Juvenile Fiction*. New York: Palgrave Macmillan, 2007.

Rose, Gillian. *Feminism and Geography: The Limits of Geographical Knowledge*. Cambridge: Polity Press, 1993.

Stepto, Robert. *From behind the Veil: A Study of Afro-American Narrative*. 1979. Champaign: U of Illinois P, 1991.

Tuan, Yi Fu. "Rootedness versus Sense of Place." *Landscape* 24 (1980): 3–8.

Valentine, Gill. "Angels and Devils: Moral Landscapes of Childhood." *Environment and Planning D: Society and Space* 14 (1996): 581–99.

Waller, Alison. *Constructing Adolescence in Fantastic Realism*. New York and London: Routledge, 2001.

Weinreich, T. *Children's Literature—Art of Pedagogy?* Frederiksburg, Denmark: Roskilde UP, 2000.

Whitebrook, Maureen. *Identity, Narrative and Politics*. London and New York: Routledge, 2001.

Wood, Naomi. "Review of *Four British Fantasists* by Charles Butler." *Children's Literature* 36 (2008): 253.

Section One

Negotiating Boundaries
Liminality, Adolescence, and Spatial Agency

Chapter One

THE OPEN GATES OF EDEN

Uncontainable Adolescence in Philip Pullman's *His Dark Materials*

KATHLEEN KELLETT

In the beginning, there was existence. Although at first chaos reigned, existence eventually resolved itself into order, with various types of matter settling into forms. This was a particularly mutable order; matter may have stayed in one form for a long time, but eventually, everything broke down to its smallest parts, dissipated, and reformed into something new. The only permanent structures were the boundaries between the multiple universes, which provided the solidity to an otherwise fluid nature. This is the genesis of Philip Pullman's multiverse in the *His Dark Materials* trilogy, in which the only constant is change itself. Pullman's nature is not static, but it is harmonious. This harmony persists even as matter begins to "understand itself," adapting into particles called Dust (Pullman, *Spyglass* 32). These particles are the most changeable matter of all, since to be Dust—to be conscious—is to learn and therefore evolve.

Among human beings, the shift of Dust from one subject to another relies upon the processes of birth, maturation, and eventually death. Though matter cannot be created or destroyed, it will not remain forever in one body, spirit, or soul. In Pullman's paradigm, the fact that identity is as impermanent as power is an absolute truth. Unsurprisingly, powerful individuals oppose such a fact. Yet the wilderness of the multiverse teems with knowledge, and anyone may discover this natural law as she grows up. That is, anyone may if she is given enough room to learn. Within the walls of a safe and secure garden, people and their changeable natures are much more manageable. Led by the Authority, the being who claims to be God the Creator, many adult characters in *His Dark Materials* attempt to both figuratively and literally contain the maturation of consciousness.

Pullman uses the narrative of the Fall of Man to reveal the impossibility of stasis for a developing human mind and body. He layers his retelling on top of the original biblical text and Milton's *Paradise Lost*, which gives the trilogy its name. I propose that the end of all of these Fall narratives—the expulsion from Eden—provides a lens through which to understand the treatment of physical space in *His Dark Materials*. The expulsion is the moment when Eve and Adam move from the limited safety of Eden to a wider and more hostile space of responsibilities and pain (Genesis 3:16–19). In the world of the trilogy, Eden is designated as a space for children, and the wilderness is the space for adults. For this reason, the prophesied second Eve and protagonist of *His Dark Materials*, Lyra, is an adolescent. If childhood is "before" and adulthood is "after," then adolescence is "during": it is the Fall itself. In spatial terms, adolescence comes *between* Eden and the wilderness: it is the expulsion, the movement between the two. Adolescence is uncontainable.

Sarah K. Cantrell argues that the physical geographies of *His Dark Materials* "force readers and protagonists to confront moments of staggering complexity and profound difference" (303). Cantrell, drawing from both Pierre Bourdieu and Pullman's own lectures about his work, discusses the "phase spaces" of the text, or the spaces that contain all potential future possibilities at once (303). The characters must remain open to the multitude of possibilities presented in these spaces. Ultimately, the decisions that the protagonists make—the possibilities that they choose to embrace—not only affect their own lives but also have a profound physical effect on each space they inhabit (307). I argue that these spaces of possibilities appear in the text as a recurring series of Falls as Lyra and her counterpart, Will, continually reenact the expulsion from Eden by opening small, ostensibly closed spaces and emerging into larger ones. Each time the adolescent characters choose one of the many coexisting possibilities, they redirect their path between the Edens they leave and the wilderness in which they arrive. The choices they make are different from those that have been approved by the most powerful adults in the text, represented by the Authority and his Church. Ultimately, the text requires Lyra and Will to abide by the "natural" course of a human lifetime, as they settle into their designated adult spaces after the long journey of their adolescence is complete. However, these adult spaces are not the same as they would have been had Lyra and Will remained on the prescribed short and narrow path as adolescents. Lyra is an adolescent Eve who uses compassion to shape her developing identity. In so doing she radically restructures the spaces of the Genesis narrative and restores the mutability of life and death.

CREATION VERSUS EXISTENCE

Anne-Marie Bird explains that because Dust is an elementary particle of consciousness that cannot be further broken down, it "constitutes a rejection of the idea of division and separation as a means of making sense of the world" (191). Indeed, Dust is fully integrated into the vast matrix of meaning that is existence—until it begins to cling to itself. When particles of Dust first condense into a personal being with an individual identity, this being immediately rejects the mutable order through which he has become. Instead, he names himself "the Authority" and forms a *cultural* order, placing himself at the top of a hierarchy contrary to the order of nature (Pullman, *Spyglass* 32). The Authority's identity formation is both a joining—a coming together and "complexification" of Dust—and a separation, because there are now boundaries between the Authority as an individual subject and the rest of existence (Pullman, *Knife* 249). As a being of Dust, the Authority's current expression of consciousness cannot last forever, but now that he has formed such a powerful identity, he does not want to lose it. The Authority builds physical borders between himself and any reminders of change in nature. These borders are not merely tools of identity formation but a desperate attempt at identity preservation.

Unfortunately for the Authority, reminders of change are everywhere. Human beings, for example, are not static creatures, and in *His Dark Materials*, human maturation occurs in highly predictable stages. Childhood and adulthood are separated by a defining moment of development. Some angels of Dust, when they realize that the Authority has lied to them about being the Creator, interfere in evolution and integrate with human consciousness, elevating these animals above the rest (Pullman, *Knife* 249–50). Although a small amount of Dust clings to children, adults are saturated in it (Pullman, *Compass* 283). The difference between these two developmental stages is reflected in the physical spaces children and adults respectively occupy. These spaces can be understood as simultaneous re-creations and inversions of the spaces in the Fall of Man narrative.

In the second Creation story of Genesis, God creates Adam *before* Eden; Eden is simply a place to hold this new creation (Genesis 2:7–9). In *His Dark Materials*, humanity similarly predates the Authority's constructed cultural spaces for them, which serve as a response to the problem of human knowledge seeking. The Authority treats the natural truths about his own and his followers' consciousness with utmost secrecy, as he fears that anyone who knows that Dust is mutable and death is inevitable will force him to accept the eventual loss of his self-granted power. The Authority's control of other subjects persists beyond Eden; the "wilderness" of adulthood is larger and more dangerous, but it is still not an unrestricted space. The only way the Authority can seem both singular and permanent to his followers is by making them believe that they are *also* singular and permanent. He manipulates his adult followers into denying their birthright to knowledge and into creating their own unnaturally enclosed spaces in a vain attempt to mimic Eden, the "blissful Paradise / of God" on Earth (Milton 4.208–9). The Authority also promises Paradise to the obedient after death, signaling a return to what he presents as the safe, peaceful ignorance of childhood, when the walls were close (Pullman, *Spyglass* 32).

In Lyra's universe humans have external souls called daemons that appear as animals. Children's daemons constantly change shape, but the daemons of adults have permanent forms that they maintain until death. This settling occurs when the full measure of Dust falls upon the developing subject. In the fictionalized account of Genesis from this universe, Adam's and Eve's daemons change shape in the Garden of Eden, but after Eve eats the Forbidden Fruit, she sees the true form of her daemon (Pullman, *Compass* 372). This narrative establishes the link between children and the prelapsarian state of innocence/ignorance. In other words, children, before the "Fall" of experience and without their full measure of Dust, are literally incomplete people. This deficit narrative of childhood consciousness introduces a tension in the text that cannot easily be resolved. The text explicitly supports an ethos of lifelong learning and change—and, as we shall shortly see, *post*-lifelong change, as well—yet the settling of daemons and Dust constitutes a definitive moment of development that establishes a stark difference between childhood and adulthood. On top of constructing prepubescent children as at least partially preconscious, the Dust-daemon relationship also naturalizes a more "settled" and stable adult identity that undercuts the narrative of continual subjective becoming. It is important to note that while I discuss the difference between natural and cultural boundaries within Pullman's invented world, in actuality *all* of these boundaries are textual constructions. The text is therefore susceptible to contradictions as it challenges many social narratives about young people while simultaneously reproducing others. Lyra at least disrupts the conflation of ignorance and innocence; even as a prepubescent child, she is not an obedient unfallen Eve, but a wild "barbarian" who is cleverer and more curious than many of the adults she encounters (34). Still, it cannot be denied that childhood is the least "whole" stage of human development in *His Dark Materials*.

Although the settling of daemons marks the difference between children and adults, daemons do not find their final form when the subject is fully grown; instead they settle during liminal adolescence. Adolescence is one of the two stages of the human life cycle that most closely reflects the mutability of all matter that the Authority shuns and fears. The other stage is death. In Pullman's natural order, human existence can be separated into three clear categories: childhood, adulthood, and diffuse postdeath. These categories have two mobile periods between them: adolescence and death (or, perhaps more accurately, the gerunds *growing* and *dying*). The developing subject has more space to explore with each stage of existence, both figuratively and physically, and the life cycle culminates in the postdeath dispersal of one's elemental particles that may now float through all of existence. Returning to Cantrell's discussion of the geography of possibility, we can read adolescence and death as the *temporalities* of possibility, and therefore the periods of existence that are most associated with "phase spaces" (303). However, the Authority superimposes his cultural boundaries onto the multiverse's natural order by imprisoning dead spirits in an unnatural world where they cannot dissolve, expand, or escape. His adult human followers, meanwhile, duplicate this process of enclosure by halting adolescence before it begins. It is this attempt to physically and metaphysically contain children that catalyzes Lyra's Fall.

EDENIC IMPRISONMENT

Elizabeth Gillhouse explains that the temptation scene is central to any retelling of the Fall, and that authors with different agendas ascribe a variety of motivations for Eve's sin, such as "desire to be God-like; desire for knowledge; being tricked or manipulated by the serpent; and desire for freedom and equality" (266). In his treatment of Lyra as Eve, Pullman clearly values the second and fourth motivations. Lyra has spent her childhood running wild around Oxford, which is her first Eden. Large yet finite, Oxford affords Lyra ample freedom to explore and be content without straying too far. However, Lyra still manages to find the forbidden places within her idyllic childhood home, just as Eve finds herself at the foot of the Tree of Knowledge. The trilogy opens with Lyra hidden in the tiny space of a closet, eavesdropping on the forbidden knowledge that the adult male scholars discuss in the Retiring Room of Jordan College (Pullman, *Compass* 4). Here, Lord Asriel (Lyra's father) and the Scholars discuss the mysteries of Dust (21). From the closet Lyra sees the promise of a much grander forbidden space—a photograph of a city in the sky above the Northern Lights—and she is filled with curiosity (23). Like the biblical Eve, Lyra is not "tempted with riches or flattery, but with the promise of wisdom, suggesting not an inferior mind but a superior intellect" (Gillhouse 265).

A desire for knowledge is not all that forces Lyra out of Oxford. Her friend Roger has been kidnapped by the mysterious "Gobblers," who have been stealing children for unknown purposes (Pullman, *Compass* 62). Little does Lyra know that her mother, Mrs. Coulter, is the head of the Gobblers, or the General Oblation Board, a Church-sanctioned organization that seeks to solve the problem of Dust, which it believes to be the manifestation of sin. Mrs. Coulter presents Lyra with a shiny new Eden in the form of her hyperfeminine flat. In this space Lyra is pampered, but she is much more contained than she ever was on the streets of Oxford. Lyra soon realizes that the paradisiac nature of Mrs. Coulter's home is an illusion. It is a place of hostility toward self-knowledge, as evidenced when Mrs. Coulter causes Lyra's daemon Pantalaimon to turn away from Lyra while she bathes (77). Lyra cannot grow in this garden. Instead she escapes to her first wilderness—the far North—in search of her friend.

In the North, Lyra finds the child victims of the Gobblers in the fortress-like Bolvangar. In contrast to the perfect enclosed Eden in Genesis, walled-off spaces in *His Dark Materials* are prisons: "They have put up buildings of metal and concrete, and some underground chambers. . . . No birds fly there; lemmings and foxes have fled. Hence the name Bolvangar: the fields of evil" (Pullman, *Compass* 187). Bolvangar's crimes against human nature are reflected in the artificiality of its "metal and concrete" walls and its dearth of animal life. The space demonstrates the dead-end barrenness that results from humanity's efforts to separate itself from the natural order in which it should be integrated. Here, Mrs. Coulter attempts to prevent conscious development by separating humans from their daemons in a practice called intercision (213). Without this crucial link between the soul and the body/spirit, Dust cannot settle on a subject during adolescence (282).

Intercision has a sexual dimension to it. When adults manhandle Lyra's daemon, her reaction is described in the language of sexual assault: "She *felt* those hands . . . It wasn't *allowed* . . . Not *supposed* to touch . . . Wrong . . ." (Pullman, *Compass* 275). The violation of a child's soul, her own personal space, is another symptom of the adult attempt to exert control over the maturing subject and to force her to remain in the conceptual space of childhood. Though the Church of Lyra's world believes in original sin, and therefore that children are not sinless, it maintains that halting the accumulation of Dust will preserve humanity in as innocent a state as possible. This imagined innocence of childhood requires sexlessness. Therefore, the Church believes that if a child has control over her own sexuality, she will fall like Eve. In Genesis, shortly after Eve and Adam become aware of their nakedness, they are condemned to a life in the wilderness, followed by death (Genesis 3:7, 3:19). In Lyra's Church, the denial and/or punishment of sexual awareness is an avenue to the denial of existential mortality; the sexually pure will be rewarded with the everlasting persistence of consciousness in Heaven. Yet sexuality also marks a change within the subject, just as death does. The "little death" of shared sexual pleasure involves a connection between two subjects, while the Authority's hierarchal order of individual power relies upon subjects' total separation.

If Eden is the lie that the Authority uses to control humanity, then Bolvangar is what a space of enforced innocence and ignorance really looks like. Innocence and ignorance are properties of childhood only according to adults—including Pullman himself to an extent, based on the child characters' lack of Dust. Yet the text also demonstrates that valorizing innocence and ignorance diminishes children and adults alike. Various child characters, including Lyra, demonstrate curiosity—that is, the desire to cast off innocence and ignorance—but children who have undergone intercision (referred to as separated children) lack inquisitiveness, insight, and ultimately the will to live. When a subject is deprived of the ability to learn, represented spatially as the ability to move from enclosed to more open spaces, then that subject ceases to exist. Separated children carry with them the specter of death, yet Lyra reacts to this embodied existential horror with empathy: "In Lyra's heart, revulsion struggled with compassion, and compassion won" (Pullman, *Compass* 216). When a separated child dies, Lyra cares for his corpse, proving that she does not fear communion with death as the Authority does (219). Lyra goes on to liberate the separated daemons from their cages and lead an escape attempt for the children awaiting intercision (261, 287). Both the children and the daemons were condemned to stay in Bolvangar so they could remain unchangingly pure, but Lyra takes her first step as the new Eve when she ensures the children's continued mobility toward experience. Lyra and the children leave the confinement of this ignorant anti-Eden and emerge into the wider world.

"THE MAJESTY AND VASTNESS OF THE UNIVERSE"

At the end of *The Golden Compass*, space opens for Lyra in an unprecedented way. Lord Asriel has learned how to breach the boundaries between universes with a machine powered by the sacrificial intercision of a child. Unfortunately, Lyra unwittingly delivers Roger to him for this purpose (Pullman,

Compass 393). Lord Asriel admits that crossing worlds may "violate fundamental laws," but he believes it is his right (376). He exists within the same restricted space as all enculturated adults in Lyra's world, but he cannot stand the confinement. Yet when he breaks boundaries, he does so with little regard for either what is right or what is true (categories that always overlap in *His Dark Materials*). Through his disregard for compassion and wisdom, Lord Asriel alters the spaces of nature, destroying both the subjective integrity of Roger and the stability of the multiverse itself (393). The violated spaces that result from such a violent act can only be spaces of suffering.

Before Lyra can find her father and Roger, the blazing light of the Aurora above her suddenly shuts off. At this moment she becomes aware of the Dust around her, swirling like "dark intentions, like the forms of thoughts not yet born" (Pullman, *Compass* 390). This is the most obvious instance of the phase spaces that Cantrell describes. Without a guiding light, Lyra must rely only on what *may* be; she chooses her path without knowing the destination. The passage of *Paradise Lost* from which the trilogy's title is drawn reflects this chaos of the unknown, when all existence is merely potential:

> Into this wild Abyss,
> The Womb of nature and perhaps her Grave,
> Of neither Sea, nor Shore, nor Air, nor Fire,
> But all these in their pregnant causes mixt
> Confus'dly, and which thus must ever fight,
> Unless th'Almighty Maker them ordain
> His dark materials to create more Worlds.
> (2.910–16)

In *Paradise Lost* this unmade space stretches between Hell and Earth, but in *His Dark Materials* these "pregnant causes" are made up of loose Dust. The Dust resists a single meaning but *could* mean anything. According to Bird, Dust's mutability "[disturbs] the value-laden binaries of innocence-experience, good-evil, and spirit-matter that lie at the core of the Fall myth" (189). This moment of many potential meanings is a necessary component of Pullman's depiction of nature. After all, in the multiverse, universes are spawned when "one moment several things are possible, the next moment only one happens, and the rest don't exist. Except that other worlds have sprung into being, on which they *did* happen" (Pullman, *Compass* 377). The Authority's unnatural order, as evidenced by the punishing Fall narrative, says that all choices must be either-or, but nature shows that the true answer is *both*.

Children with unsettled daemons also represent multiple coexisting possibilities, but in Pullman's paradigm it is not until they begin to break out of the spaces of childhood and embark upon the journey of adolescence that they can realize any of these potentials. Lyra initially navigates through the Dust guided by her desire to save Roger, but after his death her compassion reroutes her journey and changes her final destination. Faced with the hole that her father has opened in the sky, Lyra realizes that Dust—the uncontainable, the potential, the ever-changing—is not actually sinful (Pullman, *Compass* 398). As she teeters on the edge of two worlds, she exists in that moment of possibility like the unformed Dust around her. She understands that she is just a small part of a vast matrix of meaning, and she accepts that the world is bigger than she had ever been taught. She embraces the infinite unrealized possibilities before her: "So Lyra and her daemon turned away from the world they were born in, and looked toward the sun, and walked into the sky" (399). In the second Creation story, Adam may not have been born in Eden, but Eve was—and she is the first to seek meaning beyond its boundaries (Genesis 2:22). Lyra expels herself into the unknown.

UNRULY SPACES

In *The Subtle Knife*, Lyra meets Will Parry, an adolescent whose childhood has not been nearly as free as Lyra's. Will's mother is mentally ill, and he has "learned how to conceal himself" in order to stay with his mother and avoid being "placed in a home among strangers" (Pullman, *Knife* 11). When his house is invaded and Will accidentally kills one of the intruders, he is forced to leave his childhood home; its walls can no longer protect him (8). He finds an open window between his world and another, but he does not view it as an opportunity for growth or learning; he simply sees this profound boundary as a barrier behind which he can hide (15). Will yearns for a space of safety.

Instead, Will finds Lyra in Cittàgazze, a city in a uniquely uncontained world. This world is riddled with holes to other universes, created by the titular subtle knife. It is therefore an appropriate place for Lyra and Will to meet: this universe, which belongs to neither of them, is a way station on their adolescent journey with multiple windows of possibility from which to choose. However, the world itself is suffering for its permeability. Consciousness-devouring beings (or non-beings) known as Specters of Indifference seep in from the windows (Pullman, *Knife* 135). They pose a threat only to those with full Dust-infused consciousness, so as children Lyra and Will are safe. But as they near the climax of their adolescence and their entry into adulthood, they must take up residence in a less porous space that respects the natural laws. Consciousness does not give one the right to attack nature, because consciousness *is* nature.

Lyra and Will do not yet understand these truths; no adults have taught them, and so they must learn from their own experience. A large part of experience is making mistakes and recognizing one's own ability to do harm. Will, without realizing the consequences of his actions, becomes the bearer of the subtle knife, giving him the power to manipulate space and choose his own course (Pullman, *Knife* 176). This is quite a change from hiding with his mother in his house, and Will, injured from his fight for the knife, is overwhelmed with grief and fear. Pantalaimon physically comforts Will while he is in this vulnerable state, breaking the sexual taboo that forbids contact between a human and someone else's daemon (182). Once again, compassion guides Lyra's Fall: she learns more about herself and develops her sexuality through experiencing empathy for Will. She does not "sin" for knowledge alone but instead transgresses cultural boundaries to help one in need. Lyra teaches Will how to wield the knife by instructing him not to shut out his fear and pain while he attempts to open and close a window between worlds (186). Part of opening up space means letting down one's interior subjective walls as well. Pain is a loss of control over the body, which reminds one of death, and fear is a response to this lack of control. Control, however, is nothing more than the ability to prevent change, and therefore as illusory as Eden. Lyra has embraced the uncertainty of change, and she helps Will to do the same.

"IN SORROW THOU SHALT BRING FORTH CHILDREN"

Lyra and Will rapidly grow in love and sexual desire for each other, though Dust has not yet settled upon them. They are truly neither child nor adult, and they cannot be contained anywhere, even by the boundaries of life itself. In *The Amber Spyglass*, they find a group of ghosts traveling to the world of the dead, and they follow them there to complete Lyra's goal of rescuing Roger. The borders of this world reflect its unnaturalness, just as Bolvangar's did: "The ground was sloping downward now and becoming more and more like a rubbish dump. The air was heavy and full of smoke, and of other smells besides: acrid chemicals, decaying vegetable matter, sewage" (Pullman, *Spyglass* 252). Here, things rot but never transform into new life. The Authority promised Heaven as a return to Eden, where one could enjoy immortality, but instead he created a containment center that prevents death and life from ever rejoining. Again, cruel acts beget cruel spaces.

As Eve, the Mother of All, Lyra's expulsion from Eden must result in the expulsion of *all* people. She represents humanity and consciousness as a whole: they go where she goes. No amount of adult resistance can ever truly halt adolescence, just as no amount of denial can avert death. Unfortunately, the fearful adults of the Authority's culture still try to divert the course of nature; all the resulting pain that children and adolescents experience is a consequence not of the changes they undergo but of adult attempts to prevent those changes. Due to the Authority's laws, Lyra and Will must abandon their daemons to progress into the world of the dead (Pullman, *Spyglass* 283). To enter the unnatural confinement of this constructed prison, they must diminish the internal space of their body-soul-spirit. A whole person cannot fit within the Authority's most restrictive space.

Lyra leaves Pantalaimon on the shore of the lake between the living and the dead, physically separating herself into parts (Pullman, *Spyglass* 285). She endures the pain on the dead's behalf, so that she can free them from their imprisonment. This Eve, then, also has Christlike qualities in Pullman's curiously Christless Christian culture. Lyra suffers for sins that she did not commit; according to Carole Scott, Lyra's journey "parallels the Harrowing of Hell," which "melds religious, classical, and folk traditions in a modern idiom consonant with Pullman's vision of the diligent creation of a harmonious universe" (104). In other words, Pullman combines disparate narrative traditions to represent the harmony of a world where multiple meanings coexist and develop simultaneously. Through rescuing the dead, Lyra adds to this overall existential meaning by breaking down the walls that prevent the reintegration of the ghosts' myriad points of view with the rest of existence. By assuming the pain of the dead, Lyra charges herself with the responsibility of their rebirth, fulfilling the curse imposed on Eve: "I will greatly multiply thy sorrow and thy conception; in sorrow thou shalt bring forth children" (Genesis 3:16).

Will must also separate from his daemon. He has never seen her, and as he leaves her on the shore, he feels as though "something secret and private was being dragged into the open, where it had no wish to be" (Pullman, *Spyglass* 285). To Will, hiddenness has always meant safety; as long as no one looked at his mother and him, they would not be separated. Now, the raw unguardedness of adolescence, a time of existing without the protection and stability of boundaries, finally catches up with Will as he travels into death. The uncontainable qualities of adolescence and death are explicitly linked within his body and consciousness.

The wasteland and the lake are not the only boundaries of the world of the dead. Grotesque and rotting harpies stand watch over the Authority's unnatural borders (Pullman, *Spyglass* 290). Here again Pullman combines meanings from multiple narrative traditions. The harpies are obviously classical, but they are also reminiscent of Milton's Sin, the half-woman, half-serpent figure who guards the Gates of Hell (2.648–53). Indeed, the harpies are literal embodiments of sin: the Authority has instructed them to absorb the "the worst" of each ghost "till [their] blood is rank with it and [their] very hearts are sickened" (Pullman, *Spyglass* 316). One harpy identifies herself as "No-Name" (292). She is thus called because the dead, the source of all her knowledge, have no identities now that their spirits and souls have been separated. Identity requires the ability to move and change.

The Authority has built his walls well. Will cannot use the subtle knife to free them here, and his attempts to do so are described with curiously similar language to that used to describe Lyra's attempted intercision: "But the touch was wrong wherever he felt" (Pullman, *Spyglass* 312). The wrongness of violating the internal space of body-spirit-soul is reflected in the unnaturalness of the external space that houses the separated people. The world of the dead does not neatly abut other worlds as naturally occurring universes do but instead is shoved beneath them, shameful and out of sight. Yet Lyra begins to bring change to this unchanging world when she shares her identity and experiences with the dead. She tells the ghosts about her childhood in Oxford; though children in *His Dark Materials* are not as mobile as adolescents, every experience they have still adds to their knowledge and pushes them toward the moment when they break free of their first Edens. Listening to Lyra's experiences reminds the ghosts of their own lives, when forward motion was still possible (314–15). The Authority has imprisoned the dead, rendering them unchangeable, but Lyra's adolescent mobility transforms them until they are as uncontainable as she is.

This transformation is not limited to just the ghosts. The harpies, having listened to Lyra's "nourishing" stories of life, no longer wish to guard this unchanging place (Pullman, *Spyglass* 317). When Milton's Sin allows Satan out of Hell, she wonders, "But what owe I to his commands above / Who hates me, and hath hither thrust me down / Into this gloom of Tartarus profound, / To sit in hateful Office here confin'd"? (2.856–59). Similarly, the harpies realize that they owe the Authority no loyalty for their confinement. Lyra gives the harpies the power to facilitate creation by reconnecting the cycle of life and death. The harpies will escort the dead who have true stories to tell through this artificially made holding cell and out into the natural universes again. They "shall make an exception for infants who have not had time to learn anything," but everyone else—including children—is expected to have spent their lives thoroughly exploring the internal and external spaces that were open to them (Pullman, *Spyglass* 318).

Lyra explains that when the ghosts leave the world of the dead, "all the particles that make [the spirits] up will loosen and float apart," just as daemons dissolve after death (Pullman, *Spyglass* 319). However, Lyra reassures the dead that changing and ending are not synonymous. Instead, the dead daemons are intertwined with "the air and the wind and the trees and the earth and all the living things," and Lyra promises the ghosts that they will enjoy the same fate, diffuse yet "part of everything alive again" (319). The harpies lead Lyra, Will, and the spirits to a place where Will can use the subtle knife to open a window out of the world of the dead (363). It is a beautiful, natural paradise: an unguarded Eden without adult-imposed walls or rules. The ghost of Roger is the first one out of the window; though his adolescence was denied him, he regains his lost mobility in death (364). Death is as creative a process as reproduction, and it is through the re-creation of the dead that Lyra becomes Mother of All. Mary Harris Russell explains: "Freeing the dead, [Lyra] breaks out of an enclosed territory instead of being expelled from one, as was the traditional Eve" (220). In other words, this expulsion, just like the exodus from Bolvangar, the walk through the sky, and all of Lyra's journeying through the multiverse with Will, is Lyra's choice. Lyra's and Will's adolescent intentions and experiences create the spaces that await them in adulthood. If sinful intentions create spaces of suffering, then Lyra's compassion allows her to bring her dead "children" into a space of liberation.

THE LAST GATE OPENED

When the reader finally sees the infamous Authority, he is revealed to be a pathetic figure imprisoned and immobilized by his own denial of natural law. Angels carry the Authority in a crystal litter while singing praises to his false identity. The litter is the smallest and most enclosed space in the entire trilogy, but it still does not provide adequate protection to the consciousness within. Through his fear of death, the Authority has become a corpselike figure of "terrifying decrepitude, of a face sunken in wrinkles, of trembling hands, and of a mumbling mouth and rheumy eyes" (Pullman, *Spyglass* 396). After eons of punishing knowledge-seekers, he is now "demented and powerless," embodying the lack of awareness that he tried to impose on others (410). The Authority is yet more proof that subjectivity cannot be sustained by containment. Change is inevitable. That change will be growth if one has room enough, but if not, then the change will be deterioration.

Lyra and Will come upon the crystal litter after the angels have abandoned it, leaving the Authority helpless (Pullman, *Spyglass* 409). The litter's walls are covered with blood and mud; as with the wasteland outside the world of the dead, physical degradation mars the Authority's unnatural boundaries. He tries to deny the wilderness, but it encroaches anyway. There is ruination both without and within, but Lyra and Will look past the filth to the consciousness. Despite his age, the Authority is described in the terms of earliest childhood: he is "crying like a baby" when the adolescents find him, and he gazes at Lyra with "innocent wonder" (410). In a way, he has upheld his promise: he has created a small, static space of innocence and ignorance, where all knowledge is kept at bay. Though angels of Dust are never children, the Authority has made for himself a womb.

Lyra, overcome with compassion for the "suffering" Authority, fulfills her role as Mother of All once more (Pullman, *Spyglass* 410). She asks Will to set the Authority free, and Will uses the knife to break this last unnatural boundary. The Authority falls apart when he leaves the crystal litter, "a mystery dissolving in mystery" (411). Russell explains this act as "not murder but a transition between deceit seen as 'aged' and true knowledge embodied as 'youth.' Only the newest Eve, nurturing mother of us all, seeker of knowledge and truth, can provide the youth that displaces age" (221). The Authority's greatest lie—that identity is static and eternal—is the root of this "deceit," and youth is the embodiment of "true knowledge" precisely because youth is by definition finite. As long as time and life continue, adolescence cannot be halted, nor can it endure forever. The same can be said of the continuous cycle of condensation and dissipation of Dust. Therefore, although Russell says that "the Authority is a being whose end of time has come," it is important to note that, while the Authority's *identity* ends, his Dust does not (221). Instead, it is restored to its original, elemental ability to understand itself. The Authority used his boundaries to hold his identity together, but the uncontainable adolescents force him to change by expelling him from the illusion of Eden and returning him to the wilderness whence he came.

THE FALL

Now that Lyra and Will have torn down the boundaries of so many false Edens, they have one last step to take in their adolescent journey. They take refuge in the world of the *mulefa*, a conscious species vastly different from humans. For the *mulefa*, there are no divisions between nature and culture; the only boundaries are those between universes. This is also the universe into which the dead are released (Pullman, *Spyglass* 431). This world deliberately evokes Eden in its pristine natural beauty, and it is therefore the perfect setting for Lyra and Will's final Fall. However, the world of the *mulefa* also differs from the enclosed Eden of Genesis in important ways. As David Levey points out, though the dead escape the Authority's prison into this place, the *mulefa*'s home is not Paradise as a final destination; it is instead a gateway to "a goal still more expansive: the starlight itself" (26). In other words, this world is the latest in a series of spaces of possibility, teeming with meanings new, old, and new again. Choices and changes are made here. Surrounded by difference and away from human boundaries, Lyra and Will experience the remainder of their transitional adolescent time together. Sharing a picnic, Lyra holds a red fruit to Will's mouth (Pullman, *Spyglass* 465). Before the Fall in *Paradise Lost*, Eve asks herself, "What fear I then? rather what know to fear / Under this ignorance of Good and Evil, / Of God or Death, of Law or Penalty?" (9.773–75). Lyra, however, is not ignorant of any of these meaning-laden categories; she has direct experience with each one. Lyra's final Fall, therefore, is not the innocent mistake of one who does not understand the consequences of her actions. It is instead a deliberate choice of an adolescent who wishes to expand her knowledge and experience with the person she loves and desires.

Lyra and Will kiss and touch each other, confessing their love (Pullman, *Spyglass* 465). Their sexual union has extreme consequences: "The Dust pouring down from the stars had found a living home again, and these children-no-longer children, saturated with love, were the cause of it all" (470). This final step in their Fall has pulled all the Dust in the universes back from the holes that ignorant children and arrogant, fearful adults have made in nature. Lyra and Will are presented as a triumph of natural change and growth over culturally constructed restriction. This first sexual experience of adolescence erases the boundaries between the two developing subjects, fusing them without diminishing either one. Similarly, the window Lyra and Will created for the dead erases the boundaries between temporary singular identity and the multiple meanings of nature. Eve's Fall was understood as the end of paradise and the cause of death, but Lyra instead combines paradise and death by creating a space wide enough to contain them both.

THE EXPULSION

Lyra and Will have not only broken culturally constructed boundaries. Through their use of the subtle knife, they have also been responsible for many transgressions against nature. Because consciousness depends on nature, then Dust will be at risk of leaking into "the emptiness outside" as long as there are holes in the universes (Pullman, *Spyglass* 483). Lyra and Will are still very young, but now that Dust has settled upon them, they must take their place in the wilderness of adulthood. This wilderness is a much different space than the one that would have been waiting for them had they maneuvered within the Authority's boundaries, but even a comparatively free adulthood in the text is still not as mobile as adolescence. Lyra and Will must settle in their natural places, lest they end up like the Authority, running and hiding for the rest of their lives. In other words, they must return to the universes in which they were born, lest their newly reunited daemons die (484). They must also close all the windows so that Dust does not spill out again, leaving only one open for the dead (492). Lyra and Will's separation from each other is their last and most painful expulsion from Eden.

For this Adam and Eve, their future deaths are not a curse, but instead their only solace. Lyra and Will must spend their adulthoods apart in separate spaces, but one day death will make them mobile again, just as they were during their uncontainable adolescence. At that point, Lyra promises: "We'll live in birds and flowers and dragonflies and pine trees and in clouds and in those little specks of light you see floating in sunbeams . . . And when they use our atoms to make new lives, they won't just be able to take *one*, they'll have to take *two*, one of you and one of me, we'll be joined so tight" (Pullman, *Spyglass* 497). Levey argues that this state of atomic reintegration with the fewest boundaries between them represents the true meaning of "home" in the series (27). After the self-expanding journey of death, Lyra and Will become as indivisible as human and daemon. It will not be a physical and temporal ending, but rather the opportunity to keep moving and changing together. To prove this point, when their daemons come to them, Pantalaimon as a pine marten, and Will's daemon, Kirjava, as a cat, Will makes his last great connection with Lyra: "Knowing exactly what he was doing and exactly what it would mean, he moved his hand from Lyra's wrist and stroked the red-gold fur of her daemon" (Pullman, *Spyglass* 498). Lyra responds in kind, and their daemons settle on these forms (499). This is a subjective as well as a sexual connection: one final expansion of their interior spaces to encompass each other. Will and Lyra part with a promise to go to their respective Oxford botanical gardens on Midsummer Day every year (508). They cannot return to the Eden in which they loved and Fell, but they can remember it, and re-create it for a time. Yet they will also be a year older each time they return, bringing their experiences with them to rest against the natural boundary between them. The botanical garden, then, remains a liminal space, both Eden and wilderness, a vestige of adolescence to revisit in adulthood.

Cantrell acknowledges the tension of Will and Lyra's return to their respective Oxfords: "What good, after all, are Lyra and Will's bravery, growth, and struggles if their quest ends in the closure of the very spaces that allowed for their miraculous journey?" (319). Like the tension between the support of lifelong subjective becoming and the settling of daemons, this tension between the rejection of Eden and the reclosing of the protagonists' home spaces is not easily resolved. Again, it is important to recognize Pullman's own cultural biases within the construction of his "natural" laws. Yet ultimately Cantrell argues that the return is necessary because the protagonists' struggle is not complete (320). Similarly, Karen Patricia Smith locates *His Dark Materials* within a tradition of children's fantasy narratives that end with "a return to the primary world with new information, insights, and abilities to address the problems that the protagonist(s) left behind" (136). Amanda M. Greenwell also tackles Lyra and Will's return to their universes in her exploration of the text's treatment of the concept of home. She explains that, while home in children's literature is often "tied metaphorically to an innocence easily mapped onto the child," Pullman instead crafts a home for Lyra "that fosters opportunities more often associated with experience" (21). Greenwell points to Lyra's shift in viewing female scholars with borrowed patriarchal disdain to a desire to learn from, which demonstrates that Lyra's home can be a place of change, too, and that Lyra herself will continue changing it with her own experiences (32). Greenwell argues, "Home should be a place that provides shelter, but not an isolated, sheltered space" (33). In other words, Oxford may have begun as Lyra's first Eden, but it is not one anymore. Although Lyra can no longer tear through natural boundaries, she has no intention of keeping her home universe in the state the Church has left it. Lyra returns to the small space of her childhood with the insight and ability to widen her world, making room for children, adolescents, and adults to learn and grow. Hers is not a return to Paradise unchanged as the Authority promised his followers. Armed with knowledge gained over the course of her long expulsion from many Edens, Lyra vows to reshape her world into "the Republic of Heaven" (Pullman, *Spyglass* 518). This Republic will contain far more possibilities than Eden ever could.

CONCLUSION: THE WILDERNESS

Although it is pleasant to imagine Lyra's universe becoming a paradise, Eve never returns to Eden. Lyra has opened many of the Authority's cultural spaces, but there will always be fearful and power-hungry adults willing to close them back up. Change is always a threat to those at the top of social hierarchies. In subjective terms, acceptance of any mutability and mobility strikes fear into the hearts of those who believe that selfhood is like a glass of water, given shape only by its boundaries and in constant danger of being spilled. Outside the world of the text, this fear pertains not only to the sexual and intellectual growth of adolescence and death's dissolution of identity but also to racial, religious, and gender diversity. Adult cultures cling fast to their rules and the firmness of the boundaries they provide. Even the construction of childhood as an incomplete state of being, as seen in the Dust-poor children of *His Dark Materials*, reinforces a cultural hierarchy that separates and privileges adults. Collapsing these categories would require a redefinition of what it means to be a subject, but the structures of power, like those put in place by the Authority, conflate any change with the cessation of the self as both an identity and a seat of control.

Fortunately, adolescents like Lyra, who broaden the boundaries around themselves in order to expand their identities without losing them, prove that there is another way of being. Lyra and Will dedicate their lives to restoring Dust "by thinking and feeling and reflecting, by gaining wisdom and passing it on" (Pullman, *Spyglass* 491). Despite the restrictions on their movement, both culturally imposed by the continued influence of the Authority and "naturally" imposed by an author who simultaneously challenges and reinscribes developmental understandings of human maturation, Lyra and Will reach the end of the trilogy committed to continuing change. When Sin opens the Gates of Hell, Milton describes the consequence thus: "She op'n'd, but to shut / Excell'd her power; the Gates wide op'n stood" (2.883–84). Dust still falls because Lyra Fell. It broadens the inner spaces of individual subjects as they learn, and it continually returns to the broadest space of the multiverse itself until it finds a new subject, and then the process begins again. For Lyra herself, though the long journey between Eden and the wilderness is complete, the wilderness itself is still vast, and she will continue to expand her knowledge of herself and the world around her. The adolescent, in order to grow into a compassionate adult, must resist the fearful urge to create smaller, safer spaces. She must not shut the gates to the wilderness. The spaces of adolescence may not be Paradise, but Eve has long since outgrown Eden.

Works Cited

The Bible. Authorized King James Version. *oremus Bible Browser*, http://bible.oremus.org/, February 2011.

Bird, Anne-Marie. "Circumventing the Grand Narrative: Dust as an Alternate Theological Vision in Pullman's *His Dark Materials*." *His Dark Materials Illuminated: Critical*

Essays on Philip Pullman's Trilogy. Ed. Millicent Lenz with Carole Scott. Landscapes of Childhood Series, Detroit: Wayne State UP, 2005, pp. 188–97.

Cantrell, Sarah K. "'Nothing like Pretend': Difference, Disorder, and Dystopia in the Multiple World Spaces of Philip Pullman's *His Dark Materials*." *Children's Literature in Education*, vol. 41, no. 4, 2010, pp. 302–22.

Gillhouse, Elizabeth. "'Eve Was Framed': Ideostory and (Mis)Representation in Judeo-Christian Creation Stories." *Children's Literature Association Quarterly* 36, no. 3, 2011, pp. 259–75.

Greenwell, Amanda M. "Remodeling Home in Philip Pullman's *His Dark Materials*." *Lion and the Unicorn*, vol. 42, no. 1, 2018, pp. 20–36.

Levey, David. "'This Wild Abyss': The Trope of Home in Philip Pullman's *His Dark Materials* Trilogy." *Scrutiny2*, vol. 21, no. 1, 2016, pp. 18–32.

Milton, John. *Paradise Lost*. New York: Signet Classics, 2010.

Pullman, Philip. *The Amber Spyglass*. New York: Alfred A. Knopf, 2000.

Pullman, Philip. *The Golden Compass*. New York: Alfred A. Knopf, 1995.

Pullman, Philip. *The Subtle Knife*. New York: Alfred A. Knopf, 1997.

Russell, Mary Harris. "'Eve, Again! Mother Eve!': Pullman's Eve Variations." *His Dark Materials Illuminated: Critical Essays on Philip Pullman's Trilogy*. Ed. Millicent Lenz with Carole Scott. Landscapes of Childhood Series. Detroit: Wayne State UP, 2005, pp. 212–21.

Scott, Carole. "Pullman's Enigmatic Ontology: Revamping Old Tradition in *His Dark Materials*." *His Dark Materials Illuminated: Critical Essays on Philip Pullman's Trilogy*. Ed. Millicent Lenz with Carole Scott. Landscapes of Childhood Series. Detroit: Wayne State UP, 2005, pp. 95–105.

Smith, Karen. "Tradition, Transformation, and the Bold Emergence: Fantastic Legacy and *His Dark Materials*." *His Dark Materials Illuminated: Critical Essays on Philip Pullman's Trilogy*. Ed. Millicent Lenz with Carole Scott. Landscapes of Childhood Series. Detroit: Wayne State UP, 2005, pp. 135–51.

Chapter Two

EMPOWERING GIRLS

The Liminal Spaces of Schools in Nineteenth-Century Transatlantic Literature for Girls

SONYA SAWYER FRITZ AND MIRANDA A. GREEN-BARTEET

Throughout the nineteenth century, British and US girls' education experienced significant changes, leading to an increasing number of girls—those from white, middle-class families especially, but also girls of other races and classes—being sent to day schools or boarding schools, instead of being taught at home or forgoing an education altogether. The Reverend John Todd's *The Daughter at School*, published in both Britain and the United States in 1853 when educating girls at school was becoming commonplace, suggests that the superiority of a school education to a home education comes down to matters of growth and maturation: "The home education, it is said, would make [girls] amiable children; and so it would, but the difficulty is, they would be children as long as they lived" (22). Distance from the sheltering influence of home and the social independence that school fosters, Todd indicates, provide the bracing effect that girls need to mature into responsible, useful women.

By the latter nineteenth century, British and US literature for young women and girls began to engage this notion as well, highlighting how school could give young women access to liberating spaces between the domestic sphere and the wider world. In nineteenth-century school fiction for girls, the shift from home to school is often portrayed as arduous, involving loneliness, homesickness, and confusion. In girls' and women's stories, school is frequently represented as an alien location, with new customs, hierarchies, and codes of conduct to be learned and obeyed. Furthermore, because it was typically impossible, both in fiction and in real life, for school administrators to implement a "system of perpetual espionage," to use Elizabeth Wolstenholme's words, the schoolgirls in nineteenth-century fiction often find themselves negotiating school and their personal development in isolation, unattended by the authority figures whose job it is to mold and guide them (156). For those who have supervision, it is often fleeting, with teachers acting to welcome girls to school and encouraging their peers to treat them respectfully, then fading into the background. Rather than impeding or endangering the schoolgirl's progress, this lack of supervision and absence of domestic nurturing is figured in nineteenth-century fiction as useful to the schoolgirl, enabling her to think critically about her future place in the world and respond to the pressures that she faces as a girl maturing into a woman.

This essay analyzes school and educational spaces in nineteenth-century transatlantic literature, arguing that such sites are liminal spaces that provide a crucial site of autonomy for young women across racial and national divides. In the US, bildungsromans such as Harriet Wilson's *Our Nig* (1859) and Elizabeth Stuart Phelps's *The Story of Avis* (1877) portray schools and other educational sites as liminal spaces where girls can escape the confines of home and develop an empowered sense of subjectivity. Although Wilson's Frado is a Black indentured servant, and Phelps's Avis is a privileged young white woman, in school and educational spaces, both learn about themselves removed from the stifling domestic sphere. In England popular girls-school stories such as Agnes Loudon's "The Moss Rose" (1850) and L. T. Meade's *Betty, a Schoolgirl* (1894) emphasize the private, less regulated spaces of the school as crucial to girls' identity work, reflecting how girls could define and perform scholarship, friendship, and defiance, even as schools aimed to train them to adhere to broader cultural norms. While all of these texts construct school spaces as privileged spaces, they also challenge the normative representation of school as only a place of book learning. While these fictional girls do receive traditional educations, they also use school spaces to test the boundaries that limit them to the domestic sphere or to engage in personal growth in ways unplanned by adult authority figures. Thus, these works suggest that in schools nineteenth-century girls shaped their own experiences and began to claim their own subjectivities. Further, through considering a variety of educational spaces, it becomes clear that, in addition to specific spaces within the school that are peripheral to the classroom, alternative educational spaces, such as the continental art studios where Avis studies, and the school as a whole can function as liminal spaces. All of these versions of school space as liminal space are similar in the ways they provide an alternative space to the domestic sphere, freedom from dominating authority figures or peers, and crucial educational opportunities for girls. Across these diverse educational and liminal spaces, girls develop in autonomous ways: they come to know themselves. Overall, in this wide range of texts, the nineteenth-century Anglo-American school is represented as a potentially liberating interstitial space for young women and girls despite its ostensible nature as a disciplined and regimented environment.

While these seemingly disparate texts emphasize the importance of schools to girls' ability to develop independent of their families and peers, these texts also show what life in nineteenth-century Britain and the US was like for girls from a variety of backgrounds. The two examples of US literature give readers a glimpse into the lives of girls who are very different. Frado, as a Black indentured servant, is virtually enslaved and routinely beaten by her white mistress. In contrast, Avis, a university professor's daughter who is privileged on the basis of race and class, is loved and encouraged to explore her artistic interests from a young age. Both Frado and Avis[1] see school and other educational spaces as potentially empowering, as such spaces can offer an escape from domestic responsibilities. The British texts upon which we focus consider girls from various strata of the expansive Victorian middle class, including wealthy trade families pursuing social mobility and members of the genteel poor, highlighting how girls' schools could be laden with class tensions. In the face of these stresses, schoolgirl protagonists Grace and May, Betty and Lotty all value the out-of-the-way spaces within their schools that give them much-needed relief from peer pressure and social expectations so that they can grow on their own terms and develop their own strategies for handling class- and money-based problems. Considering these four texts together allows us to examine how girls across race, class, and national boundaries experienced school and how they used school spaces to develop their subjectivities.

Perhaps it goes without saying that schools, particularly those of nineteenth-century Britain and the US, are rarely seen as spaces in which young people—specifically girls—have much freedom. Novels as varied as Charlotte Brontë's *Jane Eyre* (1847) and Louisa May Alcott's *Little Women* (1869) present schools as spaces in which young girls are taught, through rigorous moral standards and a highly controlled environment, to be obedient and adhere to the strict social codes governing their bodies and behavior, ensuring that girls will grow into women capable of running their own households and raising good, moral children. Such instruction occurs primarily in the classroom, a space often characterized by demanding teachers and unwholesome social interactions between schoolgirls, where peer pressure and bullying can manipulate girls by clouding their judgment and often encouraging them to behave badly. Girls do, though, have access to other school spaces; these small, out-of-the-way spaces become important for girls' moral and emotional well-being. In such locations girls can briefly escape the trials and temptations of school life. Peripheral school spaces, including hallways, thresholds, stairwells, closets, and corners of unused rooms, can be made into liminal spaces by schoolgirls as they appropriate and redefine these locations for their personal character development.

We define liminal spaces as both literal and figurative. In architectural terms a liminal space is one that "mark[s] the boundary" between public and private spaces (Clark 42). Architectural historian Clifford Edward Clark, Jr., categorizes staircases, thresholds, and hallways as spaces that connect otherwise separate locations. Liminal spaces are literally spaces in between other spaces. Political scientist Margaret Farrar defines liminal spaces as ones that "intervene between things, especially things considered to be opposites in such a way as to unsettle them both" (20). Farrar considers connections between and among buildings, neighborhoods, and streets. The connections between these spaces suggest that there are no "singular or absolute spaces" (20). Liminal spaces can be transformed according to the needs of the individuals occupying them; those occupying liminal have an opportunity to challenge "the boundaries of intellectual and political practice" (21). Liminal spaces "resist binary classification" and are therefore sites of creative possibility and independent identity formation (Atkinson et al. 153). Mary Ann Caws asserts, "Liminal perception chooses its framework, hallowing an otherwise mundane space and setting it apart" (14); these locations become "extraordinary, and anything might happen in [them]" (14).

In the liminal spaces of a school, the girls of these texts gain some control over themselves. The characters are able to do so because each is aware of "the spatiality of human life" (Soja 5). As geographer Edward Soja contends, humans are "intrinsically spatial beings, continuously engaged in the collective activity of producing spaces and places" (6). The girls of these texts are aware—or become aware—of the limitations and the benefits of the various spaces they occupy. For example, Frado realizes she cannot escape her mistress's control in domestic spaces, while Grace comes to understand she cannot challenge her domineering peers in the classroom. As they come to understand the purposes of clearly defined spaces and the advantages of liminal spaces, they learn how to avoid spaces where they can be harmed, either physically or psychologically, and how to use spaces that can be empowering. These characters' awareness, evidenced in their thoughts and actions, of how spaces are produced and can be transformed allows the characters to use liminal spaces to challenge the codes limiting them to domestic spaces. Both Farrar's assertion that there are no "singular or absolute spaces" and

Soja's theories of "the spatiality of human life" are useful to our analysis of these characters and their experiences in schools because each highlights their awareness of space and the flexibility and potential of liminal spaces.

WILSON'S *OUR NIG*

Harriet E. Wilson's novel, *Our Nig* (1859), recounts the life of Frado, an African American girl based on Wilson. Abandoned by her impoverished white mother shortly after her Black father's death, Frado becomes an indentured servant[2] for the wealthy, white Bellmont family. A biracial child living in rural New Hampshire in the antebellum period, Frado is effectively enslaved and is thus marginalized both within nineteenth-century US society and the Bellmont home. Whereas young middle- and upper-class white girls would have been taught, both at home and school, that as adult women they would be responsible for the moral well-being of their families and therefore entitled to limited power within the domestic spaces of their homes, Frado learns that she will never be afforded such power.

Through Frado's interactions with the Bellmont family, Wilson characterizes domesticity as dangerous for African American women and girls. *Our Nig* "rejects many aspects of domestic ideology," as the "racism documented in [the text] makes it impossible for Frado to join or claim a family or fulfill the maternal and material expectations of womanhood valued by sentimental ideology" (Foreman & Pitts xxxiv). As P. Gabrielle Foreman and Reginald H. Pitts assert, Wilson's novel questions "domestic ideals that privilege bourgeois home maintenance without providing a point of entry for those who have been excluded" (xxxiv). Frado's race and class prevent her from gaining any power in the domestic sphere. While Mrs. Bellmont, like most middle- to upper-class white women, may enjoy some power in domestic spaces, Frado experiences violence and brutality, as evidenced by the many beatings she endures in the Bellmont house, specifically in the kitchen. Rather than finding solace in what is, ostensibly, her home, Frado seeks refuge in various liminal locations, which are located outside the domestic spaces of the home. In addition to these spaces, which include a hayloft and a woodpile, the schoolhouse becomes a liminal space where she is able to escape Mrs. Bellmont's brutality. There, she is able to play, learn, and know something about herself.

Throughout the antebellum period, school attendance was considered a luxury for many Black Americans. Critic Nazera Sadiq Wright explains that in most "free black households, neither parents nor children had much leisure time to dedicate" to education (25). Further, "many free black children were forced to work for wages to supplement household income" (25). While Frado is not working for wages, she is working to ensure that she has a place to live; after all, as unbearable as life as Mrs. Bellmont's indentured servant is, it is marginally preferable to the County Home, where Frado would have been sent had the Bellmonts not taken her into service. Frado's ability to attend school is dependent upon the Bellmonts' willingness to release her from service during the school term. Mrs. Bellmont claims she cannot do without Frado's constant labor and believes it is useless "to educate people of color, who were incapable of elevation" (Wilson 18). However, Mr. Bellmont, who typically stays out of domestic matters, "declared decisively that she *should* go to school" (18). His decision is significant, as it ensures that Frado attends school for three months a year for three consecutive years. It also keeps her away from Mrs. Bellmont for most of the day for three months. Mr. Belmont's declaration tacitly reminds both readers and Frado that she is more than his wife's workhorse. She is worthy of receiving an education. Further, his declaration emphasizes to Mrs. Bellmont that her power has limits: she may have control over domestic spaces, but he retains control over her and their home.

Initially, Frado finds school disappointing. She has been looking forward to attending but changes her mind when the other children shout, "See that N----r!" at her (Wilson 19). Hopeful school would provide her with a respite from Mrs. Bellmont's brutality, Frado is "chagrined and grieved," feeling "that her anticipations of pleasure at such a place were far from being realized" (19). Frado is just seven years old, and like most children she looks forward to what she hopes will be a positive experience. Wilson also emphasizes Frado's awareness of space. Knowing the schoolhouse is a location over which Mrs. Bellmont has little control, Frado anticipates she will feel safe at school, even if only briefly. The children's response to her arrival, however, reminds Frado that a young Black girl is not guaranteed safety in any public or private space; here, the hazing of newcomers that is often characterized as typical or even inevitable in school society is focused on the racial difference that marks Frado as vulnerable and affirms her marginalized status. Realizing school may be as brutal as the Bellmont home, Frado determines to leave and "never come there again" (Wilson 19). But the teacher, Miss Marsh, intervenes and kindly escorts Frado away from the taunting children and into the quiet schoolhouse. There, she calls her pupils to order and reminds them of "their duties to the poor and friendless," chastising "their cowardice in attacking a young innocent child" (19). Miss Marsh establishes clear parameters for how Frado will be treated and transforms the school into a safe space for

Frado. There, she is treated, first by Miss Marsh and eventually by most of the children, with kindness and generosity. In relative safety Frado seizes on the schoolhouse as a liminal space where she can behave as a child rather than a servant.

For Frado, several factors transform the schoolhouse into a liminal space. Most importantly, the school is entirely removed from the domestic sphere. Arguably still a feminine space, the schoolhouse is not a site of domestic labor under Mrs. Bellmont's control. Frado is expected to complete her schoolwork, and while rigorous it is not physically demanding. Although Miss Marsh may be an exacting teacher, she is also fair and kind. Also, the school is simultaneously a public and a private space. It is public in that the community children all attend the school, and they can (and likely do) report what happens at school to their parents, who may share such information with other community members. The public nature of the school, along with Miss Marsh's constant presence, ensures that the children behave differently than they would on their own. For example, they initially treat Frado kindly because Miss Marsh tells them to, but they continue to treat her kindly because they come to know that she is a merry and mirthful child (Wilson 22). The school can also be seen as a private space because the children maintain a code of silence about what happens at school; they may discuss their lessons with their parents, but they do not reveal details about the fun or the mischief they make. Finally, the schoolhouse is a liminal space because it is a space of play and rest for Frado, two activities that she is denied in the Bellmont home.

A servant, Frado is seen as a menial laborer, not an individual and certainly not a child. When she joins the Bellmont household, at age seven, she must feed the family chickens, wash dishes, and keep the woodboxes full (Wilson 17); she proves so capable at completing these tasks that her workload steadily increases. By age fourteen, she does "all the washing, ironing, backing, and the common *et cetera* of the household duties" (35). In other words, Frado singlehandedly completes most of the household work. At school she is more than a laborer; she is Frado, a young girl and student. Under Miss Marsh's guidance, in a space specifically constructed for children, Frado can behave as a child, an identity she cannot experience elsewhere. Thus, Frado transforms at school: "Day by day there was a manifest change in Frado" (Wilson 19). As she grows more comfortable at school, she becomes more playful and is "a great source of merriment to the scholars" (20–21), and "her jollity was not to be quenched" (22). Wilson emphasizes that in Mrs. Bellmont's presence, Frado "was under restraint," but at school, "among her schoolmates," she feels free to "play and tell jokes" (22). The schoolroom is significant to Frado because it enables her to behave as a child, and, at school, she is able to begin to determine who she is separate from her role as a servant.

The school's liminality is liberating for Frado because it frees her, even if only for a few hours a day for a few months out of the year, from the demands of her domestic work and gives "her rest from Mrs. Bellmont's tyranny" (Wilson 23). She does still experience verbal and physical abuse before and after school, and she must complete all her household work while attending school, or she will be beaten. The schoolhouse is also useful for Frado's social development, as it is the only space in which she is able to play and interact with other children. While she does not form lasting friendships like some of the other girls we discuss, she gradually becomes part of the school community and is valued for her "winning ways" and "antics" (19, 22). Finally, attending school proves to Frado that she is capable of "elevation," despite what Mrs. Bellmont tells her (18), as she does well at her studies. While her education is far from complete when Mrs. Bellmont refuses to allow her to attend school any longer, Frado has learned to "read and spell" and "the elementary steps in grammar, arithmetic, and writing" (23, 23–24), all of which she is able to build upon later in life. For Frado, school is a location that fulfills multiple purposes: there, she begins her education and social development; she escapes unceasing work and abuse; she is welcomed into a community of her peers and can be a child. In the liminal space of the schoolhouse, Frado learns that she has worth as more than Mrs. Bellmont's servant, and she begins to consider what her life might be like once her period of indenture is over.

PHELPS'S *THE STORY OF AVIS*

Like *Our Nig*, Elizabeth Stuart Phelps's *The Story of Avis* (1873) is set in rural New England and focuses on a precocious young woman's coming of age. The protagonists are, however, seemingly very different: whereas Frado is marginalized because of her race, age, and class, Avis Dobell lives a life of relative privilege. The daughter of a well-respected, highly educated university professor and his wife, who had hoped to become an actress before marrying, Avis is loved and never lacks for anything. Further, Avis, as a white, middle-class young woman, has more power within the domestic spaces of the home than Frado. Despite these obvious differences, Frado and Avis both begin to know themselves in educational spaces, and both question the domestic ideologies that govern nineteenth-century women's lives. While Wilson criticizes the ways domesticity excludes Black and working-class women, Phelps questions the assumption that every woman desires to be a wife and mother, arguing that some women want careers and find their traditional roles, even with the promise of limited power, stifling. Through their very different protagonists, Wilson and Phelps both challenge the demands and limitations domestic ideology places upon women of all classes and educational backgrounds.

Like Wilson, Phelps is concerned with the spaces that women and girls can access. Wilson focuses on how accessing liminal spaces helps African American women claim their subjectivity, while Phelps sees liminal spaces as especially useful to women with intellectual and creative ambitions. Liminal spaces offer women escape from domestic spaces, including the kitchen, dining room, and parlor. Escape is particularly important for women like Avis, Phelps suggests, because women who want to pursue creative or intellectual ambitions need space in which to work. As Carol Farley Kessler asserts, Phelps makes clear that it is not a lack of talent or ambition but the "absence of emotional support" and lack of personal spaces that limit women and girls' ability to produce creative and intellectual work (xxiii). For Phelps, women's domestic responsibilities, specifically marriage, "stifle creativity . . . [as] wifehood, homemaking, and motherhood . . . use all energy, all time" (xxiii). While girls spend much of their time in domestic spaces learning how to run a household, educational spaces are locations in which they can develop and pursue their own interests and begin to know who they are.

The novel is set in Harmouth, New Hampshire, a town that revolves around the college there; most male characters are professors, tutors, or students. The women of Harmouth are similarly focused on the college, especially the professors' wives and daughters. They are well educated, reading Chaucer and Spenser, speaking German and Latin, and learning physics and geology. Avis grows up in a community that prides itself on producing thoughtful, well-read, and intelligent young women. Nonetheless, despite the emphasis on learning, the educational spaces of Harmouth available to girls are decidedly domestic.

While school offers Frado respite from domestic labor, school and other educational spaces remind Avis that she is being educated purely to become a professor's wife. Avis, who is seventeen when the novel begins, has already completed "her *school* education" (Phelps 35). Therefore, there are no scenes of Avis in a traditional school, although she does refer to school. Phelps highlights other, less formal educational spaces, including drawing rooms and parlors. In these locations, which are ostensibly private and typically coded as feminine, the young women of Harmouth gather to discuss poetry, history, and philosophy. They read to one another and write essays, but they also invite young men attending Harmouth to share their work. These "clubs," as they are called, educate the young women and help them find husbands. In one notable scene, the Harmouth Poetry Club discusses Spenser, and Avis is introduced to Philip Ostrander, an eligible young bachelor working as a tutor. In a friend's drawing room, where Avis had been considering Spenser's cantos, she is reminded that she cannot simply learn about poetry; she must also learn to be a desirable wife. As she is introduced to Philip, Avis, feeling as though she has been called "to recite a lesson," becomes "timid . . . like a shrinking child" (Phelps 7), as she is made aware that her education makes her more attractive as a wife.

For Avis, educational spaces are connected to domesticity, as the goal of her education, regardless of its intellectual rigor, is to find a good husband. Even in progressive Harmouth, Avis is an anomaly, because she wants to be a professional artist, not a wife and mother. To achieve her goal, she must transgress the boundaries that limit women to the domestic sphere. Avis must train, and to do so she must learn from other professional artists. Thus, Avis asks her father to send her to Europe to study with art teachers there, but her father tells her that her dream is "nonsense" and reminds her that her "business . . . is to 'be' a studious and womanly girl" (Phelps 34). Realizing that her father thinks girls can be only wives and mothers, Avis knows she must leave Harmouth, her father's control, and the expectations of Harmouth society. At nineteen, she travels to Europe with her best friend, but rather than return as expected, Avis asks her father "that she be permitted to remain for an indefinite time, and study art" (35). That Avis makes this request from Europe suggests that she never intended to return as planned and that she feels more confident in seeking her father's permission to continue her artistic training in a liminal space over which he has no control. In Europe, where her father has little control over her, Avis determines her own future, creating educational spaces completely separate from the domestic sphere. She produces her own autonomous space and prepares for the life she wants rather than the future planned for her.

For Avis, Europe is a liminal space because, although she must still behave as befits an educated, middle-class young woman, she is completely on her own and has agency over her life: "Avis had now plunged into a life which extremely few women in America . . . found it possible or desirable to lead" (Phelps 36). The continent is a schoolroom, because there she learns how to live on her own: she finds her own lodgings and her own instructors, shops and cooks for herself, and manages the small allowance her father sends her, which she supplements by selling her drawings. In short, she learns to be independent and make her own way. Whereas she learned to be a good wife for an intellectual man in the various schoolrooms that she occupied in Harmouth, living in Europe, Avis reflects on her life and her talent on her own terms. Removed from the expectations of Harmouth society, she becomes so "sure of the beauty and the patience" of her art that she determines not "to marry" (55) in order to become an artist.

Although not schoolhouses in the traditional sense, the studios where Avis receives instruction mimic the schoolhouse. In studios, which are often "little bare" rooms in attics, "high, so high that it seemed, by putting her hand out of the window, she could touch" the sky (Phelps 37), Avis learns about art history, artistic practices, and refining her technique. In the limited physical space of the studios, Avis gains access to psychological spaces as she becomes a better artist. Further, she learns how to talk to other artists about her art, realizing in these small, quiet spaces that only other artists understand the "physiological effect" art has on the soul (38). Avis also locates a community of artists and teachers who understand her desire to become something more than she is. Much like the other characters we consider, Avis sees these studios as liminal sites, locations where she is free from all practical matters and can have "her own thoughts" and focus on "her task with a stern, ungirlish doggedness" (37). For Avis, like Frado, there is great comfort in occupying a space that is separate from the domestic sphere. Whereas Frado values the schoolhouse because it grants her the space to be a child, Avis values the studios because they allow her to give herself wholly to her art. She can think critically about her art and her future place in the world as a female artist. She can also consider how to respond to the pressures she knows she will face as a girl with a dream in the process of maturing into a woman with a career.

While Frado benefits from the camaraderie she experiences in the schoolhouse, Avis benefits from the solitude she experiences, with only her instructors to guide her. That Frado and Avis experience the liminality of educational spaces differently reflects their differing races, in particular, and their differing ages. Further, they experience work differently. Frado, as a young Black woman, has no choice but to work, even as a young child, whereas Avis must explain first to her father and then to her husband why she wants to work. School spaces have distinct meaning for Frado and Avis. Frado needs the school's liminality to experience childhood, whereas Avis needs the studios' liminality to consider her future. In studios, then, Avis has only to learn and to focus on her art, and she is able to form an identity separate from her father, her community, and other sociocultural authorities. She learns as much about herself as she does about art and realizes that "she had never lived before" (Phelps 36). In the dark corners of studios with her instructors standing behind her to offer instruction and guide her strokes, Avis slowly loses the sense of distrust that haunted her in Harmouth, and she becomes consumed with "mastering the *technique* of art with passion" (37). Through her experiences in Europe and her innumerable hours of instruction in various studios, Avis grows from a quiet, self-conscious girl into "a sublimely self-contained [young] woman" (Kelly 100). As Lori Duin Kelly asserts, Avis becomes "strong [and] independent . . . and utterly dedicated to her pursuing career" (100). She represents the "individual who operates . . . outside the bounds of conventional behavior" (100), and she has learned to challenge these boundaries in artists' studios where she is expected only to learn and create. Unfortunately, the freedom Avis finds in the studies is fleeting, and she is unable to sustain it upon returning to Harmouth. Against her better judgment, she marries Philip, who promises her, "I do not want your work, or your individuality. I refuse to accept any such sacrifice from the woman I love" (Phelps 107). Philip, however, breaks his promise, privileging his career over Avis's. Consumed by marriage and motherhood, Avis finds herself relegated to the domestic spaces she detests, unable to access liminal spaces similar to the European studios. For Frado and Avis, the escape and comfort they experience in educational spaces is limited. They are able to use these spaces to explore who they want to be, but they are unable to access similar spaces as adult women.

LOUDON'S "THE MOSS ROSE"

One of four school stories published in Agnes Loudon's 1850 collection *Tales of School Life*, "The Moss Rose" was written for an audience that is both significantly younger than Wilson's and Phelps's and also decidedly white and middle-class. Loudon's work assumes that its girl readers cannot identify with a childhood as cruel and dehumanizing as Frado's and that they require more educational guidance than the older Avis. "The Moss Rose" is thus less explicitly invested in portraying the school as a space that is empowering or liberating for girls than these US texts; instead, like many early/mid-nineteenth-century British school stories, "The Moss Rose" considers the ways school influences could be detrimental to girls who have left the shelter of a wholesome, middle-class home.[3] Anxiety about girls' welfare at school pervaded mid-century England as the middle class struggled to come to terms with the shift from home to school education for both boys and girls, and this anxiety resulted in Loudon portraying school as a space fraught with unhealthy class tensions that potentially harmed girls. Elizabeth Gargano traces this sociocultural anxiety throughout midcentury fiction by mapping the Victorians' fear of "the looming specter of educational standardization" as a reaction against the institutionalization of education for children, in which "harsh, excessively regimented classrooms" were contrasted to "a supposedly nurturing tradition of domestic instruction that dated back to Rousseau's *Emile* (1762)" (1).[4] But there was also uncertainty regarding the benefits of daughters' association with strangers and the long-term effects of prolonged absences from the home and its moral compass. For solicitous parents, the outside influence of other, less well-trained girls could foster bad habits and undermine all of the morals and values that careful teaching and nurturing at home inculcated in their daughters.

In Loudon's story Grace Harding has been sent to a "decidedly aristocratic" school by her wealthy tradesman father; there she suffers "the rude taunts and biting speeches" of her class-conscious schoolmates (108). She finds that "her father had done neither a wise nor a kind thing to her, though he thought he had done both" (108). Figuring schoolgirl society as problematic for its characters, Loudon's story constructs the classroom and other communal school spaces as hotbeds of unwholesome social interactions among schoolgirls. They are sites where peer pressure and bullying can manipulate girls, clouding their judgment and even leading to bad behavior. Thus, what become important for girls are liminal spaces "where identity can slip and reform," to use Jacob Bull's words (461); these sites momentarily liberate girls from the strictures of the school's social conventions and routines, allowing them to reflect on and navigate their situation from a space outside the microcosm of the school.

"The Moss Rose" represents schoolgirl society—particularly the communal space of the schoolroom—as fraught with the "cruel thoughtlessness" of schoolgirls (Loudon 109). In the schoolroom, Grace's classmates tease her for being a tradesman's daughter. In the classroom, the aggressive Augusta Colville, "who [is] very fond of managing and being at the head of everything" (100), also domineers over students when she takes charge of collecting the funds to buy a birthday present for the headmistress, Mrs. Vance. Instead of asking for donations from all interested parties, Augusta insists on making a list of each student and then traveling about the schoolroom to request each girl's donation individually. Augusta imposes her own social hierarchies on the communal school space by intruding upon each girl's studies to invade and judge their personal finances, deeming girls' contributions "capital" or "stingy" depending on the amount they pledge (103, 107). In contrast to the schoolroom—which is an unpleasant space, full of "noise and heat" and judgment—stands the hallway right outside, which offers privacy with its almost complete darkness and extremely narrow passages with "sharp turns, and every now and then a step up or down" (105). The hallway is a liminal space, because it stands between and mediates passage to all other spaces of the school, and for this very reason, it gives Grace peace and relief. Grace, who suffers from migraines aggravated by the schoolroom's noise, takes comfort in escaping her schoolmates and traversing the cool, dark, quiet passageway, a space of sanctuary and a haven. The hallway provides an opportunity for even more significant relief when Grace comes across the young and mistreated May Gerald, who is crying in the darkness because she is too poor to donate to the collection and has been ridiculed by Augusta for being "very stingy" (107). In the secluded passageway, Grace can talk openly with May about the cruelty of other students and the respectability of poverty. She reveals her own background as a parvenu to May and shares "how deeply [Grace] had suffered from that same false shame" when mocked by other students because of her family's position (107). In the privacy of the hallway, Grace offers the young girl a practical solution by giving her the needed money and counseling her to keep it a secret from the others.

The girls' exchange can occur only in a private, out-of-the-way setting, where the nature of their conversation and Grace's donation can remain their secret. Thus, the hallway provides a unique opportunity for each girl's personal character development. May learns not to feel the "false shame" of poverty, and Grace, who desires "to avenge [May] by scolding Augusta," realizes "that God always gave punishment where it was due, and that in avenging May, she would sin herself" (Loudon 109, 110). Furthermore, their meeting in the passageway changes both their lives by enabling them to become lifelong friends and helpmeets to one another: "not only was May entirely devoted to Grace while they remained at school, but in after years, when Grace was visited by a painful and lingering illness, May was her constant attendant" (112). This humble passageway serves as the catalyst for significant improvements in the lives of both girls, suggesting that liminality is key to the school's ability to provide girls with positive long-term outcomes.

Loudon's story is, though, somewhat didactic, as Loudon intrudes upon the narrative to emphasize that these girls are equals and that shame over trade wealth or poverty is a travesty—which contrasts sharply with the work of contemporaries including Elizabeth Missing Sewell and Charlotte Yonge, who advocated the separation of classes in schools. However, in addition to this class-conscious agenda, the geography of the school in Loudon's story implies that the conventional, organized spaces of the school are not sufficient for the complete and healthy development of the nineteenth-century girl, particularly regarding her personal identity formation. It is only through time alone together that Grace and May can hone one another's characters and, across age, class, and social standing, help each other find peace and confidence in who they are as individuals, beyond socioeconomic and cultural status. In this way "The Moss Rose" is more conditional than *Our Nig* or *The Story of Avis* in its understanding of school spaces' potential to provide girls with opportunities for independent growth and self-actualization; while a specific liminal space can accomplish this, the main spaces of the school, such as the classroom itself, can work against it.

MEADE'S *BETTY, A SCHOOLGIRL*

In the decades following the publication of Loudon's school stories, as parents viewed school education as more acceptable, the prospect of one's daughter mingling with other girls became more appealing. The types of social tribulations Loudon's protagonists faced in schools' main spaces came to be perceived less as potentially devastating to girls' character development and more as typical, character-building rites of passage. However, even in later-century British school stories for girls, the peripheral spaces of the school—those that exist on the margins of the central classroom and main communal spaces—continue to be characterized as crucial to girls' autonomous social and personal development. Later Victorian school stories for girls convey an understanding of the bedroom as a particularly important location for schoolgirls, representing this space as a significant factor in schoolgirls' character development.[5] In many stories boarding-school bedrooms figure as vital sites for girls' inner growth, especially in spiritual matters; schoolgirl protagonists such as Hester Thornton in Meade's *A World of Girls* (1886) and Molly Lavender in Meade's *Girls New and Old* (1895) take to their bedrooms to work out moral dilemmas or to pray earnestly over a troubling situation.[6] But in many stories bedrooms are also portrayed as especially useful in girls' social development, be it in the form of strengthening the bonds of intimacy with a bosom friend or in nurturing one's personal identity as distinct from the schoolgirl community.

Meade's *Betty, a Schoolgirl* (1894) demonstrates a link between personal space and social development through its protagonist's experience of her bedroom as a retreat from the bewildering, stressful experience of school. The novel focuses on Miss St. Leger's school for girls, lodged in her own home and consisting of only seven students, where Betty Falkoner, the titular character, is sent by her father to be educated after her mother dies. Though the setting for Miss St. Leger's small establishment is strikingly homelike in appearance, and Betty finds the rooms "picturesque" and "pleasant" (Meade 33, 37) instead of cold and institutional, the defining characteristic of both Miss St. Leger and her school is a strict dedication to industry that casts a severe sense of discipline on the place. After a fortnight in the school, Betty observes that this is "a house where no one had her own way for a single minute; where there was not a second of time left unemployed; where from morning to night there was . . . a rush to get things done" (Meade 71). Miss St. Leger's economy of time rules the girls' movements and behaviors in the house down to the very minute; even in the girls' bedrooms, "there was never time for talk. Even at night there was no time. Bed was meant to be slept in" (Meade 71). Like the arrangement of the bedroom in Robson's *School Architecture*, Miss St. Leger's rules preempt the pupils' experiences of personal leisure time in their bedrooms and institutionalize a normally intimate, private space.

In spite of all this regulation, Betty finds that the privacy that her bedroom affords also gives her an opportunity for a crucial respite from the whirlwind and strain of school life—not through solitude, but through friendship with her roommate, Lotty Raynham. From Betty's very first evening at Miss St. Leger's, the girls' room becomes a refuge where they can confide in and support each other. When Betty's classmates tease her in the school's preparation room, Lotty constructs their shared bedroom as a sanctuary from the communal space and the girls' harassment as she urges Betty to "escape them" by following her upstairs (Meade 41). Upon arriving at the room, which, like the entire house, is "pretty" and "neat" (41, 42), the girls further enjoy the space as a place of peace by ignoring Miss St. Leger's orders to quickly unpack Betty's things and go to bed, instead belying the alleged lack of time to talk by sitting on their beds and doing just that. The girls' private conversation transforms the bedroom into a subversive space by resisting Miss St. Leger's institutionalization of the room. It also cements the girls' friendship as Betty vents her sorrow over her mother's death and Lotty comforts and nurtures Betty like an older sister. Their confidence eventually inspires Lotty to reveal her own secrets: her mother's illness, of which none of the other girls know, and her ambitious plan to make the most of her studies so that she can pursue a career to help support her widowed mother and three brothers.

When Miss St. Leger is called away from the school by a family emergency, the novel further emphasizes the girls' bedroom as the locus of their friendship and a refuge from the communal spaces of the school, where the other girls so often make Betty uncomfortable. Temporarily released from Miss St. Leger's strict attention and indulged by the lazy and corrupt French governess, Mlle. Henri, all of the girls except Betty and Lotty quickly run amok in the schoolroom, refusing to do their lessons. Like the preparation room where Betty is first bombarded by the other girls, the classroom is a space in which the majority rules, and Betty must sit in silent turmoil, wishing that

Lotty as the eldest would "look up.... and compel the rest of the girls to be at least outwardly respectful" (Meade 92). But, whereas in their bedroom Lotty attends lovingly to Betty, she remains oblivious in the classroom: "as usual, her fingers were pressed to her ears—her shoulders hitched up high. She was bending over a difficult Latin exercise with knitted brows, absorbed in thought" (92). As Miss St. Leger's absence progresses, Lotty's single-minded devotion to study, which absorbs all of her attention in the preparation room and classroom, prevents her from standing up for Betty and for what is right among the other girls; indeed, the novel implies that, were it not for the girls' shared bedroom, Lotty's studies may well have prevented her from taking an interest in Betty at all.

The bedroom continues to provide a space for their friendship to flourish, in spite of all the tensions and misunderstandings that occur in the schoolrooms. It is here that "Lotty's dreamy eyes seemed to awake; her face became active, interested, and alert," and she can focus on and confide in Betty (Meade 170). It is here that the homely Lotty admits to her despair of winning a school prize that considers physical appearance as a criterion, which would give her the money she needs to care for her mother, and the girls scrutinize her appearance and discuss strategies for making her seem more attractive. As the day for the prize-giving draws near, the girls' bedroom becomes the headquarters for their private plan of refining and beautifying Lotty; each night Betty "brushe[d] Lotty's long black hair until it shone and glowed" and "drill[ed] Lotty, who pace[d] up and down her bedroom with measured and martial strides . . . and enter[ed] a room as if she were a soldier in a cavalry regiment, and not a gentle, young girl in her early teens" (Meade 221). When Lotty feels crushed by the certainty that their beautiful classmate Henny will receive the prize instead, Betty's evening pep talks in their bedroom "hearten [Lotty] up once more" and move Lotty to admit the "fierce" love she feels for Betty but typically "can't talk about" (Meade 224). Intimate moments such as these, which are possible only in the privacy of the girls' bedroom, strengthen the bond between Betty and Lotty, helping Betty to forget her own misery and recover from her mother's death.[7]

Ultimately, this bond strengthens Betty's character in significant ways. Betty struggles with "fear, weakness, [and] uncertainty" in her new life at school; according to Miss St. Leger, "[her] character is absolutely unformed" (Meade 176). Betty demonstrates this perceived lack of character most significantly when Miss St. Leger requests that Betty write her a report of the schoolgirls' activities during her absence, and Betty is too afraid to tell Miss St. Leger the truth about the girls' and Mlle. Henri's behavior. When Mlle.

Henri steals Lotty's prize-winning essay and gives it to another student, Betty's love for Lotty and her knowledge of the prize's importance to her friend motivate her to overcome her timidity and to stand up for her friend. Betty's openness and emotional honesty, which were fostered during the time spent in her bedroom, move her to grasp for once "the courage of [her] convictions," making her into the "good, brave child" that Miss St. Leger has hoped she would become (Meade 296). Though the climax of the novel takes place on the school's front lawn when the truth about the prize-winning essay is revealed, Betty's most significant moments of personal—and, subsequently, social—development at school happen in her bedroom. Like Loudon's "The Moss Rose" in particular, *Betty, a Schoolgirl* suggests that the communal spaces of school can provide neither the privacy nor the flexibility that these schoolgirls require to develop a complete and autonomous sense of self. Indeed, both British texts are more conservative than their US counterparts in their interpretation of school in general as a liberating place for the girl, which can be linked to their status as didactic children's stories that have less interest in addressing the nineteenth-century race and gender politics that underpin Wilson's and Phelps's examinations of the relationship between their female protagonists' individual autonomy and their exposure to school.

CONCLUSION

As it became more commonplace for Anglo-American girls to attend school, literature for young women increasingly highlighted how schools gave them access to spaces outside the domestic sphere. While girls received instruction in traditional subjects in their classrooms, in other school spaces, especially those that exist on the margins of the school, girls learned how to socialize with one another and to be independent. Liminal spaces of school, then, enabled girls on both sides of the Atlantic to claim moments of privacy and to escape the demands of the domestic sphere as well as the social pressures of school life. Wilson, Phelps, Loudon, and Meade each posit that schools are either liminal spaces or contain liminal spaces that permit girls to develop a greater sense of subjectivity than they would if they never traveled beyond the boundaries of the home. The British girls' school stories are more moralistic, reflecting specific cultural anxieties and expectations regarding British girls' public and private roles in the expanding empire. Loudon and Meade share a pointed interest in the ways the liminal spaces of the school allow girls to retreat into privacy, which figures girls' maturation as a personal, interior process, rather than solely as a product of their socialization with other girls. The British texts also differ from their American counterparts in their views regarding the limitations of communal school spaces; in framing private, liminal spaces as crucial to girls' development, both Loudon and Meade highlight the pitfalls of the conventional public schoolrooms and common areas where girls spent the majority of their time.

In contrast, the US texts are less didactic and, perhaps in keeping with the emphasis on American independence, embrace the idea that a school and its associated liminal spaces can offer girls true autonomy, even if that autonomy is limited to the spaces of the school. For her part, Phelps also identifies the privacy girls are afforded in what can otherwise be seen as public places as key to their development and growth. Such privacy allows girls to know themselves, to assert their own desires, and to be more independent. Wilson, however, is less concerned with privacy, and Frado is the sole character discussed here who seeks out communal school spaces rather than private ones. As a Black girl, Frado lacks the race and class privilege[8] that benefit the other girls. That her white teacher must instruct the white students who hurl racial epithets at her to be kind so that Frado can experience school reminded nineteenth-century readers that Black children were marginalized even within the supposed sanctity of a schoolhouse.

Despite the differences among all the girls, each text recognizes that many girls value the liminal space of the schoolhouse—and recognize that they can behave, interact with others, and even perceive themselves differently in the liminal spaces they encounter at school. Frado, Avis, Grace, and Betty are each able to foster an autonomous identity or at least begin to do so, suggesting that schools are increasingly essential to girls' development. These four disparate texts further highlight the importance of schools to girls of a variety of socioeconomic and racial backgrounds, suggesting that all girls, regardless of position in society or if they live in the United States or England, want to experience life beyond the confines of the home.

Notes

1. Traditionally, neither *Our Nig* nor *The Story of Avis* has been seen as children's literature. However, both are frequently categorized as bildungsromane. See Eric's "'This Attempt of Their Sister': Harriet Wilson's *Our Nig* from Printer to Readers" and Renée Bergland's "Women's Novels and the Gendering of Genius," which categorizes Phelps's novel as a "bildungsroman, clearly in conversation with the works of her peers" (464).

2. For further discussion on Frado's status as an indentured servant, see Miranda's essay "From the 'L-chamber' to the Woodpile: Negotiating Space in Harriet E. Wilson's *Our Nig*," *Canadian Review of American Studies*, vol. 49, no. 2, 2019, pp. 160–84.

3. Harriet D'Oyley Howe's *Clara Eversham; or the Life of a School-Girl* (1851) offers an exception to this early Victorian characterization of school by portraying the school as a provisional home in the absence of a real one: its titular character is a spoiled, uneducated, and unchurched orphan who is sent by relatives to a decidedly homelike school, where kind teachers and fellow students help her to learn "the all-importance of religion," which in turn assists her in improving her personal character and her studies (99).

4. Gargano's study is similar to this project in that she traces ideological undercurrents through nineteenth-century representations of spaces in boys' and girls' schools, including the garden/playground, the classroom, and the teacher's study. However, Gargano's discussion is much broader than the one here, covering texts published earlier as well as Victorian fiction for adults.

5. The bedrooms provided for girls in actual schools varied widely: they could be small cubicles, such as those typically found in institutions created to educate clergymen's daughters and other members of the genteel poor; or they could be larger rooms like those found in colleges and universities for older girls and young women. Either way, the standard inclusion of some kind of personal bedroom for girls at school reflects a larger cultural awareness of the schoolgirl's need for a degree of privacy in her daily life.

6. It is worth noting that using the bedroom as a space to pray or consider spiritual matters is not limited to British representations of schoolgirls. Susan Warner's *A Wide, Wide World* (1850) and Louisa May Alcott's *Little Women* (1869) and *Work: A Story of Experience* (1873) feature girls praying in their bedrooms for spiritual guidance.

7. Moments such as these also underscore how the homosocial relationships portrayed in nineteenth- and twentieth-century girls-school stories could have homoerotic overtones, as scholars such as Helen Bittel and Judy Simons have noted.

8. Neither May nor Betty is wealthy, but their families' ability to send them to school signals they enjoy a degree of class privilege.

Works Cited

Atkinson, David, et al. *Cultural Geography: A Critical Dictionary of Key Concepts.* L. B. Tauris, 2005.

Avery, Gillian. *Behold the Child: American Children and Their Books, 1621–1922.* Johns Hopkins UP, 1994.

Bergland, Renée. "Women's Novels and the Gendering of Class." *The Oxford History of the Novel in English, Volume 5, The American Novel to 1870*, edited by J. Gerald Kennedy and Leland S. Person, Oxford UP, 2014, pp. 449–65.

Bittel, Helen. "Required Reading for 'Revolting Daughters'? The New Girl Fiction of L. T. Meade." *Nineteenth-Century Gender Studies*, vol. 2, no. 2, 2006, pp. 1–14.

Bull, Jacob. "Watery Masculinities: Fly Fishing and the Angling Male in the South West of England." *Gender, Place, and Culture*, vol. 16, no. 4, 2009, pp. 445–65.

Caws, Mary Ann. *A Metapoetics of the Passage: Architextures in Surrealism and After.* UP of New England, 1981.

Clark, Clifford Edward, Jr. *The American Family Home, 1800–1860.* U of North Carolina P, 1986.

D'Oyley Howe, Harriet. *Clara Eversham; or, The Life of a School-Girl*. Wertheim and Macintosh, 1852.

E. T. M. [Eliza Theodora Minturn]. "An Interior View of Girton College, Cambridge." *The Education Papers: Women's Quest for Equality in Britain, 1850–1912*, edited by Dale Spender, Routledge, 2001, pp. 279–84.

Farrar, Margaret E. *Building the Body Politic: Power and Urban Space in Washington, D.C.* U of Illinois P, 2008.

Foreman, P. Gabrielle, and Reginald H. Pitts. "Introduction." *Our Nig; or, Sketches in the Life of a Free Black*, by Harriet E. Wilson, Penguin Books, 2009, pp. xxiii–lv.

Gargano, Elizabeth. *Reading Victorian Schoolrooms: Childhood and Education in Nineteenth-Century Fiction*. Routledge, 2008.

Kelly, Lori Duin. *The Life and Works of Elizabeth Stuart Phelps: Victorian Feminist Writer*. Whitson Publishing, 1983.

Kessler, Carol Farley. Introduction. *The Story of Avis*, by Elizabeth Stuart Phelps, edited by Kessler, Rutgers UP, 1992.

Loudon, Agnes. "The Moss Rose." *Tales of School Life*. Grant and Griffith, 1850.

Meade, L. T. *Betty, a Schoolgirl*. Grosset & Dunlap, 1894.

Phelps, Elizabeth Stuart. *The Story of Avis*, edited by Carol Farley Kessler, Rutgers UP, 1992.

Robson, Edward Robert. *School Architecture: Being Practical Remarks on the Planning, Designing, Building, and Furnishing of School-Houses*. 2nd ed, John Murray, 1877.

Simons, Judy. "Angela Brazil and the Making of the Girls' School Story." *Popular Children's Literature in Britain*, edited by Julia Briggs, Dennis Butts, and M. O. Grenby, Ashgate Publishing, 2008, pp. 165–81.

Soja, Edward. *Thirdspace: Journey to Los Angeles and Other Real and Imagined Places*. Wiley-Blackwell Publishing, 1996.

Todd, John. *The Daughter at School*. T. Nelson and Sons, 1856.

Wilson, Harriet E. *Our Nig; or, Sketches from the Life of a Free Black*, edited by P. Gabrielle Foreman and Reginald H. Pitt, Penguin Books, 2009.

Wolstenholme, Elizabeth. "The Education of Girls, Its Present and Its Future." *The Education Papers: Women's Quest for Equality in Britain, 1850–1912*, edited by Dale Spender, Routledge, 2001, pp. 153–60.

Wright, Nazera Sadiq. *Black Girlhood in the Nineteenth Century*. U of Chicago P, 2016.

Chapter Three

"THERE'S NO PLACE LIKE HOME"

Dystopian Depictions of Home in *The Giver* Quartet and the *Unwind* Dystology

DANIELLE RUSSELL

Whatever form it takes, the home looms large in children's literature. It is, arguably, the primary space associated, physically and imaginatively, with childhood.[1] As Jon C. Stott and Christine Doyle Francis note, while "there is certainly no shortage of adult literature dealing with this concept, . . . the home is even more a focal point in the lives of children than in those of adults" (223). The need for home, and all that it represents—ideally a protecting and nurturing place—is most primal in childhood. Mavis Reimer reinforces the logic of this association, theorizing that "because home normally is the site of the satisfaction of the most basic human needs for shelter and food, the depiction of stable and safe housing in narratives for children can be read as the adult promise, or hope, that the world is a place in which children can not only survive but also thrive" (iii). Home is more than a structure here; it is a (hypothetical) "contract" between adult and child with implications that exceed its physical boundaries. "'Home' to a child," Stott and Francis propose, "is not merely a dwelling place but also an attitude. For a real child or a fictional character, it is a place of comfort, security, and acceptance—a place which meets both physical and emotional needs" (223). What is being described is, of course, an ideal; the *desired* is not necessarily equivalent to the *actual* home. It depends on the people who occupy the dwelling.

The link between the family and the home in children's literature has been so strongly forged as to become (almost) "naturalized." If the child's "natural" place is within the home, by extension, it is more narrowly within the family; family homes are the mainstay of children's literature. Ann Alston is emphatic about this connection: "the home, like the family, is central to children's literature . . . home and family . . . are almost inseparable: the term 'family home' barely needs to be voiced, for home *is* essentially family" (69). The concepts have become intertwined to the point that the ideal conditions of one are difficult to distinguish from the other. "The sanctity of the family home, the warmth and domesticity implicit in the very word itself, the continuity and security inherent in the cultural—and literary—construction of family," Alston argues, "are often contrasted with the insecurity and unpleasantness of the wider world" (27). Home and family are conflated in Alston's assessment; they hold out the same "promise" Reimer identified. Home is positioned in stark contrast to all other space, space that is almost invariably depicted as physically, emotionally, and/or psychologically threatening. But what happens when the threats are contained within the home? How do authors accommodate a more nuanced depiction of the home?

The potential disconnect between the concepts of family and home and the actual experience of them is provocatively depicted in *The Giver* quartet and the *Unwind* dystology. Their "real" homes are fraught with danger and thus are sites of imposed vulnerability, and yet the male protagonists cling to the positive concepts associated with the idea of home as a key aspect of their survival "strategies."[2] The movement toward self-definition and personal security for Jonas and Connor—Lowry's and Shusterman's central protagonists—begins in their family homes and, by necessity, expands into a hostile world that heightens the need to achieve an alternative home. Jonas and Connor initially appear to have the "continuity" and "security" identified with the family home, but unspoken threats destabilize both family and home.[3] Jonas discovers that the harmony of his entire community hinges upon his obligation to pay the terrible price of being the Receiver of all memories. Connor discovers that his parents have signed the unwind document giving the government the authority to dismember him and redistribute his body parts. The threats to Jonas and Connor originate within the state, but they are enacted within their respective homes: both sets of parents actively lie to their sons, withhold vital information, and align themselves with the state. In doing so they abdicate responsibility for their sons and transform the family home from a sanctuary to a site of disempowerment. Survival, for Jonas and Connor, will require more than mere physical escape; it will necessitate reconceptualizing both home and family.

HOMEWARD BOUND: THE PITFALLS OF DWELLING IN AN INTIMATE INSTITUTION

Home is a complex place: it can take multiple forms and serve multiple functions. As both a concept and an experience, it, paradoxically, confines, constricts, contains, and comforts. Structure *and* inhabitants are the foundation of the home, but it is "built" from more than tangible materials; intangible concepts and emotions play a key part in the creation of a home. It carries emotional implications—whether positive or negative—and reverberates with psychological and intellectual symbolism. Commonly associated with women, and by extension, children, the home is frequently assumed to be a site of stasis. All too often, the home is labeled a "feminine" space with the potential to inhibit (if not outright emasculate) its male occupants. It is both desired and despised in literature. In stark contrast to the wide-open ("masculine") world, with its vastness, movement, and potential danger, the house is identified as providing intimacy, stability, and security.

The private/public spatial paradigm emerges from a particular moment in Western history. Pia Christensen and Margaret O'Brien provide a concise summary of the process:

> During the nineteenth century in Europe and North America the gradual separation of the work place from the home led to the emergence of the "home" as a prime physical and spatial location for people's social and emotional lives. The home became a key context for the family which came to represent "the modern domestic ideal" of parents and children living together forming a nuclear family. (3)

In many ways the idealization of the home is a response to the depersonalized and institutionalized experience of public space. More than fulfilling the basic human need for shelter and sustenance, the home became a "sanctuary" fulfilling key psychological and emotional needs. Except when it did not: literature in general is replete with examples of "good" and "bad" homes; nor does Children's Literature shy away from such depictions. The key distinction is that child characters are rarely left in those "bad" homes. Whether through self-determination, timely intervention or a plot twist, deliverance from the "false" to a "true" home is the dominant pattern; the initial home is ameliorated, or a substitute home is found/created.

For Jonas and Connor, the need for a genuine home is a direct response to the depersonalized and institutionalized experience of their initial homes. At first glance Jonas's home is a protective and nurturing space—his parents were vetted before he was assigned to them, daily rituals ensure calm continuity, and the community's "it-takes-a-village" policy ensures that his "best interests" are being met—but a key development exposes it as a more constrictive and totalitarian institution. "The Ceremony of Twelve," in which he is "selected" (unlike the others who are assigned jobs) to be the "Receiver of Memory" ruptures Jonas's sense of familiarity and the familial: all of the rules he has unthinkingly followed—rules for the "greater good"—no longer apply (Lowry, *The Giver*, 76). Prior to the ceremony, Jonas drew comfort from the fact that "the community was so meticulously ordered, the choices so carefully made" (Lowry, *The Giver* 61). As the new Receiver, Jonas comes to the painful conclusion that, while the policy of sameness has eliminated suffering and pain, it has also eliminated genuine emotion and the possibility of choice. The price of communal harmony, Jonas learns, is a diminishing of its humanity. The sanitized lives they live belie some brutal truths. Witnessing his father "releasing" a baby—an act of infanticide because twins are not permitted—destroys Jonas's sense of security and trust. Home, he discovers, conceals a threat; it is an instrument for ensuring the "sameness" the Committee of Elders has carefully constructed and meticulously maintain.

Social control, in Connor's world, at least for those between thirteen and eighteen, also entails a sinister cooperation between the family and the state. Inappropriate social behaviors or attitudes (aka being a teenager!) have deadly consequences in the *Unwind* dystology. "The Bill of Life" which ended the "Second Civil War" grants parents the right to "retroactively 'abort' a child. . . . on the condition that the child's life does not 'technically' end. The process by which a child is both terminated and yet kept alive is called 'unwinding'" (Shusterman, *Unwind*, 1). Semantics and science support state-sanctioned murder. The possibility is not a secret, but the actual termination of parental responsibility is typically hidden until the last moment. Unbeknownst to his parents, Connor has found the "Unwind order. It had been signed in old-fashioned triplicate. The white copy was already gone—off with the authorities. The yellow copy would accompany Connor to his end, and the pink would stay with his parents" (Shusterman, *Unwind*, 6). Brutal bureaucracy at its finest; no need to hide the paper trail. Once the official form is submitted, the parents are also disempowered: "an unwind order [is] irreversible" (Shusterman, *Unwind*, 6). The policy leaves no space for sober second thoughts. Parents and children must "live" with the consequences of their "choices."

The threat of unwinding is itself sufficient grounds to question the security of the home for a teenager. It is clearly not inviolable. For Connor, the imminent loss of home has both physical and emotional implications: "Home. Connor wonders how he can call the place he lives home, when he's about to be evicted—not just from the place he sleeps, but from the hearts of those who are supposed to love him" (Shusterman, *Unwind*, 5). Family and dwelling are interconnected for Connor; the sheltering space is both the physical structure—the place he sleeps—and the familial structure—the "place" he is loved. Connor recognizes the ideal as he braces for the reality of expulsion from it. The feeling of home, paradoxically, is found in "one of those dangerous places that make adults shake their heads, grateful that their own kids aren't stupid enough to hang out on the ledge of a freeway overpass.... It's not about stupidity, or even rebellion—it's about feeling life.... For Connor, life on the edge is home" (Shusterman, *Unwind*, 4). It is an indication of the feelings and behaviors that have cost him his home. Simply being a teenager, however, renders Connor vulnerable; the generational conflict is intensified by the fact that one "side" is armed with a license to kill.

The nature of their homes renders Connor and Jonas vulnerable; their liberty is impinged, their lives are imperiled, and they are bound to their homes by authoritarian leaders. The paradigm of private/public space is shattered in both series. Jane Carroll's assertion that the "home is at once a personal, localised place and a microcosmic version of the world" has sinister ramifications in the lives of Connor and Jonas (19). "The personal is political" is illustrated in chilling fashion. Society's values and demands encroach on the sanctity of the home, in turn distorting the structure of the family. Home, a true home, must be located/created outside of their original family homes; Connor and Jonas are compelled to flee, but that flight is ultimately focused on a goal. The pair of characters are homeward bound but on their own terms.

FAMILY TIES AS ALIBIS:
THE DANGERS OF DOMESTIC SPACES

In Western culture the concept of the nuclear family has become so entrenched as to be (almost) naturalized. The concept of a "normal" family shapes social and legal expectations. Literature, and children's literature in particular, seemingly affords a safe space in which the nuclear family can be explored or outright critiqued. Alternative families will be discussed in a subsequent section of this chapter, and I return to the status of the nuclear family in the final section. The reader's initial encounter with Jonas and Connor, however, finds them firmly entrenched within the two-(heterosexual)-parent model of the family. Jonas will soon begin to question the validity of that model. Connor is on the brink of being violently severed from it; he is painfully aware of the reality behind the facade.

The "perfect" community in which Jonas lives has only one type of family: a father and mother who have been carefully matched by the Committee of Elders. This matchmaking does consider the compatibility of the spouses, but the focus is on the subsequent "family unit." Members of the community who lack "the essential capacity to connect to others . . . required for the creation of a family unit" remain single (Lowry, *The Giver*, 10). Every family is the same in Jonas's community: "two children—one male, one female—to each family unit" (Lowry, *The Giver*, 11). And it has a shelf life: "When adults of the community become older, their lives became different. They [are] no longer needed to create family units. Jonas's own parents, when he and Lily [are] grown, would go to live with the Childless Adults" (Lowry, *The Giver*, 128). Families fulfill a practical function; when it is completed, they are dismantled. Contact between grown children and their parents is neither expected nor encouraged. Efficient but emotionless, the "family unit" serves the needs of both the children—ensuring a nurturing and protective space when it is most required—and those of the larger community—ensuring that its members are equipped to participate in the smooth continuation of society.

Connor's family is not socially engineered like that of Jonas, but it is nonetheless shaped by external social pressures. The government provides a convenient solution to the inconvenience of parenting a teenager. In Connor's case the dismantling of family, at least his part in it, is an imminent threat. The unwind orders have been submitted, obliterating any sense of security he may have had. Fleeing the family home, Connor dreams of a time when his parents did provide the space of comfort and security:

> he was at a cabin . . . with his parents. . . . [His] leg had fallen through a rotted board on the porch nto spiderwebs. . . . His father was there to pull him free, and carry him inside, where they bandaged his leg. . . . His father told him a story. . . . It wasn't the story but the tone of his voice that mattered, a gentle baritone rumble as calming as waves breaking on a shore. Little-boy-Connor drank his cider and leaned back against his mother pretending to fall asleep. . . . His whole being flowed into the cider cup, and his parents placed it gently on the table, close enough to the fire to keep it warm forever and always. (Shusterman, *Unwind*, 16–17)

A dream helps Connor access the maternal and paternal reassurance he craves; at the heart of his dream is the concept of the loving and nurturing family. Outside of the door, however, is the harsh reality that it now exists only in the space of dreams: his father is waiting with the police to enforce the unwind order. Rather than being "placed gently" and kept "warm forever and always," Connor finds his parents have irrevocably displaced him. Despite the real and present danger his family has unleashed on him, old dreams are hard to resist: two years into his struggle to survive, "the feeling of normalcy—the thoughts of family" at another family's dinner table "somehow [make] the word [mom] surface like an unexpected belch" (Shusterman, *Unsouled* 242). Connor is mortified, but the "slip" signals that the desire for a return to his family still resonates within him—the dream endures despite the betrayal.

Technically, both sets of parents are doing the right thing based upon society's standards. Their acts are in the "best interest of the child"; thus, being a "family" is their alibi. They do not deviate from social norms, nor will they permit their sons to do so. The parents do not calculate the cost of that compliance: results are of greater significance. Alston's assertion that "the family unit is a disciplinary institution which conforms to state-promulgated ideologies" provides an apt description of Connor's and Jonas's original families (10). They reflect and (attempt to) reinforce the norms and laws of the larger social group. In this context the family home is an extension of the state, which blurs the line between public demands and private desires. Flight is the only option available to Connor and Jonas. Escape from physical threats to existence is their primary catalyst, but both boys will discover that flight becomes a quest for a "true" home.

BODY AS BORDER:
DEFENSIVE MANEUVERS AS SELF-DETERMINATION

The catalyst for action in both series is a threat to the autonomy of the boys' personal space. In each case the border under attack is the body. Connor has been consigned for dismemberment. Jonas, while not facing a literal death sentence, is experiencing a psychic "dismemberment" as his newfound knowledge violently severs him from his community. A border, theorize Jessica Elbert Decker and Dylan Winchock, is "more than a line: it is a physical limit.... It locates the division between things, their beginnings, and their endings" (1). The most primal border is the body. It is "the first border that each human being encounters," notes Filippo Menozzi (33). Body as border separates internal and external realities. Discovering the reality of those "beginnings" and "endings" is a pivotal part of early childhood; navigating the implications of those divisions dominates adolescence (and, one might argue, adulthood).

Maintaining the integrity of their personal borders becomes a matter of life and death for Connor and Jonas; vulnerable to a variety of violations, each character discovers it must be actively defended. In the case of Connor, bodily violation is state sanctioned: the policy of unwinding is a real and present danger. It grants his parents the legal right to transfer control of *his* body to the government. Between the ages of thirteen and eighteen, children in Connor's country can have no real expectation of personal autonomy: the boundary between state's rights and personal rights has been obliterated. One border is superseded by another, highlighting the fact that, as Decker and Winchock persuasively argue, "with every border drawn a structure of power materializes alongside it" (2). Hierarchies establish and reinforce power dynamics; while such structures are often hidden, in Connor's world there is no attempt to mask the generational power imbalance. In point of fact, public awareness of the power imbalance is a means of social control.

The power imbalance is not specifically generational in Jonas's community: life assignments after childhood (the Ceremony of Twelve) determine the degree of power and knowledge an individual can access. Both adulthood and childhood are monitored and shaped by the Committee of Elders. In the process of imposing "sameness," the body is chemically denaturalized: once puberty occurs, all citizens must take "the treatment for Stirrings"—pills which must be taken for "all of your adult life" (Lowry, *The Giver*, 48, 49). Jonas has heard of the pills, but they fall "into that uncomfortable category of 'being different.'... Always better... to talk about things that were the same" (Lowry, *The Giver*, 48). Jonas, however, "liked the feelings" and wants "to feel the Stirrings again" (Lowry, *The Giver*, 49). This desire will be permitted as part of his assignment of Receiver. It is linked with his ability to see color (not part of "sameness") and receive/transmit memories.

Jonas occupies a unique space in a community shaped by the concept of homogeneity. It is, to some degree, a space of privilege, but it comes at a horrific price. To ensure the peaceful function of the community, Jonas must hold all the memories—the good, the bad, and the ugly; he experiences the physical, psychological, and emotional aspects of what were once communal memories. The burden of knowledge extends to Jonas's discovery that the seemingly benign "release" to "Elsewhere" of the elderly, the smaller of a set of twins, and those who cannot abide by the community's rules is in fact murder. Witnessing his father "releasing" a baby, Jonas connects it to the memory of a soldier dying: "*He killed it! My father killed it!* Jonas said to himself, stunned at what he was realizing" (Lowry, *The Giver*, 188). Intensifying the horror, his father uses "the special voice he uses with Gabriel," saying "Bye-bye little guy" as he puts the dead baby in the trash chute (Lowry, *The Giver*, 185, 188). As painful as witnessing his father's act of infanticide is, it does empower Jonas. The catalyst for his flight from the community is his father's announcement that he has voted for Gabriel's release: "It's bye-bye for you, Gabe, in the morning" (Lowry, *The Giver*, 207). Desperate to prevent the baby's death, Jonas improvises an escape plan that ultimately saves them both: by the end of the series, they will achieve genuine homes and loving families.

The desperate quest to preserve his life begins with an expulsion from what Connor once found to be a genuine home and loving family. The frustration of dealing with teenage angst or the angry-young-man syndrome, and the highly publicized, widely accepted "solution" of unwinding, offers an easy out for his parents. As a practice, personal space does not exist for teenagers like Connor; the public—parents, society, and the government—have laid claim to the most personal space of all: their bodies. "Borders, in whatever form they may take," observe Decker and Winchock, "are always political" (2). Ideology seemingly overwhelms individuality in this society; there is no overt policy of "sameness," but there is an implicit code of appropriate behavior: Don't annoy the adults! The initial act of running away is thus a personal political choice—an instinctive refusal to recognize the "legitimacy" of the public decree.

Connor's experiences while on the run will inadvertently become political on a public platform. Labeled the "Akron AWOL," he becomes a symbol of resistance and the stuff of urban legend. Stories of his exploits circulate widely, the antics exceeding his actual actions. It can be construed as another act of appropriation—Connor has no control over his story—but he recognizes the space of hope the myth creates. Apprehended and taken to the "Happy Jack Harvest Camp" to be unwound, Connor, "hobbled by leg shackles, constricted by handcuffs," with "armed Juvey-cops . . . on either side, in front of and behind him," is "publicly humbled for all to see" (Shusterman, *Unwind* 266). The intent is to render him a spectacle of powerlessness—his bound body a message to all the teens in the camp. The result is spectacularly different: "The staff's own announcement that they've taken down the Akron AWOL does not deflate the spirits of the Unwinds there. Instead, it takes a boy who was only a rumor and turns him into a legend" (Shusterman, *Unwind* 266, 267). What was simply a story offering vicarious resistance is transformed into a tangible symbol; it opens a new space in the harvest camp: the space of hope.

Despite his efforts to deflate the stories circulating about him, Connor discovers "it's no use—no amount of downplaying the story can convince the others that the Akron AWOL is not some larger-than-life action figure" (Shusterman, *Unwind* 270). The legend fulfills a need, fills a void, for the other Unwinds. Connor recognizes its symbolic value as he is being taken to be unwound:

"Hands off me, I'll walk by myself," he orders the guards, and they instantly release him, perhaps surprised by the authority in his voice.

> He . . . strides forward. . . . He decides that he will neither run nor dawdle. He will neither quiver nor fight. . . . And in a few weeks from now, someone, somewhere, will hold in their mind the memory that this young man . . . faced his unwinding with dignity and pride. (Shusterman, *Unwind* 304)

At this point Connor is trying to store the memory for the "someone" who will receive his body parts. It is an attempt to rewrite the narrative of his personal ending: a moment not of fear and defeat but of "dignity and pride." The significance of his performance is not lost on the other Unwinds. Defying their guards, "this volatile gathering of kids" "just stand there—maybe they can't stop this, but they can witness it. They can be there as Connor strides out of this life" (Shusterman, *Unwind* 307). They, like Connor, claim the only power they can: the power to redefine the events they cannot otherwise alter. The repetition of "strides"—a more defiant term in this context than "walks"—suggests that his audience appreciates the significance of Connor's internal choice—his final act of self-determination.

Self-determination in its strictest sense—choice without coercion or compulsion—is not achievable for Connor or Jonas. They do not create the conditions that shape their survival strategies, but they do choose how to respond to those conditions. Jonas abandons the original plan he formulated with the Giver out of necessity. Determined to save Gabriel, he devises a desperate escape plan focused on getting to "Elsewhere" in the hope that it will mean freedom. Connor's "plan" to thwart destruction is even more dangerous. He concedes that he cannot avoid being unwound but sets in motion a plan to reunify his parts: "Connor honestly didn't have much faith in it, because it had too many moving parts. Far too many things could go wrong" (Shusterman, *Undivided* 337). The plan requires switching labels on body parts and all of the body parts being purchased in a black-market auction by the Admiral. The possibility of success is further undermined by the fact that "even if all that came together, there was no telling if Connor would. No one had ever tried to physically reassemble an Unwind from his own parts" (Shusterman, *Undivided* 337–38). The pursuit of "autonomy" for Connor is literally played out on (and in) the space of the body.

DEFENDING THE DOORWAY: AMELIORATING THE HOME

Self-determination is a precarious process for both Connor and Jonas; the "worlds" they live in are constructed in such a way as to negate the very possibility of self-interested actions. They need to recognize that they actually inhabit a much wider world *and* be prepared to protect the space of possibility it opens up. It is akin to the "defence in the doorway," theorized by Jane Suzanne Carroll. Carroll explores "one of the great narrative set-pieces in English literature"—the defense in the doorway—which occurs "when the boundaries of sacred spaces are threatened, transcended, or transgressed" (22). The family home proves indefensible on a number of levels, for a variety of reasons. Focus shifts to a defense of a different space: the bodies of Gabriel and Connor are substituted for the "sacred, enclosed, demarcated space of the hall or the house" identified by Carroll (22). Initially, Connor and Jonas can only resort to flight: they must escape in order to protect "sacred [bodily] spaces" that are in danger of being "transgressed." In time, however, each character will be more proactive in his resistance to the attacks on the spaces he holds sacred. Paradoxically, physical threats reinforce the importance of the individual body in both series; the probability of annihilation leads to a sharpened awareness of the value, if not sanctity, of the most primal of personal spaces: the body.

In its initial iteration, survival is a practical problem for Jonas and Connor. Basic human needs—protection from the elements, escape from predators and the search for sustenance—drive their quests for shelter. Once these essential requirements are fulfilled, each character can refine his goal: more than a dwelling, each is seeking a home that affords not only a place of safety but a space in which he can thrive. They are desperately in need of a place of connection and a connection to place. The structure is not as significant as the experience. Home, Holly Youngbear-Tibbets proposes, "is a created place, secured not by nativity, entitlement, or endowment but by the continual and careful creation and recreation of ties to place" (36). Home is a process. It can act as a buffer between the individual and a hostile environment, but it must be sustained. Creating some type of home, rather than merely discovering one, is crucial to physical and psychological survival. Jonas and Connor must look beyond their past definition of what constitutes a home. The process requires creativity and tenacity (and a little bit of luck!).

Jonas's frantic flight from his community is left in suspension at the end of *The Giver*. "Using his final strength, and a special knowledge that was deep inside him," Jonas struggles to control the sled "that seemed to lead to the final destination, the place that he had always felt was waiting, the Elsewhere that held their future and their past" (Lowry, *The Giver* 224). "Seemed" and "felt" open a space for uncertainty, if not outright doubt; "Elsewhere" is a vague and paradoxical place containing "their future and their past." Jonas is certain "that below, ahead, they were waiting for him; and that they were waiting, too, for the baby" (Lowry, *The Giver* 225). The reader may be less certain. Readers are given the space for two distinct options: Jonas and Gabriel perish in the elements, or the miraculously appearing sled carries them to a place of warmth and music. The third book in the quartet resolves that tension: Jonas and Gabriel do indeed find a genuine community. In time, each of the boys will play an integral role in the defense of that community.

Despite his youth Jonas becomes "Leader," chosen by "the people he loved . . . to rule and guard them" (Lowry, *Messenger* 20). He embraces the community that embraced him in his time of need. It is an emotional connection that moves beyond gratitude to a deeper bond. Welcomed into the community, Jonas in turn essentially welcomes the community into himself. It becomes intimately connected to his identity. Nostalgia is not a burden he carries: "He had never tried to go back, never wanted to. This was his home now, these his people" (Lowry, *Messenger* 21). While this response could be construed as a logical reaction to a hostile environment, the arrival of "huge wooden crates . . . each one filled with books" suggests to Jonas that his prior community is undergoing a positive change. The books strike him as "a kind of forgiveness" that sets him free and signals that "they were rebuilding themselves into something better" (Lowry, *Messenger* 33). What was chance becomes choice: Jonas blindly ran "Elsewhere," but he chooses to remain *somewhere*—in his newfound home. Jonas focuses not on what was lost but on what is found and then fostered.

Unlike Jonas, Connor must maintain constant vigilance. He *is* being actively pursued and experiences greater difficulty in finding a protective, welcoming community. A modern version of the Underground Railroad does lead Connor to a haven perversely named the Graveyard (where decommissioned airplanes house Unwinds eager to avoid a similar fate); here he encounters the formidable Admiral. This soon-to-be surrogate father proclaims: "This will be your home until you turn eighteen or we procure a permanent sponsor willing to falsify your identification. Make no mistake about it: What we do here is highly illegal, but that doesn't mean we don't follow the rule of law. *My* law" (Shusterman, *Unwind* 181). The paternalistic approach is particularly necessary here given the circumstances. Hunted and haunted, the desperate teenagers need to be comforted *and* contained. The community is a decidedly different one from the village Jonas inhabits. It is nonetheless a community, asserts the Admiral: "We are a community here. You will learn the rules and you will follow them, or you will face the consequences as in any society. This is not a democracy; it is a dictatorship. I am your dictator. This is a matter of necessity. It is the most effective way to keep you hidden, healthy, and whole" (Shusterman, *Unwind* 182). Connected by the shared goal of survival—arguably the basic purpose of any community—the occupants of the Graveyard are expected to adhere to common rules. It is an unapologetically authoritarian home. Vulnerable to intrusions from the larger society, the "legitimacy" and "autonomy" of this community are tentative at best. The Admiral's approach is to outlast: Unwinds regain their legal status at age eighteen and can return to mainstream society. Community, in this context, is temporary.

By the end of the novel, there will be both new leadership and a more nuanced policy; the Admiral yields his position to Connor. Addressing the new arrivals, Connor is both welcoming and inspiring:

> "You're all here because you were marked for unwinding but managed to escape, and, thanks to the efforts of many people, you've found your way here. This will be your home until you turn seventeen and become a legal adult. That's the good news. The bad news is that they know all about us. . . . They let us stay because they don't see us as a threat." And then Connor smiles. "Well, we're going to change that." (Shusterman, *Unwind* 332)

Like the Admiral, Connor identifies the Graveyard as a temporary home, but unlike the Admiral, Connor speaks from the experience of being an Unwind. He expresses gratitude to those who aid the fugitives, and he opens a space for activism. He offers them a choice: "Some of you have been through enough and just want to survive until seventeen.[4] . . . I don't blame you. But I know that some of you are ready to risk everything to end unwinding once and for all" (Shusterman, *Unwind* 335). For those who are willing, what Connor is calling for is a revolution: "We'll infiltrate harvest camps and unite Unwinds across the country. We'll free kids . . . before they even arrive. We will have a voice, and we will use it. We will make ourselves heard" (335). Rather than imposing (self-defensive) passivity on its inhabitants, Connor's version of the Graveyard opens a space for action. The spirit of community with its emphasis on collective responsibility, fostered by the Admiral, is extended to the larger "community" of Unwinds. The space of the Graveyard is not changed, but it is driven by a different motivation: collective responsibility under Connor's guidance becomes proactive, not reactive.

Connor seemingly recognizes that in order to fulfill a potentially nurturing and life-affirming function, the home must be approached as a process rather than as a structure. Home as a self-contained space is neither possible nor desirable in Connor's world. Closed borders may appear to offer security, but there is a danger of protection shifting to imprisonment. Stasis has the potential to be psychologically crippling. Connor taps into a different potential found in the home: its political potential. Marginalized by their society, the renegade Unwinds have been discounted, discredited, and disempowered. Life on the margin is clearly a precarious state, but it can also be empowering. It can be a space of resistance, contends bell hooks, in which "we are transformed . . . we make radical creative space which affirms and sustains our subjectivity" ("Choosing the Margin" 209). Operating within the margins, the Unwinds assert the subjectivity denied to them by the mainstream community. Hideout becomes headquarters; victims become activists.

Threats to subjectivity take a decidedly different form in *The Giver* quartet, but Jonas must also transform the margin into a space of resistance to ensure the continued existence of the home he loves. The roots of the community itself are found in the margin. It begins as "a gathering of outcasts. Fleeing battles or chaos of all kinds . . . each of the original settlers . . . made his way to this place. They . . . found strength in one another, . . . formed a community" (Lowry, *Son* 290). Displaced and downtrodden, the initial inhabitants recognize the value of a sanctuary open to all who need it. Nurturing and life-affirming, the village is a space of healing. In the final novel, however, there is a danger of complacency obscuring a lurking threat to that tranquility: Trademaster, an evil entity, has returned determined to corrupt the community.

The task of confronting, and vanquishing, Trademaster will be shouldered by Gabriel, but Jonas's role as Leader has required overcoming what is arguably a more insidious "evil"—basic human jealousy and possessiveness: "from time to time, as the years passed, people muttered that they shouldn't let newcomers in; the village was becoming crowded, and it was hard, sometimes, for the newcomers to learn the customs and rules. There were arguments and petitions and debates" (Lowry, *Son* 290). The threat is muted—particularly when compared with the threats Connor faces—but hardly insignificant. It pivots on the question of what the community represents. The attempt to redefine its boundaries—rigid, not porous; closed, not open—is an attempt to alter the very identity of the community. Diplomacy is Jonas's weapon: "Gently but firmly [he] reminded the villagers that they had all been outsiders once. They had all come here for a new life. Eventually they had voted to remain what they had become: a sanctuary, a place of welcome" (Lowry, *Son* 290). He appeals not only to their reason but to their emotion, convincing the inhabitants to keep the community a compassionate space. In so doing Jonas maintains the "radical political dimension" of the home bell hooks identifies ("Homeplace" 42). hooks's specific focus is on the importance of the home in the African American community, but her argument is applicable to Jonas's emphasis on the home as "the site where one could resist" (42). Resistance takes the form of being "affirmed in . . . minds and hearts" (42). Insistence on the dignity of all is a political act; in defending his vision of the community, Jonas takes a clear political stance.

Connor's family home is not a "sanctuary" or "place of welcome," *because of* political acts. Government policies do not remain outside the house. In fact, they have become instrumental in how that house functions. Despite the dangers associated with the dwelling, Connor cannot resist the pull of the space and what it represents. He is compelled to return and hand-deliver the letter he wrote to his family while on the run: "He wonders if they'll invite him in, and if they do, will he accept?" (Shusterman, *UnDivided* 232). He both desires and fears the prospect. His parents' betrayal evokes a healthy sense of caution, but Connor has forgotten the external dangers that lurk in the shadows. He is captured outside the home by a bounty hunter who anticipated the irresistible appeal of "coming home." The desire for home renders Connor vulnerable at this point, but it proves to be a hard habit to break.

Captured, unwound, and rewound, Connor nonetheless invokes "homey" imagery when attempting to articulate his feelings when he emerges from a medically induced coma. There is a disconnect between Connor's thoughts and his speech; he resorts to symbolism to communicate: "'Fireplace,' he says. 'Cocoa. Blanket.' 'Are you cold?' 'No,' he says, happy to have found the right word. It inspires him to hack through the thicket to find more words. 'I'm warm. Safe. Grateful'" (Shusterman, *UnDivided* 339). The conversation echoes his earlier memory of being comforted by his parents in which "his whole being flowed into the . . . cup, and his parents placed it gently on the table, close enough to the fire to keep it warm forever and always" (Shusterman, *Unwind* 16–17). The fact that the initial memory is promptly followed by his father exposing him to the Juvey-cops does not negate Connor's need for a sense of safety, comfort, and love. He has, momentarily, gratified this desire through the makeshift but loyal "family" in the hospital with him: the Admiral and Risa. In their company Connor *is* home.

The final moments of the dystology raise the specter of the family home again. His parents and younger brother appear at the massive rally Connor is headlining to force the government to revoke unwinding. The crowd quickly becomes a violent mob upon recognizing them. Connor instinctively chooses to save them:

> He throws his arms around both his mother and his father and holds them with all the strength he has. Lucas, pulled in by their gravity, joins them in this odd and awkward familial embrace, and for Connor

it's as if the crowd and the police and the world have gone away. But he knows they haven't. They're all there, waiting to see how this hair-trigger reunion will end. (Shusterman, *UnDivided* 371)

The tension is defused by this scene of reconciliation. Connor is clear that it is a performance with a purpose—"I'm doing this to save your lives"—but his response to his brother opens up the possibility of a new space: "'Can we go home now?' Lucas asks. 'Soon,' Connor tells him gently. 'Very soon'" (Shusterman, *UnDivided* 372). It is a protective gesture that transitions into deeper emotional territory. It is clear that there is a great deal of healing to be done, but Connor does not dismiss the idea of a home. The final image of the dystology is of "Connor Lassiter hold[ing] his family like he'll never let them go" (372). It is a symbolic homecoming.

Connor does not establish a new home or transform his old one in terms of home as structure, but home as process is a different story. As the reader leaves him, Connor is in the process of reestablishing a connection with his family of origin and his community. Connor's defense of the home is more abstract than that of Jonas (who has a physical home and community at stake), and yet both characters are insisting on the right to define their homes as part of that defense. Both transform the margin into a space of resistance in order to ensure their continued existence. Evil, in the form of the Trademaster and the baser self-interest of some inhabitants, stalks the village in *The Giver* quartet; a collective effort and insistence on the power of love and hope are required to defeat it. Evil takes a political and scientific form in the *Unwind* dystology; again, a collective effort and insistence on the redemptive power of love and hope will be required to defeat it.[5]

WORKS IN PERPETUAL PROGRESS: RECONCEPTUALIZING THE FAMILY

The nuclear family as the model family is so entrenched in children's literature as to seem inevitable. Mother, father, children bound together in a domestic circle of mutual love and concern—a sanctuary from the world's pressures and dangers. Protection is found in both the physical structure and the familial structure. Christensen and O'Brien recognize this potentiality, observing that "home can become a haven where parents can ensure their . . . [children] are safe and protected, provided with comfort and care, and safeguarded in their health and well-being" (5). In this scenario dwelling and occupants "work" in harmony in the best interests of the child. There is also the potential for disharmony, acknowledge Christensen and O'Brien: "These images are untrue when . . . risk from the outside world can be recognised as exaggerated and the home is revealed as the primary context for the abuse to children" (5). For Jonas and Connor, the risk is both within and outside the home and family. The ideal is critiqued in both series; outside forces and conflicts complicate the experience of the nuclear family. Ultimately, however, the ideal is modified rather than outright rejected. Jonas's and Connor's struggles for survival are mitigated by the formation of alternative families, but both characters remain associated with the nuclear family.

The Giver quartet covers a longer span of time than the *Unwind* dystology, in which the events transpire in two years. Jonas is thirteen when he flees with Gabriel; by the end of the collective narrative, he is a grown man with a wife and two children. In fact, he has "relinquished leadership to others so that he could take up an unburdened life with his family" (Lowry, *Son* 279). Readers are given a brief glimpse of Jonas interacting with his children as he "kissed their sweaty little necks and called night-night affectionately" (Lowry, *Son* 335). Jonas is firmly established as a "family man" at this point, but there are signs of his protective, if not paternal, instinct much earlier. The child Jonas volunteers to care for Gabriel at night. "I know how to feed and comfort him, and it would let you and Father get some sleep," he tells his mother (Lowry, *The Giver* 145). The concern is directed toward his own family, but it will become more focused on Gabriel. Patting the restless baby's back as a comforting gesture, Jonas unconsciously transfers a soothing memory to Gabriel; when they subsequently battle the elements and physical pain, it will be a conscious choice. Disheartened, Jonas "wept because he was afraid . . . that he could not save Gabriel. He no longer cared for himself" (Lowry, *The Giver* 218). He summons a memory of sunshine; "for a fleeting second he felt that he wanted to keep it for himself. . . . But the moment passed and was followed by an urge, a need, a passionate yearning to share the warmth with the one person left for him to love" (Lowry, *The Giver* 221). Protection takes the form of self-sacrifice. In his mind, Jonas's suffering is inconsequential in comparison to that of Gabriel. His instinct is outward; his response is driven by emotion.

Connor displays a similar protective impulse driven by emotion, not reason. As is the case with Jonas, Connor's reaction to the plight of a baby puts him in greater danger. He overhears a boy inform his mother, "We've been storked again," and "going against all sense of self-preservation, Connor bolts straight for the porch" (Shusterman, *Unwind* 62). The addition of a baby is a complication that endangers not just Connor but his companions (Risa and Lev). It is linked to a similar experience when Connor was seven and *he* informed his mother, "We got storked again" (Shusterman, *Unwind* 74). "Again" is not quite accurate: the baby "had been passed around the neighborhood for two whole weeks," including by Connor's parents. Connor is witness to the baby's death. It is buried as "Baby Lassiter," and Connor realizes that the people crying at the funeral "were the ones, just like my parents, who had a hand in killing it" (Shusterman, *Unwind* 75). It is an early lesson in the inhumanity of which humanity is capable. It is also a key moment in his development of his own sense of morality. Waiting in a temporary safe house, Connor holds the sleeping baby, "and right now, in this place and at this moment, there's something so comforting about holding it in his arms, he's thankful he saved it" (Shusterman, *Unwind* 112). The use of "it" undercuts but does not negate the paternal image. Reckless as the action is, it is crucial to Connor's sense of self in a society that has legally stripped him of his selfhood.

Jonas experiences a similar struggle to assert his selfhood in a community engineered to eradicate individuality. Significantly, this process hinges upon Jonas looking beyond the boundaries of the self. The adult Jonas laments the fact that "Gabriel—a toddler with no past, a child who deserved a future" had "no one" but him (Lowry, *Son* 279). He explains to his wife: "I was a boy. I couldn't be a parent to him. I didn't know what that meant. The people who raised me did their best, but it was a job to them" (279). Jonas focuses on absence: what he wasn't, what he didn't know—a negative reflection of his self. His age and lack of being properly parented, in Jonas's eyes, negate his "paternity," but from Gabriel's perspective, he is "the closest thing he had to a father" (Lowry, *Son* 332). The boy's quest is to find his mother; his father (figure) has always been with him.

Aside from saving Gabriel's life and bringing him to a place of safety, there is a strong indication that Jonas has helped (if not saved) his former community. Each of these actions is possible only because of the alternative family Jonas forms with the Giver; it counters the failings of his given family. One of the memories Jonas receives is of an extended family celebrating Christmas; it is his first lesson in love. He wishes "we could be that way, and that" the Giver could be his grandparent (Lowry, *The Giver* 158). The family in the space of memory feels "a little more complete" to Jonas, and he tries to access it in the space of reality (158). The question "Do you love me?" prompts a lesson in "precision of language" from his parents:

> "Your father means that you used a very generalized word, so meaningless that it's become almost obsolete," his mother explained carefully.... "You could ask, Do you enjoy me? The answer is Yes," his

mother said. "Or," his father suggested, "Do you take pride in my accomplishments? And the answer is wholeheartedly Yes." "Do you understand why it's inappropriate to use a word like love?" . . . Jonas nodded. "Yes, thank you, I do." . . . It was his first lie to his parents. (Lowry, *The Giver* 159–60)

They focus on the rational use (or to be precise, nonuse!) of the word. Jonas focuses on the emotional connection represented by the word. This bittersweet connection is found in his relationship with the Giver, who tells him, "I love you, Jonas," just as they must part. "Your role now is to escape. And my role is to stay" (Lowry, *The Giver* 202). For the sake of the community, to give its occupants a chance at true selfhood, Jonas must go alone. In response to his plea to accompany him, the Giver reminds Jonas, "If I go with you, and together we take away *all* their protection from the memories . . . the community will be . . . thrown into chaos" (Lowry, *The Giver* 195–96). Jonas weakly protests, "You and I don't need to *care* abut the rest of them," but concedes that "of course they needed to care. It was the meaning of everything" (Lowry, *The Giver* 196). The concept of love is revealed to Jonas through the transfer of memories, but the importance of love is reinforced by the Giver's compassion and concern, not just for Jonas but for their community.

Connor's lesson in the necessity of looking beyond his own needs and desires comes from a more cantankerous father figure than the Giver. The Admiral is a no-nonsense man who articulates his affection and concern through his actions. He appears in Connor's times of need offering sound advice and whatever protection he can. The Admiral has a particular gift for defusing Connor's self-destructive anger—"Connor has to laugh. Leave it to the Admiral to make sense of the senseless" (Shusterman, *UnWholly* 247). More importantly, he has the ability to redirect that anger into positive actions. Telling Connor, "You must educate yourself," and to "man up, get the hell out of my limo, and save these kids' lives" is precisely the pep talk Connor needs (Shusterman, *UnWholly* 248, 249). He is supportive but will not coddle Connor; the Admiral demands that Connor act on behalf of his community.

The threats to Connor's community—the policy of unwinding in particular—shape that community. While individual adults are a crucial part of the resistance movement, it is largely composed of teenagers. Communities of necessity become communities of choice as Connor moves from being merely reactive to being proactive. He leads a community of resistance determined to change the system that persecutes them. "For *mature* self-identity," argues Marilyn Friedman, "we should . . . recognize a legitimate role for *communities of choice*, supplementing, if not displacing, the communities and attachments that are merely found" (92). Defense from, defiance of, an oppressive mainstream society for Connor and Jonas hinges upon discovering likeminded, supportive allies. In the period of crisis, both characters must reject their nuclear families as a self-defensive response to circumstances beyond their control. Communities of choice enable them to confront and alter those circumstances. Initially, it appears to be a case of the new community displacing the original, familial one. By the end of the narratives, however, the nuclear family will have a resurgence.

Just as the home is both structure and process, so too is the family both an identifiable unit and a series of processes. There are boundaries to the space of the family demarcating those who are members from those who are nonmembers, and establishing the nature of the relationships between members. For both Jonas and Connor, incursions by those in power have denaturalized their familial relationships. In the case of Jonas, the denaturalization is almost literal: in the interest of "sameness," all babies are socially engineered and then assigned to "parents." He struggles to explain their "origins" to a nine-year-old Gabriel. "'Why did my parents let you take me?' he had asked. 'You didn't have parents,' Jonas had explained. 'Everybody has parents!' 'Not in the place where we lived. Things were different there'" (Lowry, *Son* 273). Recalling that there were "birthmothers," Jonas fuels Gabriel's desire to find his family. Five years later, the prospect prompts Jonas's concern; as he explains to his wife, "'I worry about what he'll find, if he goes searching.... He wants a family, and there won't be one. He was a—' Frowning, he searched for the right description. 'He was a manufactured product,' he said at last. 'We all were'" (Lowry, *Son* 280). The community's insistence on order and logic demands the eradication of the disorder and emotion it distrusts and fears.

A different kind of social engineering distorts the family in Connor's society: the unwinding procedure alters adolescence from a time of self-discovery by testing and stretching boundaries to a period of heightened anxiety and fear for actual survival. The law seemingly empowers the parents, granting them the absolute authority over their children. In fact, the law undermines parental authority by shifting responsibility for family relationships first to their children—meet expectations or be dismembered—and then to the government—discipline our child as you see fit. Rescuing a boy from being unwound, Connor makes the parents document their motivations: "'Disrespect and disobedience.' Those are always the first reasons. If every parent unwound a kid due to disrespect, the human race would go extinct in a single generation" (Shusterman, *UnWholly* 75). The confrontation drives home the fact that unwinding is an abdication of responsibility, exercised in an impulsive act:

> "We were desperate," says the mother with a high quotient of self-righteousness. "Everyone told us that unwinding was the best thing to do. Everyone." . . . "So, in other words you decided to unwind your son because of peer pressure?" Finally the two of them crumble, feeling the appropriate weight of shame. The father . . . suddenly bursts into tears. It's the mother who holds it together enough to offer Connor one last excuse. "We tried to be good parents . . . but there's a point at which you give up trying." "No, there's not," Connor tells her. (Shusterman, *UnWholly* 76)

The act of betrayal is socially sanctioned and widely encouraged. The problem is not the family alone. Liberating individual children is not a strategy that will overturn unwinding; for that, the counterattack will need to be multifaceted. It will also require a revitalized family that focuses less on the power to include or exclude and more on the intimate space of the family—mothering and fathering versus motherhood and fatherhood, action rather than institution.

Significantly, Connor does not confront his own family, but he does write them a letter while in a safe house. It is done at the insistence of Sonia—the price everyone she helps must pay. The act, but not the actual letter, will be crucial to the dismantling of unwinding. Connor's letter is lost, but others do reach their intended recipients: "Of the various people touched by the 1411 letters . . . more than a thousand find reading the words of their lost son or daughter to be a life-changing event. In a population of hundreds of millions, such a small number . . . is a mere drop in the bucket . . . but enough drops can make any bucket overflow" (Shusterman, *UnDivided* 300). The "reconnection" of parent and child happens on an individual level, but it sparks a national conversation. The voices in the letters are a key element in the grassroots movement. Connor's personal refusal to allow himself to be sacrificed sets in motion various forms of resistance—liberation raids, acts of violence, political and social campaigns denouncing unwinding, the discovery of alternative medical technology—but the crucial one is the re-empowerment of the family.

Speaking at the rally on the capitol steps, Connor recognizes that it is "the galvanizing of millions—not to wage acts of violence or revenge, but to hold their ground against the institutionalized murder that has defined a generation" (Shusterman, *UnDivided* 369). In the midst of this political rally, he also recognizes his family: "They came to the rally. They didn't even know he'd be here, but they still came!" (Shusterman, *UnDivided* 370). This spark of hope is threatened by the angry mob. Tensions are high, and Connor must decide in a split second if he will ameliorate the family—the family who betrayed him; as mentioned earlier, he tells his father he is hugging them to save their lives. On one level, it is a pragmatic response, but "he knows it's more than that. It is as if his embrace can rewind them—not into the family they once were, but into the one they may still have a chance to be.... They will have to fight for his forgiveness. They will have to earn it. But if they survive today, there will be time for that" (Shusterman, *UnDivided* 372). He is cautiously optimistic and clearly still values the family despite the pain it has inflicted. Tensions around the family are not resolved, but the final tableau is a striking image of a unified family (372). It opens a space of possibility; a space for love, compassion, forgiveness, and growth.[6] It is a family in process.

The village affords Jonas a similar emotional buffer from a threatening world. It is clearly a sanctuary associated with family. Sliding down the hill toward "places where families created and kept memories, where they celebrated love," Jonas "was aware with certainty and joy that . . . they were waiting for him . . . and . . . the baby" (Lowry, *The Giver* 225). It is all that his old community was not: rich in memory and emotion, and welcoming of newcomers. While this is an accurate comparison, Jonas does draw strength from his past. In his agony "he began to recall happy times. He remembered his parents and his sister. He remembered his friends, Asher and Fiona. He remembered the Giver. Memories of joy flooded through him" (Lowry, *The Giver* 223). It is a credit to Jonas's emotional complexity that he can give what he has not received (except from the Giver): love. Speaking with his wife, Jonas recalls his parents' inability to articulate love: "'They didn't know what that meant. They said the word was meaningless.' 'They did their best,' Kira said, after a moment, and he nodded" (Lowry, *Son* 280). It is a small but significant gesture. He does not fault them for what they did not know and therefore could not give. Acceptance of his past frees Jonas from its negative aspects, but his present is threatened by an evil presence.

Unlike Connor's situation, where collective action is required, Jonas's problem can be resolved only by an individual's action. The boy he was willing to sacrifice himself for must shoulder this burden. Gabriel begs Jonas to come with him, but Jonas must refuse: "Years ago, Gabe, when I took you and ran away, there was a man I loved and left behind. I wanted him to come with me but he said no. He was right to refuse. It was my journey and I had to do it without help. I had to find my own strengths, face my own fears. And now you must" (Lowry, *Son* 367). It is a rite of passage that must be faced alone. Love is empowerment; the protective impulse must yield to self-governance. As the Admiral encouraged Connor to believe in himself—"We are all tested in this life.... The measure of a man is not how much he suffers in the test, but how he comes out at the end" (Shusterman, *UnWholly* 248)—so does Jonas encourage Gabriel to have faith in his abilities. Gabriel is fearful but determined as he approaches Trademaster. Again, in a time of need, strength is drawn from the connection to loved ones; "armed" with his paddle carved with the names of his friends and Jonas, Gabriel mentally adds Kira, Matthew, and Annabelle, and "finally he said his mother's name—Claire—aloud, adding it to the list of those who cared about him" (Lowry, *Son* 372). Gabriel is a solitary figure defending his community, but he is not alone in the struggle. At the pivotal moment in the confrontation, Gabriel tightens his grip on the paddle and

> felt the place where the name Jonas had been carved. The ... paddle was infused with all of them: the ones who cared about him, the ones who at this moment were sending strength to him.... He suddenly felt something unfamiliar beneath his fingers.... He felt the rounded curve of a *C*. An *L*. And then the four letters that followed. (Lowry, *Son* 385–86)

Love, *familial* love, ultimately empowers Gabriel to defeat Trademaster. The addition of his mother's name to the paddle expands the masculine community symbolized by the names of his friends and father figure. The appearance of Claire's name inserts a maternal space on the paddle and in Gabriel's life.[7] As for Jonas (and Connor), it is the experience of an alternative family that enables Gabriel to overcome a threat to self and his community of choice.

INCONCLUSIVE CONCLUSIONS: EXPANDING THE SPACE OF THE FAMILY

Images of the family in process dominate the final moments of *The Giver* quartet and the *Unwind* dystology: Claire tells Jonas she sees her son approaching, and Connor clings to his parents and brother. Biological connections seem to dominate—Jonas is in the background, Risa is on the stage above Connor; neither the Giver nor the Admiral is referenced—but the alternative families cannot be discounted. They have served vital functions when the biological family could not. The communities of choice that Jonas and Connor form counter the vulnerability imposed upon them by their original families. They open a space for forgiveness, for renewal and acceptance of the initial family.

Lowry and Shusterman critique but do not reject a conservative model of the family and the family home. Child characters must flee but never leave behind the desire for a "return" to home. Ann Alston argues that this is true of children's literature in general:

> The texts may question behaviour, but they cannot stray into the realm of parents and children not loving each other, for this I contend is too radical: it would break the traditions of family as represented in children's literature, for this literature, despite its apparent changes is inherently conservative. (63)

Whether or not it is possible to break from the "traditions of family" is beyond my discussion, but it is clear that neither Lowry nor Shusterman chooses to do so. They toy with the possibility but ultimately reinforce the tradition. The boundaries are pushed, but that border is not crossed. Readers leave the newly connected families on the edge of possibility—Lowry and Shusterman do not depict what happens next.

Notes

1. As the Introduction to this book indicates, nature and school are also strongly associated with childhood. Home, with its expectations of protection and nurturance, however, trumps the other two as the most "appropriate" space for children.
2. While the characters do not expressly articulate these strategies, their flights from harm implicitly entail a quest for a space of safety—not just a movement *away from* danger but a *desire for* a sanctuary. Significantly, the pursuit of that desire extends beyond personal safety, ultimately incorporating communal salvation.
3. This chapter focuses on the experiences of Jonas and Connor, rather than the larger group of characters found in each series. The focus is on the overall narrative, and as a result the individual texts do not receive equal attention.
4. The age has been lowered from eighteen to seventeen.
5. Unwinding is not abolished, but all signs point to it happening.
6. Connor's letter supports this optimistic reading: it starts in anger, moves to revenge, but ends in love (*Unwind*, 109–10).
7. As does the inclusion of Kira's name.

Works Cited

Alston, Ann. *The Family in English Children's Literature*. New York: Routledge, 2008.
Carroll, Jane Suzanne. *Landscape in Children's Literature*. London: Routledge, 2011.

Christensen, Pia, and Margaret O'Brien. "Children in the City: Introducing New Perspectives." Ed. Christensen and O'Brien, *Children in the City: Home, Neighborhood and Community*. New York: Routledge, 2003. 1–12.

Decker, Jessica Elbert, and Dylan Winchock. "Introduction: Borderlands and Liminality across Philosophy and Literature." Ed. Decker and Winchock. *Borderlands and Liminal Subjects: Transgressing the Limits in Philosophy and Literature*. New York: Palgrave Macmillan, 2017. 1–18.

Friedman, Marilyn. "Feminism and Modern Friendship: Dislocating the Community." Ed. Eva Browning Cole and Susan Coultrap-McQuinn. *Explorations in Feminist Ethics: Theory and Practice*. Bloomington: Indiana UP, 1992. 89–97.

hooks, bell. "Choosing the Margin as a Space of Radical Openness." Ed. Jane Rendell, Barbara Penner, and Iain Borden. *Gender, Space, Architecture: An Interdisciplinary Introduction*. New York: Routledge, 2000. 203–9.

hooks, bell. "Homeplace: A Site of Resistance." *Yearning: Race, Gender, and Cultural Politics*. Toronto: Between the Lines, 1992. 41–49.

Lowry, Lois. *Gathering Blue*. New York: Houghton Mifflin Harcourt, 2000.

Lowry, Lois. *The Giver*. New York: Houghton Mifflin Harcourt, 1993.

Lowry, Lois. *Messenger*. New York: Houghton Mifflin Harcourt, 2004.

Lowry, Lois. *Son*. New York: Houghton Mifflin Harcourt, 2012.

Menozzi, Filippo. "Ethics at the Border: Transmitting Migrant Experiences." Ed. Jessica Elbert Decker and Dylan Winchock. *Borderlands and Liminal Subjects: Transgressing the Limits in Philosophy and Literature*. New York: Palgrave Macmillan, 2017. 21–40.

Reimer, Mavis. *Home Words: Discourses of Children's Literature in Canada*. Waterloo, ON: Wilfrid Laurier UP, 2008.

Shusterman, Neal. *UnDivided*. New York: Simon and Schuster, 2014.

Shusterman, Neal. *UnSouled*. New York: Simon and Schuster, 2013.

Shusterman, Neal. *UnWholly*. New York: Simon and Schuster, 2012.

Shusterman, Neal. *Unwind*. New York: Simon and Schuster, 2007.

Stott, Jon C., and Christine Doyle Francis. "'Home' and 'Not Home' in Children's Stories: Getting There—and Being Worth It." *Children's Literature in Education* 24.3 (1993): 223–33.

Youngbear-Tibbets, Holly. "Making Sense of the World." Ed. Susan Hardy Aiken, Ann Brigham, Sallie A. Marston, and Penny Waterstone. *Making Worlds: Gender, Metaphor, Materiality*. Tucson: U of Arizona P, 1998. 31–44.

Section Two

(Re)Active Engagement
Childhood Forays into the Production of Space

Chapter Four

TAKING IT TO THE STREETS

Production of Space in Louise Fitzhugh's *Harriet the Spy*

RICHARDINE WOODALL

The study of the production of space in Louise Fitzhugh's *Harriet the Spy* brings into view a much-needed new perspective on the subjects of children, children's literature, and the adult-child binary. Social and literary critics often contend that adults try to colonize children through their literary productions. However, this is not a universal principle; there is a vocal group of critics who insist that children are active agents participating in the production of culture, although an imbalance of power exists between children and adults (Flynn 255–56).[1] Agency here denotes the ability of children to act in cultural productions (256). Fitzhugh's novel supports the position that children participate in producing their culture, and one method she uses is Harriet's production of social space. Another method is character focalization; she uses this narrative technique to combine a limited third-person narrator with Harriet's own idiosyncratic voice as Harriet works spying on her neighbors and recording her observations in her notebook. In this way Fitzhugh offers the reader unprecedented access to Harriet's mental spaces, to the uncensored thoughts of her blunt, candid, and impetuous heroine. Fitzhugh uses these two methods to demonstrate that although some adults in the novel try to control Harriet mentally and physically they are ultimately powerless to colonize Harriet's ability to think space or to act in space. As one can see, Harriet herself is not colonized, since she is free to undertake her spying activities as a way to be.

We tend to limit our conception of space to that which we can touch or apprehend physically and visually. For example, there is a plot of land near a moderately busy road. We can see and even touch the grass and the trees growing on the land. We might decide that this would be a wonderful place for a playground. It is vital that we understand that in this very act of visualizing in our mind a future playground, we are thinking space. Similarly, Fitzhugh's protagonist not only trespasses into tangible public, private, and "adult" spaces but also thinks space and actively produces new social spaces. Furthermore, Fitzhugh creates space in which Harriet socially dwells, observes, and forms relations, and such production and creation of space involve the reader. The author, her characters, and the child reader show space as a necessary condition of existence. Space is not limited to physical places such as a playground, because literature also produces social space. Space itself is neither a container such as a jar nor a thing such as an organism, but it is the precondition for all such things and beings to be regardless of whether they are fictitiously or materially in space, which becomes clearer as the meaning of space itself develops within the context of Fitzhugh's work.

The study of Fitzhugh's depiction of space enables us to better understand and interpret the potential power of children's literature. Empirically, Harriet repeatedly transcends the divide amongst home, streets, school, and "playground," all of which are public spaces that Fitzhugh shows through her characters, Harriet in particular. Harriet is in the ceaseless process of transcending the conventionality of social space for a fresh mode of it that was previously hidden. Harriet is, for example, reenvisioning and reinterpreting already-existing phenomena, such as class and gender roles; through this process Harriet produces space. However, she is able to reinterpret and reconfigure in a fresh way only by virtue of the ever-present space. In essence, space is one of these existential structures that define humans such that it makes their relations with others possible; and without it, existence of any kind is impossible.

Adults expect children's existence to be shaped in such spaces as the school, the home, and the playground. The home is a structure in which humans dwell; and for many children, the home is their first intimate space, their first dwelling place, their first coming to consciousness, and to self-consciousness. In *The Poetics of Space*, Gaston Bachelard argues that "our house is our corner of the world. As has often been said, it is our first universe" (4). However, social life necessitates that we leave our homes for a multitude of reasons; for example, educational life requires that we go to schools; economic life requires that we go to work. Empirically, the streets are concrete conduits from one location to another. Most contemporary adults in privileged Western societies do not expect to find children in the streets except when they are in transit; however, Fitzhugh takes her heroine out of the domestic space and into the public space as streets, repeatedly. Fitzhugh shows that in the streets Harriet gains a more critical understanding of social space. Harriet does not merely act and react to her social, economic, and political conditions, but her perceptions, emotions, and intellect are working, and at times painfully so. Fitzhugh demonstrates explicitly that, by means of her notebook and as coeditor of her school's paper, Harriet is producing social space.

MAPPING AND FUSING: CHILDREN'S LITERATURE AND THE NEGOTIATION OF SPACE

There are two essential ways in which most literary and social critics understand the relationships among space, children's literature, and the child reader. The terminology of mapping and fusing distinguishes between the two methods. Mapping is the process of associating elements from one thing with elements from another; however, the individuality of the entities remains the same. In contrast, when things are fused, the individual parts become a whole such that individuality is lost. As a metaphor for the literary process, fusing indicates the considerable power that the author can wield to try to extinguish the individuality of the child reader. The choice of mapping or fusing to describe the author's act of bringing together material and literary spaces in order to shape child readers existentially is to understand differently the power inherent in the relationship between children's literature and children. Fitzhugh's method in *Harriet the Spy* is mapping.

Published in 2015, *Space and Place in Children's Literature, 1789 to the Present* is a very important collection of essays that raises questions about space, children, and children's literature. Maria Sachiko Cecire, along with others, recognizes that "the field of children's [literature] . . . is always in conversation with space" (6). For example, in his contribution to Cecire's text, Peter Hunt recognizes that an author can "map the significant [outer] spaces . . . onto the child-focalizers' inner sense of space" (35). One of Fitzhugh's most noteworthy accomplishments is mapping the outer spaces of the real New York City with the inner spaces of New York City in the novel. As Kathleen T. Horning demonstrates, we can trace Harriet's spy routes in the novel with material places in the real city of New York (17). Sara Fischer's study of child readers and place offers considerable insights into this relationship. Fischer interviews several adults about their "middle childhood" reading experiences (1476). One of the interviewees is named Violet. Violet states that reading Fitzhugh's novel as a child enabled her to conceptually reposition herself from her condition as a Jew in a predominantly Catholic midwestern American state by fantasizing about the rich diversity of New York City (Fischer 1480). Violet's response to reading *Harriet the Spy* demonstrates that children's literature has the potential to enable the child reader to imaginatively project into space. Fitzhugh's method of opening up space in her novel is one that nurtures and enables the growth of Harriet as an individual thinker and a full participant in her social environment. Harriet's ability to map out and think radically and originally about her neighborhood fosters in her intellectual rigor and political engagement. Harriet's projections into social space are potentially freeing, and this can open up space conceptually for the child reader as well.

Fitzhugh discloses the very real imbalance of power between the author and the child reader. Peter Hunt argues that a "children's book is a negotiation of the space between the adult writer and the child reader, a complex negotiation of an inevitable, and often radical, imbalance of power" (23). He continues, "The normal slight bias towards the writer . . . is accentuated by the writer's superior experience of the medium and the mechanics of the interchange. For some critics, this imbalance of power has been seen as fatal to the project of children's literature" (23). In this view, to the detriment of children's literature, some authors try to convince child readers that their imaginary constructions are true representations of the real world outside of the text, and this act of fusing enables authors to exercise power over children.

Perry Nodelman and Mavis Reimer link this power imbalance to adults' colonization of children:

> Children's literature then represents a massive effort by adults to *colonize* children: to make them believe that they ought to be the way adults would like them to be, and to make them feel guilty or downplay the significance of all the aspects of themselves that inevitably don't fit the adult model. (82)

The term "colonize" advances the perspective that children's literature is a method used to exert adult power over child readers. This word "colonize" carries with it the history of the often-brutal means by which one country establishes and maintains control over another; the analogy is that adult authors of children's literature act like a colonizing country when they wield their inevitable and indomitable power over the child reader. However, even if the analogy is true, then it behooves us to examine it more insightfully and by so doing give some consideration to the dynamic nature of the colonial encounter. This is not to deny that there is an imbalance of power between the colonizer/adult and the colonized/child. However, there is ample evidence suggesting that the colonizer and the colonized are both affected and changed in substantial ways. Furthermore, the colonized is not simply dominated and victimized by the encounter with the colonizer. Ania Loomba's *Colonialism/Postcolonialism* offers a critical and nuanced discussion of the complexity of this colonial problem. Loomba draws upon the writings of Homi Bhabha to argue that we must question ideas that promote "a static model of colonial relations in which 'colonial power and discourse are possessed entirely by the coloniser' and therefore there is no room for negotiation or change" (49). It is important, therefore, that we consider that the colonial encounter is not one-dimensional, that is, the colonizer alone has and wields power. To the contrary, as Loomba argues, "colonial authority, like any other, is legitimised through a process during which it constantly has to negotiate with the people it seeks to control" (51); that is, colonial power does not necessarily flow from the top down (Loomba 1–57). The point here is not to prolong this analogy, but to bring into view that the imbalance of power between children and adults is not the end of the process or the relationship. Furthermore, children are not always passive receivers of children's literature for a multitude of reasons (Flynn 256), and one such reason is because children are thinking beings in the world and always projecting as thinking into space.

SOCIAL SPACE AND THE PRODUCTION OF SPACE

Social space is an essential relationship humans have with others in the world. Social space is not possible without space itself, because space is not an entity; rather, it is a condition of any entity. We find space in every form of social life, such as economics, politics, and literary art. These activities are all in space; these spaces are all empirical and historical. The precondition, however, for all these various forms of social space is space itself. Analogously, time is another existential structure of humans; time will not stop if we take a clock off the wall and break it, nor will space disappear if we destroy the chair or the table. Time is not the clock, and space is not the chair or the table, but they make possible the chair and the table. Indeed, the clock, the chair, and the table are possible only because of space. Space is thus a primordial structure in which humans dwell and in which they work through their existence (Nuyen 37). The production of space is not the sole domain of any human being. When we dismantle a backyard shed and replace it with another, plant or garden, or walk to the school or the playground, the experience of space is already presupposed. Space is thus a structure of being in the world that enables humans to be among things and with one another. We cannot understand social life without thinking about space regardless of whether such an understanding is basic or refined.[2]

In *The Production of Space*, Henri Lefebvre argues that space is an essential form without which social space is not possible:

> (Social) space is not a thing among other things, nor a product among other products: rather, it subsumes things produced, and encompasses their interrelations in their coexistence and simultaneity—their (relative) order and/or (relative) disorder. It is the outcome of a sequence and set of operations, and thus cannot be reduced to the rank of a simple object . . . social space is what permits fresh actions to occur, while suggesting others and prohibiting yet others. (73)

Space is the condition for the existence of all things in social space. Humans do not produce existential space; to the contrary, space "subsumes" all production—and this includes necessarily adults' production of children's literature; thus, social life in all of its different forms is not possible without space. Lefebvre brings into view another important idea we need to understand. Social space "is what permits fresh actions to occur." Humans are creative and productive; they are always projecting into space. Through perceptivity, intellectuality and emotivity (the structures of consciousness itself), humans bring into being fresh new ways to be. Social spaces are produced as a direct result of people living and working in a certain place; like the palimpsest, social spaces are layered with meaning and history (Cecire et al. 9).

SPACE IN *HARRIET THE SPY*

Fitzhugh has a penetrating understanding of social space. She very carefully organizes her fictional world spatially. Harriet lives in a three-storey house. Throughout the novel Harriet runs up and down the stairs in her house; Harriet and Ole Golly's rooms are on the third floor in the attic (200). Harriet's parents occupy the second floor; on the main floor is the kitchen, the cook's domain. In this way, the novel draws our attention to the social distinctions in the Welsches' household. Fitzhugh also directs her reader to recognize the class divisions in the state of New York. Mrs. Golly is Ole Golly's mother. Mrs. Golly lives in Far Rockaway in Queens, New York (12). It is a lower-middle-class neighborhood. In comparison, Water Mill is a playground for the very rich. The houses in Water Mill cost millions of dollars. Harriet's family vacationed there in the summer. There are other class divisions in the novel that are signaled by characters' addresses; some of the most expensive real estate in New York City is located in the Upper East Side. Rachel Hennessey lives on the corner of York and East Eighty-Fifth Street. Harriet lives a life of privilege on East Eighty-Seventh Street in Manhattan (3). Harriet's spy route is located in her Upper East End neighborhood. Carl Schurz Park is steps from her house; it sits on acres of land and boasts waterfront views, shady paths, and plenty of green space. Thus, the social space in which Harriet dwells is one of affluence and leisure.

Fitzhugh is peeling back the surface of the urban landscape and taking her heroine deep into the structures of her society; the home, the school, the playground and other private and public spaces are not simple backgrounds in the novel. The knowledge that Harriet acquires from navigating the streets of New York City on her own is such that the spaces of childhood are potentially subversive and transgressive. She comes to see the vulnerability and even folly of adults as well as the strength and cruelty of children. Fitzhugh's novel makes a strong case that children are capable of successfully engaging in positive and negative behavior that can change lives and change societies. Through processes of observations, questions, and analyses, Harriet attempts to take apart and open up the social conditions in which she dwells in order to see and understand their constituent parts, including causality.

The space of Harriet's becoming is New York City. New York City is layered with sociocultural meaning. New York City is a world capital, an economic powerhouse, a city of immigrants, and a cultural mecca for those dreaming of fame and fortune. Keith O'Sullivan and Pádraic Whyte understand that the myth of New York is central to its very survival. They write:

> The mythology of New York has helped maintain its resilience and survival in reality. Despite the hardships experienced by New York and its inhabitants ... the myth of New York as a place of opportunity and possibility, where all individuals have a chance to realize their potential, has endured. (1)

New York City is also a space of reinvention and renewal. Frank Sinatra's "New York, New York" encapsulates the cultural myth and historical lure of New York City. Sinatra sings that he is taking his "vagabond shoes" to New York because "if I can make it there / I'll make it anywhere." New York City thus facilitates the rags-to-riches narrative. New York City is mythologized as an emancipatory space in which an individual can potentially free oneself from sociocultural dogma (O'Sullivan and Whyte 4). Fitzhugh's selection of New York City as the setting for Harriet's sociopolitical development is central to Harriet's production of social space.

Harriet roams the streets of New York City with minimal adult supervision, spying on her neighbors and sneaking into their private spaces. In this way Fitzhugh gives Harriet a great deal of urban mobility and social freedom. The contemporary reader might be alarmed by Harriet's unsupervised freedom, particularly in such a large urban center as New York City. As Sonya Sawyer Fritz argues, Fitzhugh's novel was published prior to the "culture of fear" that has produced overprotective parents (85). Published during a very different cultural landscape, Fitzhugh "creates and celebrates a city space that mentors children ... [and offers] models of childhood competence and autonomy" (86). New York City clearly shapes Harriet's agency, her understanding of social space, and her projections into space.

Harriet the Spy opens with Harriet trying to teach her friend Sport how to "play Town" (3). She explains the layout of the town and the professions of the people who live and work there. Her town consists of a filling station, the Carterville General Hospital, a farmhouse, and a police station; the citizens of her town interact with one another as policemen, bankers, writers, bank robbers, pregnant mothers, and farmers. Crouched down in the dirt of the courtyard of her Manhattan home, Harriet is an urban planner. The novel uses the space of "play" as a means of guiding Harriet to perceive the various structures shaping social life. It enables Fitzhugh to demonstrate that children have quite a sophisticated understanding of domestic life, economic disparities, and power relationships in social space. In Harriet's game normative gender relationships are reinforced: there are women's names and men's names, and married women have babies (6). Violence is also a condition of social life in the game. Men with guns rob and beat several of the town's inhabitants (6). Despite the fact that it is Harriet's creation, in Town, men have economic power, physical power, and political power. Harriet tries to convince Sport, to whom she is explaining the game, that playing Town is "fun" (5).

The game Town motivates Ole Golly to expose Harriet to the world: "'I'm going to take you somewhere. It's time you began to see the world. You're eleven years old and it's time you saw something'" (8–9). The reader should observe that Ole Golly's intention to show Harriet the world is another instance of creating space, since Ole Golly is projecting her intention into space in the absence of which there could never be any such intention. Every character is in space; all actions are in space. However, in response to Ole Golly's pronouncement, "Harriet felt a twinge of guilt because she had seen a lot more than Ole Golly thought she had" (9). This is an important revelation in that children oftentimes know more than adults attribute to them.

In particular, Harriet already transcends Ole Golly's understanding of her experience in the world.

Ole Golly takes Harriet and Sport to visit Mrs. Golly. Harriet fills her diary with observations of the trip to Far Rockaway and of Mrs. Golly. Many of Harriet's comments are cruel and unsympathetic, as Perry Nodelman has noted. Nodelman's rebuke of Harriet has some merit: "Harriet's desire to stand back and observe makes her arrogant about the failings of others.... Harriet's lack of compassion allows her to see others unfiltered by kindness, it is inhumane" (136). Harriet's lack of kindness and compassion for the failings and devastating conditions of others is quite explicit in the novel. Harriet writes, for example, that Mrs. Golly is "the fat lady . . . rather stupid" (15). The illustration of Mrs. Golly is a cruel, exaggerated caricature (17). Harriet writes in her notebook,

> I THINK I WOULD LIKE TO WRITE A STORY ABOUT MRS. GOLLY GETTING RUN OVER BY A TRUCK EXCEPT SHE'S SO FAT I WONDER WHAT WOULD HAPPEN TO THE TRUCK. (21–22)

This episode reveals that it is not reasonable to attempt to relegate Harriet to certain "child-appropriate" social spaces. Harriet's guardian, parents, and teachers do not own space. Adults in Harriet's life might try to police her, but their efforts at best are only partially successful. Harriet has seen more of the world than Ole Golly knows. Harriet's perceptions and interpretations of the world are independent of the adults around her. She is conscious of the world and perceives things in space. Harriet dwells in the world as a condition of being. Space is liberating. No one human can occupy the space of another. In Mrs. Golly's house, for example, there were four humans: Mrs. Golly, Ole Golly, Sport, and Harriet. These four humans occupy the same time, but each occupies their own space. Harriet demonstrates the impossibility of any adult colonizing her psychologically. Materially, of course, humans can colonize social space, but space as a primordial structure is outside of humans' power and control. Harriet is an exceptional character because not only does she resist those who attempt to overpower her, adults and classmates alike, but also Harriet produces social space as a necessary condition of being-in-the-world. Harriet does not require the permission of any individual to project her own perceptions and interpretations of the world into space. However, as Harriet is beginning to understand, social space is relational; we are always in space with the other. The novel reveals the difficulties of all of its characters, creating social space in which conflicts with others are inevitable.

Ole Golly visits her mother every week, which suggests that she has a sense of duty (20). Furthermore, Harriet recognizes sadness in Ole Golly's face (19). Ole Golly seems to view her mother with cruelty and contempt as well. "Behold, Harriet," Ole Golly said, "a woman who never had any interest in anyone else, nor in any book, nor in any school, nor in any way of life, but has lived her whole life in this room, eating and sleeping and waiting to die" (18). Harriet is aghast; she "stared at Mrs. Golly in horror. Should Ole Golly be saying these things? Wouldn't Mrs. Golly get mad? But Mrs. Golly just sat looking contentedly at Harriet" (19). Many characters in the novel are cruel and narcissistic, particularly the very wealthy. For example, in one telling scene in the novel, Harriet is questioning her mother, Mrs. Welsch, about romantic love, and she wants to know how her mother felt when she met her father. Mrs. Welsch remarks, "'I haven't the faintest idea what anyone else feels.'" In response to her mother's reply, Harriet thinks, "My mother . . . doesn't think about other people much" (102). Neither Mrs. Golly nor Mrs. Welsch seems to care much about others. These women are so consumed with themselves that the needs, wants, and desires of others are of no concern to them. Unlike Mrs. Golly and Mrs. Welsch, Harriet is sensitive about Mrs. Golly's feelings when Ole Golly criticizes her. Fitzhugh therefore demonstrates Harriet's sensitivity and care for the other; she is not inhumane, as Nodelman contends.

Harriet is a keen observer of her social space. She is perceptive, intellectual, and emotional, but these attributes are underdeveloped, not refined. She perceives, reasons, and uses her senses to try to understand her environment, particularly the sense of sight. However, she sees but does not always understand the significance of what she sees. She feels but does not understand what she feels. Early in the novel, in response to Harriet's exuberant declaration "I want to know everything, everything. . . . Everything in the world, everything, everything. I will be a spy and know everything," Ole Golly replies, "It won't do you a bit of good to know everything if you don't do anything with it" (24). Here, Harriet simply doesn't understand that it is impossible to know everything, since she is a finite being in finite space; hence, she doesn't understand her own finiteness. Harriet is a keen observer; she is perceptive, intellectual, and emotional, but these attributes are not mature.

When Ole Golly leaves to get married, Harriet writes in her notebook, "I FEEL THERE'S A FUNNY LITTLE HOLE IN ME THAT WASN'T THERE BEFORE" (132). Harriet feels heartache and emptiness; however, she doesn't have the language yet to articulate her feelings clearly. Later in the novel, after she is treated cruelly by her schoolmates, Harriet writes the following disturbing entry.

> SOMETHING IS DEFINITELY HAPPENING TO ME. I AM CHANGING. I DON'T FEEL LIKE ME AT ALL. I DON'T EVER LAUGH OR THINK ANYTHING FUNNY. I JUST FEEL MEAN ALL OVER. I WOULD LIKE TO HURT EACH ONE OF THEM IN A SPECIAL WAY THAT WOULD HURT ONLY THEM. (241–42)

Harriet's self-analysis is a direct consequence of dwelling in space with others. In the entry above, Harriet is responding to her condition without reasoned thought; she is consumed with anger and vengeance. Perhaps for the first time in her eleven years, she is becoming aware that social space is interrelational and that her social behavior, such as writing, can have consequences.

Harriet's development in the novel depends on space in two fundamental ways. She inhabits social space with others. She records her observations and interactions with her world in her diary. However, she is more than a chronicler; she does not record only what she sees factually and faithfully. In many of her earlier entries, she reacts emotionally to what she sees in the world. When, for example, her notebook is discovered, her classmates retaliate by ostracizing her from the group; in turn, Harriet responds and hurts her friends (Fitzhugh 216–21).

The discovery of her diary has far-reaching consequences. One result is that her relationships with her friends are undermined. Another outcome is that the boundaries between her imagination and the real world are ruptured. Previously, Harriet imagined violence, such as when she recorded her desire to run down Mrs. Golly with a truck. However, after her private thoughts become public, Harriet herself becomes caught up in escalating violence. A case in point, Harriet's desire to inflict pain on her classmates is actualized (243–44). And although taunting Rachel Hennessey that she does not have a father, putting a frog in Marion Hawthorne's desk, or chopping off a chunk of Laura Peter's hair (243–44) might seem like amusing "childish" pranks to some readers, the violence Harriet manifests can be compared to the brutality perpetuated by the robbers against Mr. Charles Hanley and Old Farmer Dodge in the game Town. *Harriet the Spy* is an unflinching and honest portrayal of the viciousness that is part of social life. This is a feature of the novel that also seems to supports Nodelman's criticism:

> Not only Harriet does not change . . . nobody does . . . the Dei Santis continue on as they were to begin with, Mrs. Plumber keeps thinking

only of Mrs. Plumber, the Robinsons are still perfect, and Harrison Withers gets a new cat. Harriet writes, "HEE HEE. THEY AIN'T GOING TO CHANGE HARRISON WITHERS." They ain't going to change Harriet either; at the end she has her friends and notebook back, and she has settled down to playing god just as she did at the beginning. Only now, she knows she does it. (136–37)

If we look closely at the last several pages of the novel, the reader can see that although Harriet's writing continues to be unfiltered, she does change; and there is some hope, albeit limited, that she will become kinder and more compassionate in her future intersubjective relations.

Harriet's more important development is as a sociopolitical thinker. Harriet begins to think more critically about social conditions and to penetrate beneath the surface of her observations. In the first chapter of the novel, for example, she watches people on the subway on the trip to meet Mrs. Golly; she records her observations of her fellow passengers in her diary.

FAT LEG ... ONE CROSS-EYE ... HORRIBLE LOOKING LITTLE BOY AND A FAT BLONDE MOTHER ... I DON'T THINK I'D LIKE TO LIVE WHERE ANY OF THESE PEOPLE LIVE OR DO THE THINGS THEY DO. (11–12)

These observations lack insight; they remain on the surface. She records only what she perceives visually. A little further into the novel, Harriet writes in her diary about Sport's living conditions. She writes:

SPORT'S HOUSE SMELLS LIKE OLD LAUNDRY, AND IT'S NOISY AND KIND OF POOR-LOOKING. MY HOUSE DOESN'T HAVE THAT SMELL AND IS QUIET LIKE MRS. PLUMBER'S. DOES THAT MEAN WE ARE RICH? WHAT MAKES PEOPLE POOR OR RICH? (52)

In both entries, she observes the effect of poverty on people. However, in the latter entry, she asks questions about the causal factors of economic disparity; she is beginning to recognize that people's material conditions have a direct impact on their social lives. She is struggling to understand not only her socioeconomic condition but also the conditions of those around her. Harriet is entering into social spaces beyond those of her class, and in so doing she is confronted with economic inequalities.

There are many characters living lives of economic hardship in the novel, and many of them are instrumental to Harriet's education, particularly those teaching at her school. For example, Miss Angela Whitehead is the present dean of The Gregory School. Early in the novel, Harriet writes this about Miss Whitehead: "THE OTHER DAY I SAW HER IN THE GROCERY STORE AND SHE BOUGHT ONE SMALL CAN OF TUNA, ONE DIET COLA, AND A PACKAGE OF CIGARETTES. . . . SHE MUST HAVE A TERRIBLE LIFE" (23–33). In a later entry in her notebook, she writes in the same blunt manner about another teacher: "MISS ELSON WAS TRAILED HOME FROM SCHOOL THE OTHER DAY AND IT TURNS OUT SHE LIVES IN A REAL RAT HOLE OF AN APARTMENT" (291). The conclusion of the entry, however, is different from some of her previous ones; it reveals that Harriet is searching for the causes, for the truth of poverty. "MAYBE THE SCHOOL DOESN'T PAY HER ENOUGH MONEY TO LIVE IN A GOOD PLACE. THERE WILL BE A SIZZLING EDITORIAL ON THIS NEXT WEEK" (291). Unlike her earlier, uncritical and insensitive, observations about the teacher Miss Whitehead (22–23) and the people on the subway (13), she now recognizes that employers might be hoarding resources and keeping workers destitute. Poverty still repulses Harriet; however, her reactions to it reveal growing intellectual and critical thinking. Harriet's growth into a complex thinker is possible only because of space: her trespasses into "adult" social spaces, her thinking space, her production of social space.

As the novel develops, Harriet is becoming a more penetrating reader of the social, political, and economic structures around her. By the ending of the novel, Harriet is developing empathy for the conditions of others, and this is also refuting Nodelman's contention that she has not changed. Janie and Sport are her friends. Whereas Janie comes from a rich family, Sport comes from a poorer one. Janie wants to be a scientist, much to the dismay of her family, and although Sport wants to be a football star, he is a domestic laborer in his household. The simplistic gendered relationships Harriet produced in her game Town are more complex in the social and real world. Furthermore, despite Janie's and Sport's different economic conditions, Harriet recognizes their common vulnerability, and she tries to better grasp and understand their existence, not just intellectually but also emotively:

> She looked at each of them carefully in the longish time it took them to reach her. She made herself walk in Sport's shoes, feeling the holes in his socks rub against his ankles. She pretended she had an itchy nose when Janie put one abstracted hand up to scratch. She felt what

it would feel like to have freckles and yellow hair like Janie, then funny ears and skinny shoulders like Sport. (299)

Although categorized socially as a child, Harriet displays a level of maturity and thoughtfulness Mrs. Golly and Mrs. Welsch lack. The final entry in her notebook reads, "NOW THAT THINGS ARE BACK TO NORMAL I CAN GET SOME REAL WORK DONE" (300).

What does she mean? Presumably, "back to normal" is in reference to the restoration of her relationships with her friends. However, what is meant by getting real work done? She has used the word "work" before. In chapter 2, for example, Harriet is about to bound upstairs to get dressed for spying (41). However, just before she races up the stairs, the cook says to her, "go out and play." Harriet is indignant; "I do not go out to PLAY, I go out to WORK!" (39–41). From Harriet's perspective, the cook's use of the word "play" is condescending and reductive. Harriet understands her activities as work, as productive and essential to her thirst to know everything. Harriet's work not only deepens her knowledge and understanding of the structures of social space but is also central to her participation in the production of space.

Harriet participates in an entire social, economic, and political system. Fitzhugh's sometimes unlikable and unrepentant heroine enables readers to see the cruelty, violence, and selfishness of which human beings, adults and children alike, are capable. However, unlike some characters in the novel that do not think about others, such as Mrs. Golly and Mrs. Welsch, Harriet's notebook is evidence that she does think about others, albeit sometimes unflatteringly and insensitively. The heroine is not a victim of her society as much as she is a product and producer of it. This penetrating and critical examination of social life is possible in part because of the novel's understanding of social space.

SPACE AND THE POSSIBILITY OF CHILDREN'S LITERATURE

Critics of children's fiction often think that adults have a tremendous amount of power because the majority of this literature is written by them. Marian Thérèse Keyes and Áine McGillicuddy argue convincingly, "Adults, whether as authors, illustrators, publishers, teachers or parents, wield enormous power in the choice of what is written, published and selected for the child reader," (9) and "One of the distinct qualities of children's literature is that it is a genre that is both heavily monitored and tightly controlled for didactic purposes" (11). However, *Harriet the Spy* requires that we rethink this position. The adult author is not a godlike figure dispensing knowledge and colonizing the child reader. Fitzhugh's novel demonstrates quite the opposite; it represents children as active participants in the production of social space. Children's consciousness of themselves and of social life cannot be controlled by adults in an absolute way regardless of how powerful the adult might be.

As a social practice, children's literature is in process; it has changed over time and will continue to change in accordance with multiple forces—social, political, and cultural—shaping social life (Heywood 19–31). A hallmark of many fictional texts for children, especially those texts published since the 1960s and 1970s, is resistance to and sometimes outright rejection of adult authority and dominant ideologies. Keyes and McGillicuddy also recognize this potential feature of children's literary texts when they contend, "Children's literature offers the possibility to explore and promote new ideas that question, resist and undermine the status quo," and that children's fiction "also enjoys a greater freedom than literature for adults to be rebellious, illogical and irreverent" (11). Children's literature is a social practice that exists in social space. It is only from within social life that humans—adults and children alike—can project into space in rebellious, illogical, and irreverent ways that reproduce social space.

Harriet always participated in social space. Even before she became aware of it, she was already involved in producing social space because she is necessarily in space as a condition of being in an ontological sense. Harriet writes in her journal in preparation for becoming a writer. She, however, fails to understand that she already is one. Harriet is herself an author of oral and written narratives. As the storyteller of Town, school editor, and journal writer, she is an active producer, and not a mere consumer, of literature for children. Adults write most of the literature for children; however, this literature is not the only type of texts to which children have access. Furthermore, adults are not the only producers of children's knowledge, consciousness, and self-consciousness. In addition, as *Harriet the Spy* illustrates, both children and adults can have an adumbrated understanding of their existence and of their participation in and production of social life.

Ole Golly asks Harriet what is the good of knowing everything if you don't do anything with that knowledge. The same can be asked of agency in the absence of understanding how one's actions participate in and produce social space. Harriet's observations of others can be crude. This is not only because her observations can be cruel, as Nodelman argued, but also because they are unrefined. She often writes without critically thinking about the sociopolitical structures of social space and without understanding that she is in space with others. She sees and observes social disparities but does not understand how she herself, even at the age of eleven years, contributes to and produces them. As Harriet's perceptions, intellect, and emotions become more refined, she begins to recognize that her writing produces social life in a potentially negative or positive way. Harriet promises to write an editorial building upon her reasoning that the teacher Miss Elson might live in a rat hole of an apartment because of inadequate pay. Thus, writing for Harriet is a pursuit of the truth of underlying causes and structures of social life (Stahl 163). This editorial makes a strong case that it is very meaningful for children to understand not only about space but also that social space permits fresh action to occur; because children dwell in space irrevocably, it is within their power to act thoughtfully and critically if they decide a situation in social life requires change. Harriet's positive and negative participation in social space is possible only because of space itself.

SPACE AND POTENTIAL CHILD READERS OF CHILDREN'S LITERATURE

Critics of children's literature often speak of the need for children to have agency and of bringing children to voice; however, in such discussions, children's agency and children's voice are in the abstract. Harriet has considerable agency and has at least two platforms from which to come to voice—her journal and the school newspaper. However, she often fails to understand the implications and potentiality of her social privilege and social mobility. Is bringing children to agency or to voice in the absence of critical thinking and self-consciousness evidence of children's power? Children's agency should be grounded in perceptivity, emotivity, and intellectuality, that is, consciousness itself. Agency in the absence of understanding the reason for one's actions, the aim of one's action, and the purpose of one's actions is to act blindly. As the novel develops, Harriet's journal entries become more thoughtful and insightful. She begins to write with a purpose. Miss Elson still lives in a "rat hole," but Harriet is now searching for sociopolitical causes. She also seeks to deepen the awareness of other child readers of her editorial, for example, about the economic and social implications of injustice and inequality in their own social spaces.

The development of children's understanding not only that they are in space but also that they are already participants in the production of social space conveys much more than "adult *ideas about* . . . children," as Cecire et al. argue. The ability of literature to participate in opening up children's awareness of space conveys to them knowledge about potentiality and becoming, that is, their existential condition itself. Fitzhugh's penetrating understanding of space in her novel demonstrates the inter-relational structures that yoke Harriet, her classmates, and adult figures into a whole; the whole consists not only of human characters but also of social, political, and economic demarcations affecting both children and adults existentially. Social life in all of its different modes affects adults and children, and children, like adults, also partake in the production of social space.

Notes

1. I would like to acknowledge the unknown reader for directing me to both Flynn and Sarah Fischer's articles.
2. I would like to acknowledge Tyrone Tull for our fruitful discussions about space.

Works Cited

Bachelard, Gaston. *The Poetics of Space: The Classic Look at How We Experience Intimate Places*. Translated by Maria Jolas, Beacon Press, 1969.

Cecire, Maria Sachiko, Hannah Field, Kavita Mudan Finn, and Malini Roy. "Introduction: Spaces of Power, Place of Play." *Space and Place in Children's Literature, 1789 to the Present*, edited by Maria Sachiko Cecire et al., Ashgate, 2015. 1–19.

Fischer, Sarah. "Readers as Place-Makers: The Experience of Place in the Literacy Life-Worlds of Middle Childhood." *Environmental Education Research*, vol. 23, no. 10, 2017, pp. 1476–88.

Fitzhugh, Louise. *Harriet the Spy*. Yearling, 1964.

Flynn, Richard. "What Are We Talking about When We Talk about Agency?" *Jeunesse: Young People, Texts, Cultures*, vol. 8, no. 1, 2016, pp. 254–65.

Fritz, Sonya Sawyer. "'New York Is a Great Place:' Urban Mobility in Twentieth-Century Children's Literature." *Children's Literature and New York City*, edited by Pádraic Whyte and Keith O'Sullivan, Routledge, 2014, pp. 85–96.

Heywood, Colin. *A History of Childhood: Children and Childhood in the West from Medieval to Modern Times*. Polity Press, 2002.

Horning, Kathleen T. "Spying on Louise Fitzhugh." *Horn Book Magazine*, May–June 2014, pp. 13–17.

Hunt, Peter. "Unstable Metaphors: Symbolic Spaces and Specific Places." *Space and Place in Children's Literature, 1789 to the Present*, edited by Maria Sachiko Cecire, Hannah Field, Kavita Mudan Finn, and Malini Roy, Ashgate, 2015, pp. 23–37.

Keyes, Marian Thérèse, and Áine McGillicuddy. "Introduction: Politics and Ideology in Children's Literature." *Politics and Ideology in Children's Literature*, edited by Marian Thérèse Keyes and Áine McGillicuddy, Four Courts Press, 2014.

Lefebvre, Henri. *The Production of Space*. Translated by Donald Nicholson-Smith, Blackwell Publishing, 1991.

Loomba, Ania. *Colonialism/Postcolonialism*. Routledge, 1998.
Nodelman, Perry. "Louise Fitzhugh." *American Writers for Children since 1960: Fiction*. Ed. Glenn E. Estes. *Dictionary of Literary Biography*, vol. 52, pp. 133–42. *Zenodo*, https://zenodo.org/record/3363727#.YiE8J5ZOlzp.
Nodelman, Perry, and Mavis Reimer. *The Pleasures of Children's Literature*. 2nd ed., Longman, 1996.
Nuyen, A. T. "From Bauhaus to the House of Being: Some Heideggerian Reflections on Architectural Styles. *Popular Culture Review*, vol. 10, no. 1, 1999, pp. 37–51.
O'Sullivan, Keith, and Pádraic Whyte. "Introduction." *Children's Literature and New York City*, edited by Pádraic Whyte and Keith O'Sullivan, Routledge, 2014, pp. 1–5.
Sinatra, Frank. "New York, New York." *YouTube*, uploaded by Sound Smart, 26 September 2010, https://www.youtube.com/watch?v=gcxGp-2p5aQ.
Stahl, J. D. "Louise Fitzhugh, Marisol, and the Realm of Art." *Children's Literature Association Quarterly*, vol. 24, no. 4, 1999, pp. 159–65.

Chapter Five

RACE AND SPACE IN DANIEL JOSÉ OLDER'S *SHADOWSHAPER*

CRISTINA RIVERA AND ANDREW TREVARROW

> "Paint a mural. Start a battle. Change the world."
> —DANIEL JOSÉ OLDER

Latinx characters who lead, wield magic, conquer evil, and are the destined hero at the end of a story rarely appear in children's and young adult literature; this phenomenon speaks to a larger conversation about the absence, if not exclusion, of genuine diversity for the next generation. The epigraph above captures the artistic yet subversive energy generated through contemporary diverse novels. What emerges, then, is a creative art form that takes up the dominant status quo by fighting the uphill battle of generating books that contain holistically diverse characters and that create spaces for readers to understand and empathize with people from all cultures. Brown bodies in narratives for children and young adults most often replicate minority positions and disenfranchised identities in our everyday world. Therefore, we must also stop to consider what construction of the Latinx human experience children's and young adult literature currently creates within the imaginations of young readers. This chapter engages the complexities of representing diverse characters—specifically Puerto Rican characters—in the young adult novel *Shadowshaper* (2015), and in both the metaphorical and real-world spaces they navigate. We employ a careful selection of narrative analysis to both deconstruct the narrative situations of Older's text and to reenvision this predominantly white theoretical framework. Through this lens, we work to discover how Older utilizes urban fantasy as a distinct space that allows brown bodies to exist freely, more authentically, and encourages the kind of empathetic reader-response experienced by the array of white characters that came before in this genre. Ultimately, our objective is to explore, through contemporary scholarship on Latinx identities and Puerto Rican environments, how *Shadowshaper* creates a narrative space that compels its readers to imagine its Afro-Puerto Rican heroine, diverse characters, and the communities with whom the characters interact.

Shadowshaper is the first book in Daniel José Older's *Shadowshaper Cypher* trilogy and one that conveys the especially relevant themes of this collection: in general, the relationship between space and identity and, more specifically, how the adolescent protagonist conceptualizes and claims her own spaces. These concepts are ubiquitous in the novel, which follows Sierra Santiago, an Afro–Puerto Rican teenager living in present-day Brooklyn. Sierra is tasked with painting a giant mural protesting a gentrification attempt that her community calls the Tower, "a five-story concrete monstrosity on a block otherwise full of brownstones" (Older 2). In the process of countering this assault on her community's physical space, she discovers an unknown but empowering space created by the act of shadowshaping, an ancestral magic that runs in her family and their larger Afro-Latinx community. As she learns about herself and the secrets that her family kept from her, Sierra also learns that she too can harness the magic through her paintings and drawings. Shadowshapers generate various art forms (murals, stories, songs, tattoos, and other forms of artistic expression) and work with like-minded spirits, asking them to physically take over their works of art. Shadowshaping is therefore a way of transforming art into active beings devoted to protecting the physical spaces in which this magic and its wielders exist. By using this magic, "you give [these spirits] form, they work for you—with you, ideally, toward your goal. And they know that, so they show up ready to work" (Older 137). As the murals, previously painted by her community for generations, fade into nothing because of an evil force, so do the memories and spirits of the loved members of the community depicted in the murals. With the help of another teen shadowshaper and her closest friends, Sierra must urgently protect and restore the spaces of her neighborhood through art and learning her own supernatural powers. *Shadowshaper*'s narrative perspective of Afro-Latinidad, and furthermore a Puerto Rican identity signifier called trigueña, creates a much-needed space for positive and popular representations of brown identity in urban fantasy.

Books like *Shadowshaper* are crucial to expanding and reinvigorating the US literary landscape. Not only does the construction of the Latina body and US Puerto Rican identity in *Shadowshaper* generate spaces of positive brown recognition, but the use of art as the magical presence in the novel also connects significantly to the Puerto Rican community, as it is used increasingly on the island itself to reclaim broken and disenfranchised spaces. Hurricane

Maria devastated Puerto Rico in September 2017, causing the majority of the island to lose power, and destroying buildings, homes, cars, roads, and the island's own natural vegetation. The hurricane was one of the strongest in recorded history, and its impact is still felt on the island. Despite the fact that this catastrophic event caused massive destruction, leaving Puerto Rico in disarray, a stronger movement of street art rose out of the flooded and ravaged terrain. Prior to Maria, street art existed in Puerto Rican culture on the island; however, since Maria people have used street art to reinvigorate Puerto Rican culture and solidarity. Now art installations can be found in cities everywhere around the island. And while *Shadowshaper* was published in 2015, three years before Hurricane Maria, it encapsulates the culture's ties to street art and community and, at the same time, captivates readers through its fantastical narrative elements.

BRIDGING THE IMAGINATIVE GAP: EXPANDING THE SPACE OF CHILDREN'S LITERATURE

Ebony Elizabeth Thomas's *The Dark Fantastic: Race and the Imagination from Harry Potter to the Hunger Games* (2019) compellingly asserts, as is implied by the subtitle, that the ever-growing popularity of YA literature does not account for the vast cultural differences of the audiences consuming them. "When people of color seek passageways into the fantastic," Thomas writes, "we have often discovered that the doors are barred. Even the very act of dreaming of worlds-that-never-were can be challenging when the known world does not provide many liberating spaces" (2). She points first to the statistics about diversity in children's publishing reported annually by the Cooperative Children's Book Center (CCBC); she writes, "The center has found every year, over 85 percent of all books published for children and young adults feature White characters—a statistic that has barely moved since the 1960s" (Thomas 4). She also notes that the CCBC report shows "a troubling trend of books that feature diverse characters not being written by authors from that background, leading to questions about who has the right to tell diverse stories" (5). In 2018, for example, we found that the center reports that only 207 (5.6%) of the 3,682 books received that year featured a Latinx protagonist (or featured Latinx identity prominently in the story) and were authored by a Latinx person (CCBC).

Beyond these present-day disparities, stereotypes, caricatures, and marginalized identities have historically been "persistent problems" in children's and YA literature. Thomas observes, "Many diverse characters that actually *do* show up on the page, on a tablet, on a television or movie screen, or on the computer are often problematic" (5). This systemic contradiction feeds into what she describes as "the diversity crisis in children's and young adult literature" (7). *Shadowshaper* is a considerable warrior in the movement for brown and black representation through the US Latinx experience in speculative fiction—or more specifically the urban fantasy genre. Older's work counters the stereotypes, caricatures, and marginalized positions typical of urban fantasy in order to reclaim brown representation in what have been white literary spaces. Furthermore, he also makes space for Latinx artists whom Rocio Isabel Prado characterizes as having "only seen their culture depicted by way of Americanized cheapened fast food, advertisements, xenophobic politicians, and shallow representations" (206). Writers like Older "are trying to escape restraints of these offensive portrayals of Latin[x] identity in the hopes of creating truly meaningful art" (Prado 206). It is an approach that mirrors the Afrofuturism movement of a developing African diaspora culture (Thomas 9). *Shadowshaper* presents humanizing characteristics in a story that follows the marginalized positions of diasporic Puerto Ricans, in a space where only white, magical and/or strong hero characters are traditionally and typically found.

Thomas echoes other scholars who emphasize the continued need for space to talk about underrepresentation and misrepresentation of characters of color in children's and young adult literature, and her analysis has immediate implications for conceptualizing adolescence, race, and space therein. Thomas uses the term "imagination gap" to identify this practice of erasure and distortion in speculative fiction, which includes an array of subgenres, including urban fantasy. Thomas proposes the concept of the "imagination gap" to refer to the ongoing failures within publishing and educational institutions, where strong and even humanizing representations of black and brown bodies just don't make their way to readers. "When youth grow up without seeing diverse images in the mirrors, windows, and doors of children's and young adult literature," she cautions, "they are confined to single stories about the world around them and, ultimately, the development of their imaginations is affected" (6). Thomas then offers the following provocation:

> Maybe it's not that kids and teens of color and other marginalized and minoritized young people don't like to read. Maybe the real issue is that many adults haven't thought very much about the racialized mirrors, windows, and doors that are in the books we offer them to read, in the television and movies we invite them to view, and in the fan communities we entice them to play in. (Thomas 7)

In short, Thomas argues, there are too few Black and brown characters in speculative fiction (and in general), too few Black and brown authors receiving the opportunity to write stories that center their own voices and experiences as people of color, and too few opportunities for real black and brown readers to pick up a book and be incentivized to read by its hopefully humanizing representations. These disparities, in addition to negatively impacting nonwhite readers, also limit the extent to which white readers have opportunities when reading to conceptualize the consciousness of and learn about unfamiliar cultures. Ultimately, these disparities are the results of systemic and collective failures of imagination.

CHALLENGE ACCEPTED: AFRO-LATINX CHARACTERIZATION IN DANIEL JOSÉ OLDER'S *SHADOWSHAPER*

Taking up Thomas's argument, there is an urgent and immense need for humanizing brown and Black representation in children's and young adult literature. Diversity for the sake of diversity is not going to cut it. It is clear from examples such as the public controversy over Angie Thomas's *The Hate U Give* (2017), one of the titles of Banned Book Week 2018 for being "anti-cop" and containing "graphic material," that authors and publishers must integrate nonwhite racial representation into all genres of fiction and nonfiction for young readers (ALA). It is also crucial that they consider how these already-marked characters portray identity and how specifically brown and Black characters are read. As the presence of Latinx characters and cultural icons increases, we must be mindful of the nuances of their emerging representations. It is important not only to have characters that look like people of different cultures and backgrounds but also to examine the way that texts represent the diversity of their perspectives and ways of being. This section thus explores how *Shadowshaper* narratively portrays what it means to be Afro-Latinx and Afro-Latina through Older's depictions of adolescence, race, space, and mobility, while addressing the production of fictional brown and Black bodies for the ever-increasing paperback market.

Much rests on the shoulders of Older's urban fantasy trilogy, which, in anticipation of Thomas's call to arms in *The Dark Fantastic*, features Black and brown characters in speculative fiction; originates from a Latinx author; and offers humanizing representations of youth of color in urban spaces. In turn, and sometimes simultaneously, it offers Latinx and non-Latinx readers opportunities to experience strategic empathy through narrative—a term we will explore in greater detail in a subsequent section. Even though it seems like an ideal book to address the imbalance Thomas identifies, the broader issue of featuring Latinx characters and experiences in YA literature is still a complex and delicate one. Scholars have a responsibility to consider how potential audiences might understand and conceptualize Latinx adolescents and their environments. Doing so necessitates examining the complicated nature of Latinidad in the United States and the undercurrents of racism and colorism within the diasporic Puerto Rican culture that *Shadowshaper* portrays through its characters and the way they navigate spaces.

One strategy Older uses in *Shadowshaper* in anticipation of his audiences' socially prescribed responses to brown and Black characters is to introduce Sierra as most young adult novels present their protagonists: devoid of physical racial markers. Initially it seems odd, given the cover's explicit portrayal of Sierra as Afro-Latina (and possibly *trigueña*—skin color being between black and white), and given the general tendency for YA authors to caricaturize characters of color immediately. The first third of the book contains only rare descriptions of her physical appearance and markers of culture. It is not until chapter 12 that the audience discovers the color of her skin, her curves, and her "wild, nappy hair" (Older 78). By doing so the text creates a rhetorical situation with the audience, weighing the importance of Sierra's general adolescence over the color of her skin.

When Older eventually provides his first physical racial characterization of Sierra, he uses her skin color, body type, and hair texture to signal her status as Afro-Latina—and her departure from the typical white protagonist of young adult literature. Sierra recalls a time she chatted online with "some stupid boy" and "described herself as the color of coffee with not enough milk" (Older 79). She sits, contemplating why she described herself that way, and realizes that she has internalized this deficit characterization ("not enough milk") "somewhere deep inside her" (80). Hegemonic whiteness is invading her neighborhood; however, it is invading the space of her own mind, too. Hereafter, Sierra becomes more conscious of whiteness and its colonizing presence in her community.

Older's depictions of Sierra are in direct dialogue with popular characterizations of real Afro-Latinas. On the island, it is "better" to be born with lighter skin. There is an unfortunate underlying belief that one's skin tone reflects how much European blood someone has, and therefore how much value someone has, due to a long history of colonialism, whitewashing of Caribe indigenous culture, and the integration of African slaves. For Puerto Ricans, and much of the Caribbean region, "[the] implicit message is that phenotypically, the dark-skinned body is defective, unattractive, undesirable, but sexually enticing and therefore, a social embarrassment" (Rivera 164). These racial markers are nothing new for scholars who research the way Latina women's appearances become marked through their rebranding for US audiences; Sierra, and perhaps the reader, however, must learn to navigate this ideological space. Sierra's character engages with this ideology from the outset of her first explicit characterization as an Afro–Puerto Rican. Myra Mendible asserts that "in showcasing the Latina body as a site of knowledge production, we claim a space for Latinidad that is invariably gendered, hybrid, and transactional." Noting that "embodied selves rarely comply with the terms or theories that attempt to define them," Mendible highlights "the interstices where lived reality and public fantasies converge." The "ethnic" self is relational, "constructed through discursive and bodily mediations that signal its relative status" (5). The Latina body, she writes, is inseparable from a culture of erotic politicizing: it becomes a fantasy of the hegemonic male gaze—consumed, a space to be occupied.

Sierra's character answers this kind of objectification in a myriad of ways. On the surface level, Sierra's physical characterizations as a young, dark-skinned, curvy, wild- and nappy-haired Latina do nothing to subvert the image of the overly imagined Latina body as a "public fantasy." She resembles a Latina archetype, "packaged and marketed as an alter/native 'type' available for consumption and sale" (Mendible 13)—through the literal purchasing of a book that displays a light-skinned, Black, young woman on the cover. Here, "ethnic" beauty is neither reinforced nor negated, rather it is incorporated and made into a spectacle of diversity and inclusion (Mendible 13). Sierra's "ethnic" image becomes the commodification of difference, and Afro-Latinidad becomes a commodity, eerily resembling the dynamics of race and space in present-day Brooklyn. In other words, Older grants the audience introspection on how brown bodies navigate a realistic US city and exposes difference through the characterization of a body that still contains a sense of whiteness. It is as if there is a correlation between the notion of safety in whitewashing a city (implications of gentrification) and the whitewashing of purely darker-skinned characters because it might be easier to sell books that way.

Considering that the novel takes a risk putting a Black-presenting, young female character on its cover, therein lies a call and example for authors to tap into the mainstream, popular YA paperback industry with diverse characters, narratives, and cultural spaces. Sierra's physical characterizations in other scenes do subvert the image of the Latina body as a "public fantasy" by compelling readers to engage with discourses of racism and dehumanization in Sierra's life, thus opening potentially subversive spaces. When Sierra visits a local recently gentrified coffee shop, for example, the narrator announces her thoughts: "every time Sierra went in, the hip, young, white kid behind the counter gave her either the don't-cause-no-trouble look or the I-want-to-adopt-you look. The Takeover (as Bennie had dubbed it once) had been going on for a few years now, but tonight its pace seemed to have accelerated tenfold. Sierra couldn't find a single brown face on the block" (Older 81–82). The extent to which the narrative jumps into her consciousness and utilizes a narrated monologue compels readers to reimagine the affluent "takeover" of her community as stripping away what was once familiar to her. This colonizing gentrification of urban space likely resonates with many nonwhite readers from similar communities while at the same time encouraging white readers to reconsider this cultural-political aspect of space. Since this scene expands on notions of gentrification the novel continuously touches upon, it also draws attention to the vast variations of Latinx folk and the whitewashing of their attempts to assimilate into US. cities. However, this phenomenon is nothing new in the conversation of border crossing into US spaces.

The multifaceted but still realistic characterizations of Sierra's Afro-Puertoriqueña-ness vivify early discussions about Latinx populations situated within the US. These articulations parallel Afro–Puerto Rican identity with Gloria Anzaldúa's foundational framing of Mexican and Mexican American identities in *Borderlands/La Frontera*. She explains that the spaces on either side of the physical Mexican-US border contain large populations of Mexican and Mexican American individuals from "mixed" communities and that, because of the spaces they inhabit, they must also navigate invisible borders. These spaces contain various conflicting ideologies, rituals, and power structures. Those who navigate these spaces are pressured to assimilate to modern US societal customs, language being one of the major racial markers of how "American" one presents. However, in an age where migration into the United States is now prevented at a higher rate and those who dare to do so are treated violently, instances of reclaiming power through language find their way into publications reaching the shelves. Anzaldúa writes, "By the end of this century, Spanish speakers will comprise the biggest minority group in the U.S.... But for a language to remain alive it must be used" (Anzaldúa 259). This statement implies that by producing more texts in English, even if there is Latinx representation, something is inevitably lost.

Older does not shy away from including Spanish text in the novel, which speaks accurately to the ostensibly diverse and Spanish-speaking populations that consume popular YA books. In Sierra's search for Lucera, the figure who bridges the material and spirit worlds, her grandfather, their community's leader, gives her a clue, which he writes in Spanish. It becomes the most significant line of the novel, because it holds the clue to finding the original power of the shadowshapers. The note reads, "Donde mujeres solitarias van a bailar" (32). The use of this phrase elevates the status of Spanish in the novel, which differs from many other texts that produce ostensibly diverse characters. Here, the idea of "Spanish-impaired" is reformulated, and, as the novel continues a negotiation of nondominant language in a pop-culture-esque genre, the phrase also aesthetically binds the Spanish language to art and power—both the figurative power of shadowshaping in the novel and the power of voicing a culture more authentically. As a Latina recognizing the complicated nature of Latinx representation in popular culture, Mary Beltrán states, "Latina/os unfortunately have been marginalized in English-language [US pop culture] television story worlds, to a degree that is only beginning to be countered. We have often been invisible—simply not there—and misrepresented when we do appear" (23). Older counters this invisibility by establishing Spanish as the gateway through which Sierra finally accesses her full powers.

Anzaldúa argues that Latinx people should recognize the parts of their identities that exist outside of their experiences in US society. In "From Trigueñita to Afro-Puerto Rican," Maritza Quiñones Rivera takes up Anzaldúa's framing of mestizo, or being of mixed race, and applies a similar approach to being *trigueña*, or a Puerto Rican whose skin color is between dark and white. Rivera pulls from her own experiences as a *trigueña* growing up in Puerto Rico. She describes instances where she was too light-skinned for her darker-skinned boyfriend and then, years later, was too dark for her lighter-skinned boyfriend, which resonates with some of Sierra's experiences in *Shadowshaper*. Rivera recognizes through her reflections that she sheltered these cultural forms of racism because of her desire to protect the larger picture of being Puerto Rican. Ultimately, she suggests that being Puerto Rican is an amalgamation of colors, backgrounds, and histories, which are not well known. She writes:

> To publicly acknowledge racial differences is a threat to the island's class—and color—blindness, where individuals—regardless of their social, economic, and racial/ethnic background—are ostensibly able to realize their potential and achieve economic and social mobility. In other words, *todo el mundo es igual sin trato especial*. For some, this assertion has become a protective shield, diverting attention away from the persistent societal denial of African heritage among Puerto Ricans. Afro-Puerto Ricans have to negotiate their blackness silently, while protecting their Puerto Ricanness, their common denominator, in an often-antagonistic racial environment. (Rivera 163)

Considering this common acknowledgment of marked African identities within the larger Puerto Rican community, *Shadowshaper* does justice as it flips these firmly entrenched cultural stereotypes (maintained by people *still* colonized, we might add) by presenting a strong *trigueña* character within the realm of the dark fantastic.

It is clear that Older does not shy away from introducing various cultures of Caribbean ancestry in this novel. Sierra and her family are Puerto Rican, while Robbie is Haitian; the characters describe cultural similarities from this region—such as the shared heritage of the Taínos, or natives that inhabited many of the Caribbean islands. The narrative also portrays various qualities of other characters that directly connect to Puerto Rico, such as Sierra's brother's band, Culebra—named after a tiny island off the coast of Puerto Rico. Here, otherwise "foreign" worlds like Puerto Rico occupy significant space within the narrative: by introducing new histories and representations of the Caribbean into the white-dominated literary landscape of YA literature, *Shadowshaper* demonstrates productive and humanizing ways for diverse experiences to enter these spaces.

DECOLONIZING THE NEIGHBORHOOD

"Languaging" is another immensely important component of creating humanizing spaces and representation by allowing the authenticity of cultural qualities to stand out. In his 2019 Conference on College Composition and Communication (CCCC) keynote address, Asao B. Inoue states that "problem-posing is an ongoing process of interrogating the paradox of judgment, how we see, hear, or feel, how we language the world into existence, how we are simultaneously right and wrong, and how that languaging makes and unmakes us simultaneously." Language produces the way people of color exist in the world around them. In terms of representing diverse characters—and particularly in terms of appropriating Latinx characters, cultures, and themes—the language, dialects, expressions, scripts, inflections, words, and rhetorical situations that authors use to construct their story worlds are what creates space for minoritized identities to exist. A valid question to raise—considering *Shadowshaper*'s success—is how and to what extent it contributes to developing a "language" in popular culture that accurately represents Latinx identity and experiences.

Not only does Inoue complicate how language produces social constructions for people and communities of color (and marginalized positions in general), but he also addresses the production of sheltered, dominant discourses (primarily in the classroom) that propagate "cages" or spaces in which racism primarily gets overlooked. He states:

> The metaphor of the cage of racism reminds me of the famous "iron cage" metaphor coined by Max Weber in 1905. . . . What Weber was describing was the way in which Capitalist societies, particularly in the U.S. with its strong Protestantism, created conditions in which people self-govern their actions and beliefs, even their desires through overdetermined structures in the market economy. This is due to the fact that no matter what you as an individual believe or do, you always are implicated and circulate in market economies that dictate the nature of the cage around you—that is, dictate your own self-governance, your boundaries and desires. You are always beholden to the market . . . the market of White language.

These metaphoric cages not only speak to Thomas's exposure of the absence of diverse texts in popular children's and young adult speculative fiction but also connect nicely to Older's efforts to change the way these dominant structures within US society influence and continue repressive ideologies.

Older's characterizations of the novel's mysterious antagonist, Professor Wick, are in dialogue with these potentially colonizing attributes of language. He is one of the only white characters in the novel and resembles a Foucauldian panopticon, secretly watching Sierra from the Tower (representing "The Takeover"). At the end of the novel, readers learn that Wick—who has devoted his career to researching Indigenous history and spirituality, and their connection to the supernatural—has been killing the shadowshapers and siphoning away their magic for himself, threatening Sierra and her Afro-Latinx community's ties to their ancestors' spirits. In line with the European colonization of Puerto Rico, Wick's character appropriates their artistic and peaceful form of magic, resembling the historical relationship between the Spanish conquistadors and the Taíno, the notably peaceful Indigenous tribe of the Caribbean. During the Spanish Inquisition, conquistadors forced the Taíno into slavery in order to take what the land and its people had to offer. With this came the loss of the Taíno's way of life, which is tied to mysticism of the land and their belief in spiritual magic.

Sierra ultimately confronts Wick in the Tower and uses her powers to destroy him, restoring her community's connection to the spirits. Their battle taking place atop the Tower further compels readers to consider the politics of race, space, and colonialism, and Sierra's role in protecting her neighborhood from further exploitation positions adolescents as capable change makers. Older writes:

> Sierra was Lucera, a fierce spiritual warrior like her abuela. She was stepping into her destiny. The spirits' intentions unified with hers. They were righteous, these spirits, and ferocious. They were not about to see the world destroyed at the hands of some old fool like Wick. No. They, Sierra and the spirits, would not be manipulated, dogged, oppressed. Not after so many years of struggle. (Older 280)

This climactic battle scene fantastically parallels the colonization of Puerto Rico, where European colonizers introduced hegemonic ideologies of whiteness that still oppress their communities today. Sierra recognizes that this white, male character has stolen her community's culture and, when defeating him, yells: "It is my world! . . . And you tried to take it from me. Tried to tear my own heritage away" (Older 287). She speaks for herself and, by extension, for Afro-Puerto Ricans.

The use of space as a metaphor in the final battle suggests the inseparability of culture and the physical spaces that people inhabit, since physical spaces are always already cultural. Sierra's evolution into Lucera, the bridge between the material and spiritual worlds, revitalizes her community, and Older's depictions of that process reinforce this message. He writes:

> Sierra didn't know which thoughts were hers and which were the spirits'. . . . She raised her left hand. If there was no vessel for her to transmit spirit into, she would be the vessel. . . . Everything flashed and light flushed out the world, as if the sun had exploded. Sierra's limbs were barely moving; ancient rivers gushed through her body, an ocean raged inside her heart. She might have been floating. . . . She had to remind herself to breathe. *Become one.* One wasn't a person: It was a state. One with the spirits. Their purpose, energy, power, ferocity had all unified with her body. She was no longer the conduit; she was the form, the vessel. She, they, had become one.
>
> "*WICK!*" Sierra's voice boomed across the building, echoing back and forth amidst the empty light fixtures and dusty piping. Her voice carried the voices of a hundred thousand souls in it; a whole history of resistance and rage moved with her. (Older 280–81)

By accepting her new role as Lucera, a spiritual, border-crossing goddess, Sierra represents a convergence of Latinx identity, experience, and community. She exorcises Wick, a figure of hegemonic whiteness, and reclaims her and her community's physical and culture spaces. The scene contains an empowering message of personal agency and political resistance, and Older imagines it through the heroic actions of his adolescent, Afro-Latina protagonist.

SEEKING A SPACE FOR EMPATHY: BROWN AND BLACK BODIES IN NARRATIVE SPACES

Narrative theory serves both as a tool and as a general framework with which to understand and analyze the various aspects of narrative storytelling, including its parts, processes, and effects. While narrative theory has historically been a predominantly white discipline, it nonetheless highlights useful structural implications for diversity in children's and young adult literature. Rhetorical narratology grants introspection into the process of reading and interpretation, creating an organized approach into readers' experiences and encounters with texts. In *Somebody Telling Somebody Else: A Rhetorical Poetics of Narrative* (2017), James Phelan argues from a rhetorical narratological perspective that "narrative is less about its materials (narrators, characters, events, techniques and so on) than about how tellers use them to influence their audience in particular ways" (1). His rhetorical approach is useful to our project because it emphasizes the importance of the role of the author—not in the sense that a text's supposed meaning adheres to an author's intentions—but in the sense that the rhetorical dynamics between authors and readers are a critical component for analyzing the potential effects of narrative. In our case, those potential effects include the extent to which Older's depictions of adolescence, race, and space compel readers to empathize with the story's narrator, Afro-Latinx characters, and the larger Puerto Rican US experience.

Furthermore, it is also important to analyze how authors and readers, through narrative, imagine what it means to be Afro-Latinx in the United States today. Thomas argues Black and brown folk must contend with a disenfranchising collective imagination on a daily basis, which is connected to the "long-entrenched lack of diversity" (3–4). The way authors write about Afro-Latinx youth gets shaped not only by their own experiences and familiarity with these marginalized communities but also by their conceptualizations of their implied readers, the experiences of these readers, and the readers' prior familiarity (or lack of) with Afro-Latinidad. In order to ensure that representations of diverse characters continue providing positive images and experiences of the cultures they represent, we must engage with how texts are written. Phelan explains that narrative is an action:

> a teller using resources of narrative to achieve a purpose in relation to an audience. The second both complements and complicates the first: the presence of somebody else in the narrative action is integral to its shape. In other words, the audience does not just react to the teller's communication; instead the audience and its unfolding responses significantly influence how the teller constructs the tale. (2)

In this sense the implied readers of children's and young adult literature help constitute a narrative's profile. The responses that authors like Older anticipate from their readers, consciously and unconsciously, are integral to the content and structure of their storytelling. In order to understand the impact of these rhetorical dynamics for readers, we find using Suzanne Keen's concept of *authorial strategic empathizing* useful for identifying spaces in the text where readers can connect productively with nonwhite characters.

"Narrative empathy," Keen writes, "intersects with identities in problematic ways. Do we respond because we belong to an in-group, or can narrative empathy call to us across boundaries of difference?" ("Narrative Empathy" 83). She coins the term *strategic empathizing* to "[indicate] the intentional (not always efficacious) work of narrative artists to evoke emotions of audiences closer and further from the authors and subjects of representation" (83). Keen's rhetorical framework is explicitly invested in the identities of authors and readers, both real and implied, through what she describes as a "metaphor of nearness/distance [but that] also correlates with familiarity/strangeness and sameness/otherness" (83). This framework is especially useful for analyzing *Shadowshaper* because, while its readers may be infinitely diverse, its author is a person of color; its diverse, featured characters are predominantly people of color; and its plot emphasizes identity and experience in an explicit way. Readers with identities both similar to and dissimilar to the featured characters are thus called to respond through emotional and cognitive engagement.

This call suggests that diverse narratives themselves are immensely important because they encourage readers to empathize with nondominant characters or situations with which they may not already be familiar. Older's depictions of nonwhite characters' physical/cultural spaces reflect an array of Puerto Rican realities. Readers' interactions with these depictions are spaces that bridge complex, diverse characterizations of Afro-Latinx identity and experience within the novel with the common stereotypes about them outside of the novel. When, for instance, Sierra sneaks into the Columbia University Library to learn more about who the shadowshapers are and what the mysterious Professor Wick has to do with her family, she enters a space that she already understands is somewhat separated from her world. Older writes:

> Sierra had never seen so many books. *Economic Development in the Third World*, one title proclaimed loudly from a display table. *Studies in Puerto Rican Literature* said another. It'd never occurred to her there was such a thing as Puerto Rican literature, let alone that it would be worthy of a thick volume in a Columbia University library. A smaller paperback was called *Debating Uncle Remus: An Anthology of Essays and Stories about the Historic Southern Folktales*. (Older 48)

The passage addresses economic and educational disparities that Latinx communities sometimes face in the US, while simultaneously directing the reader to contemplate other real-world issues. The first title suggests a connection between poverty and the still-colonized country of Puerto Rico. The second surprises Sierra; people outside her neighborhood seldomly acknowledge Puerto Rican culture, and they never do so in a meaningful way. And the third implies a connection between the Black community, slavery, and Puerto Rican history: Spaniards brought Africans to Puerto Rico (and many other Caribbean islands) as slaves, just as they did in the mainland US. This narrative positioning anticipates familiarity from some of its informed readers (an example of *bounded* strategic empathy); encourages learning for others who do not perceive themselves as insiders to Sierra's understanding or experience (an example of *ambassadorial* strategic empathy); and capitalizes on any reader's general, human experiences of feeling like an outsider in an unfamiliar place (an example of *broadcast* strategic empathy). Similarly, the familiarity of just "being an adolescent" maintains space for disinvited readers to engage with the text. "Though we are prone to notice the delineations of class, gender, sexuality, and ethnicity that mark a text as for one audience and not so much for another," Keen explains, "an effort of strategic empathizing may also be bounded by the toggle switch of experience.... Nothing prevents a reader who has not shared an experience from exercising the role-taking imagination while reading a remote or forbidding work, but some works do not extend the invitation to all potential readers" ("Narrative Empathy" 83). In other words, readers are compelled to respond to texts based on their perceived experiences of mutuality with characters, whether the readers and characters are actually members of the same in-groups or not. Older utilizes multiple forms of authorial strategic empathizing in *Shadowshaper*, and passages like this one demonstrate how books, including genres like urban fantasy, can utilize diverse representation productively.

Readers encounter explicit representations of Puerto Rican culture in other spaces, too, such as when other characters share aspects of their communal history with Sierra that are new to her, too. For example, Sierra's friend Robbie (who is also a shadowshaper) explains that even though his cultural background is Haitian, they share a similar heritage with Puerto Rico:

> Sierra: "Why they always gotta draw Indians lookin' so serious? Don't they smile?"
> Robbie: "That's a Taíno, Sierra."
> Sierra: "What? But you're Haitian. I thought Taínos were my peeps."
> Robbie: "Nah, Haiti had 'em too. Has 'em. You know..."
> Sierra: "I didn't know." (Older 125–26)

Encountering this dialogue, different groups of readers may position themselves with Sierra as insiders, learning as she does, or they may position themselves with Robbie as insiders, already knowing this information. The way Older conveys this information is not overtly didactic and allows engagement on multiple levels.

This narrative tactic aligns with Older's assertion for his own works, which he discusses in an interview with Frederick Aldama. Aldama's *Latino/a Children's and Young Adult Writers on the Art of Storytelling* (2018) explicitly examines the role and impact of Latinx experiences and epistemologies in children's and young adult literature. "There's a long tradition of fiction (and media generally)," Older notes, "that focuses on urban landscapes filled with simplistic representations of Latinos—and people of color generally. There's a kind of reclamation that needs to happen to get back to the truth of what it really means for people of color to live in the city. That's a complex truth that I seek to capture in my work" (qtd. in Aldama 170). This iteration of strategic empathizing is also linked to the ways in which authors, publishers, critics, teachers, and other gatekeepers can call for allyship around issues of diversity and equity. For example, non-Latinx readers may not be able to understand wholly the experiences of Latinx people and communities; however, by reading Latinx young adult literature, they can develop an ethical understanding of and feeling toward Latinx experiences.

Older also incorporates opportunities for readers to discover not only ways that Puerto Ricans are a part of large US city spaces but also how these spaces cultivate positive representations of brown and Black characters.

Utilizing magical realism, Older emphasizes that the sacred magic of shadowshaping is brought to the United States exclusively from Puerto Rico. The description of Sierra's grandfather's shadowshaping legacy reads as a communal space: "It's like a whole spirit world in Brooklyn that Abuelo was in touch with. He was deep with them. Came over from PR with a buncha spirits, I guess, and then kept it going the whole time he was here" (109). Puerto Rico is the originating place of magic that can save the world from evil and malice. Through the use of magic, Brooklyn's urban landscape transforms from containing stigmatized representations of Latinx folk to one that contains something special brought from "La Isla de Encanto" (Island of Enchantment)—a nickname that Puerto Ricans often use. This maneuver is a strategic choice, compelling the reader to reconsider spatial and racial expectations.

CAN I SEE ME? LATINAS NAVIGATING SPACE

Aspects of characterization provide useful access points for analyzing the dynamics and processes of representing diverse characters in *Shadowshaper*. Sierra's characterizations would feel relatively empty without Older's rhetorical positioning and foregrounding of teen experience. Older's characterizations of Sierra and fellow artist Robbie's budding romance, for example, offer numerous contact points for various readers. The scene where they dance together at a club likely resonates with a large audience, whereas the detailed descriptions of their interactions highlight their culturally specific tenacity: "He took her arm, raised it up, and placed his other hand on her hip. 'Ooh! I love a little belly fat on a girl.' / 'Shut up!' Sierra laughed and felt the blood rush to her face. 'No one asked for your opinion'" (Older 125). The dialogue presents a culturally relevant machismo about Robbie, and the exposition reinforces Sierra's physical characterizations as a voluptuous Latina. The passage thus invites different kinds of responses from its readers, continuing to perpetuate the commodification of Latina bodies, but doing so without contradicting or negating the positive spaces that Sierra has been navigating. In other words, her agency here demonstrates that she doesn't need validation from Robbie or even the reader.

The text also provides ample descriptions of the spaces the Puerto Rican characters navigate. When visiting the Columbia University Library for the first time, Sierra meets Nydia, the head librarian of the Anthropology Archives. Older's characterization of Nydia provides immense US cultural significance for people of color in predominantly white spaces: academia and libraries—both of which are institutions that are also the gatekeepers of knowledge. When Sierra questions Nydia about how she got the position, because she looks so young, Nydia responds, indicating that she is thirty-three, "And I got a seven-year-old and a nine-year-old. But thanks for the compliment. Black don't crack, ya know? And anyway, we Boricuas age at our own dang pace. You Puerto Rican, right?" (Older 50). Not only is this one of the first instances where the audience gets insight into Sierra's cultural background, but it also depicts a woman of color paving the way for the next generation of marginalized youths of color to enter these "white" spaces.

Older's characterization of the library space also provides a counternarrative that Latinx people belong and can excel in academic spaces. Nydia says:

> "I love books and I wanna be around 'em all day, even if it's in some dingy basement at a stuffy old university on the Upper West Side." True to her heritage, the head librarian talked a mile a minute. "Eventually, Imma open my own library up here in Harlem, but like a people's library, not just for academics. And it'll be full of people's stories, not just jargon scholar talk. This is like practice, really, and to boost my standing in the eyes of certain potential founders." (Older 50)

This quotation demonstrates the capacity with which Older's diverse characters navigate white, dominant spaces and even reclaim them throughout the book. It also addresses Thomas's argument at the beginning of this chapter: there are too few opportunities for real Black and brown readers to pick up books and read humanizing representations of people of color within realistic spaces.

CHANGING WORLDS: (RE)PAINTING THE LITERARY LANDSCAPE

Significantly, Thomas references Older in the introduction to *The Dark Fantastic*, agreeing with his own position statement as an author, creative writing professor, and activist himself. He discusses an issue that is largely overlooked in academia and in publishing, which is that calling for diversity is not enough:

> The question industry professionals need to ask themselves is: "How can I use my position to help create a literary world that is diverse, equitable, and doesn't just represent the same segment of society it always has since its inception? What concrete actions can I take to

make actual change and move beyond the tired conversation we've been having for decades?" (Older qtd. in Thomas 5)

Older alludes not only to authors but to editors, sensitivity readers, educators, librarians, and so on. It begs all of us to take up the lack of diversity in children's and young adult literature and address the larger social issue this erasure produces. Sierra's magical heroism allows readers to experience Puerto Rican identity, cultural and historical markers, and identify where racism may still exist in our own familiar spaces.

To extend the metaphor of the cage introduced earlier, it is crucial to consider what's missing when authors write urban fantasy primarily about white folk. In an interview for *The Guardian* in 2015, Older specifically states that his purpose for writing *Shadowshaper* and other novels centering diverse characters is to "generally fuck shit up." He makes the case that authors are responsible for generating texts that emulate realistic representations, even (or especially) in fantasy worlds. He states:

> We're doing something very political by deciding whose life matters, where we're going to focus things, and who we erase from the picture. . . . When we create worlds based on this world that don't include diversity, we're lying. . . . We're not being honest as authors. Even if it's infused with magical powers, or zombies, or whatever you'll have, we should still be trying to tell the truth. Then, it becomes a question of what truth, how are we telling it, and whose truth do we take the time to repeat? (Older qtd. in Ford n.p.)

The rhetorical dynamics of Older's authorship certainly have their own impact on readers. His portrayals of Afro-Latinx identity and experience are shaped by his anticipation of readers' familiarity (or lack thereof) with Latinx cultures. *Shadowshaper* is honest. It acknowledges negative stereotypes about Latinx communities and combats them with realistic depictions. It centers brown lives, experiences, and spaces, packaging them in culturally specific urban fantasy.

Works Cited

Aldama, Frederick Luis. *Latino/a Children's and Young Adult Writers on the Art of Storytelling*. U of Pittsburgh P, 2018.
Anzaldúa, Gloria. "How to Tame a Wild Tongue." *Herencia: The Anthology of Hispanic Literature of the United States*, edited by Nicolás Kanellos, Oxford UP, 2002, pp. 254–61.

Beltrán, Mary. "Latina/os on TV! A Proud (and Ongoing) Struggle over Representation and Authorship." *The Routledge Companion to Latina/o Popular Culture*, edited by Frederick Luis Aldama, Routledge, 2016, pp. 23–33.

Broadnax, Jamie. "What the Heck Is Afrofuturism?" *Huffpost*, 16 February 2018. Accessed 4 February 2020.

Carlowicz, Mike. "Puerto Rico Landscape Ravaged by Hurricane Maria." *NASA*, 28 September 2017. Accessed 4 February 2020.

Cooperative Children's Book Center (CCBC). "Books by and/or about Black, Indigenous and People of Color 2018–." *School of Education, University of Wisconsin-Madison*, https://ccbc.education.wisc.edu/literature-resources/ccbc-diversity-statistics/books-by-and-or-about-poc-2018/, 27 October 2020. Accessed 25 February 2021.

Diaz, Shawn Michael. "Why Santurce Es Ley Is Puerto Rico's Best Cultural Festival." *Puerto Rico Revealed*, 10 August 2014. Accessed 4 February 2020.

Ford, Ashley C. "Daniel José Older Creates Female Black Heroes to Make Fantasy More Real." *Guardian*, 29 June 2015. Accessed 4 February 2020.

Inoue, Asao B. "How Do We Language So People Stop Killing Each Other, Or What Do We Do about White Language Supremacy?" *Conference on College Composition and Communication*, Pittsburgh, PA, 14 March 2019.

Keen, Suzanne. "Narrative Empathy." *Toward a Cognitive Theory of Narrative Acts*, edited by Frederick Luis Aldama, U of Texas P, 2010, pp. 61–93.

Mendible, Myra. "Embodying Latinidad." *From Bananas to Buttocks: The Latina Body in Popular Film and Culture*. U of Texas P, 2007, pp. 1–28.

Older, Daniel José. *Shadowshaper*. Scholastic, 2015.

Phelan, James. *Somebody Telling Somebody Else: A Rhetorical Poetics of Narrative*. Ohio State UP, 2017.

Prado, Rocio Isabel. "Inexact Revolutions: Understanding Latino Pop Art." *The Routledge Companion to Latina/o Popular Culture*, edited by Frederick Luis Aldama, Routledge, 2016, pp. 205–13.

Rivera, Maritza Quiñones. "From Trigueñita to Afro–Puerto Rican: Intersections of the Racialized, Gendered, and Sexualized Body in Puerto Rico and the U.S. Mainland." *Meridians: Feminism, Race, Transnationalism*, vol. 7, no. 1, 2006, pp. 162–82.

Thomas, Ebony Elizabeth. *The Dark Fantastic: Race and the Imagination from "Harry Potter" to the "Hunger Games."* New York UP, 2019.

"Top Ten Most Challenged Books Lists." *American Library Association*, 26 March 2013, www.ala.org/advocacy/bbooks/frequentlychallengedbooks/top10. Accessed 4 February 2020.

Chapter Six

THE WIDE, STARLIT SKY

Childhood Space and Changing Identity in the Work of Laura Ingalls Wilder

JOYCE McPHERSON

In the first decades of the twentieth century, several conventions in children's literature defined the space that children occupied. Earlier works tended to privilege home as a child's proper sphere, and journeys away from home concluded with a return to that space in a type of circular progression. Also, the focus was often on events rather than on the child's interior perspective, so that space was consistently projected outward rather than inward. In 1935 Laura Ingalls Wilder published *Little House on the Prairie*, a novel that would exemplify a new path in children's literature. She transforms the traditional space for children from a defined building or place to the wide-open frontier through the creation of a linear progression of journey-home-new journey. This new space reveals the reality of nature, rather than a romanticized pastoral idyll common to earlier children's books. In addition, Wilder validates the interior space of the child protagonist by relating emotions and thoughts through a close third-person perspective. This interiority invites the child readers into the story's world to experience and evaluate their impressions, a move away from a didactic approach and toward the child reader as an independent evaluator. Indeed, Wilder includes interactions with Indigenous people that give readers the opportunity to consider complex issues. An analysis of *Little House on the Prairie* reveals an inflection point in children's literature in the 1930s as perceptions of childhood space and identity began to change. Wilder challenges the discourse begun by earlier authors to create insights on both adult expectations of where children belong and the growing awareness among child readers of their freedom to explore.

REMAPPING THE SPACES OF CHILDHOOD: LINEAR PATTERNS

In *Poetics of Space*, Gaston Bachelard seeks "to determine the human value of the sorts of space that may be grasped," and he coins the term "eulogized space" (Bachelard & Jolas xxxv). This eulogized space is significant to Bachelard's conception, because space receives meaning from lived experience, and its existence is crystallized in a moment of time. Moreover, Bachelard validates imagination, which he defines as an embodied relational state of openness that enables the experience of space. Wilder's semi-autobiographical novel achieves this definition of space as a physical place that may be grasped and eulogized. Perhaps more importantly, her linear pattern of successive locations for her child protagonist demonstrates an innovative understanding of childhood spaces realized through imagination. A deeper understanding of Wilder's approach to children's literature reveals a remapping of the spaces of childhood.

Wilder's linear theme is significant since adult perceptions of childhood space have impacted the genre of children's literature from its inception (Nikolajeva 79). In the English-speaking world, several conventions in children's literature had been established by the third decade of the twentieth century. One of the most prominent was the home-journey-home plot as can be seen in a sample of books such as *The Wonderful Wizard of Oz* (1900), *Five Children and It* (1902), and *Peter Pan in Kensington Gardens* (1906). According to Perry Nodelman and Mavis Reimer, "many versions of the generic story try to persuade young readers that despite its boredom, home, representative of adult values, is a better place to be than the dangerous world outside" (200). The security and protection of home is a common theme for this time period, perhaps as an effort on the part of adults to place children in safe spaces. Wilder, however, is an iconoclast in regard to the sanctity of the conventional home. She does not privilege one space (home or away-from-home) over the other; she creates a narrative space for her readers and invites them to explore the possibilities for themselves.

Little House on the Prairie begins with a journey, which leads to a home and finally advances to an open ending with a fresh journey. Ironically, though "house" or the geographic location is identified in several titles in Wilder's series, none of them is permanent. The family leaves the first home in *Little House in the Big Woods*, abandons the cabin in *Little House on the Prairie*, and spends only two years in a dugout in *On the Banks of Plum Creek*. This pattern of temporary homes bounded by journeys reveals important issues about childhood space. The home-journey-home paradigm is often cited as an adult attempt to colonize children and urge a joyful acceptance of the constraints of childhood (Nodelman & Reimer 96). Classic literature of earlier periods that concluded with a homecoming, like *The Wizard of Oz*, tended to communicate morals concerning the goodness of home and the danger of journeys. In *Little House on the Prairie*, however, Wilder turns this idea on its head as Laura embraces the independence of the new journey at the conclusion of the novel. This inversion of the typical pattern was intentional. Wilder based her children's novels on her adult manuscript *Pioneer Girl*, which was written as one long narrative without chapter breaks. For the children's series, Wilder chose where each novel should begin and end within that original narrative. She broke from the traditional structure of home-journey-home and crafted a journey-home-journey pattern for *Little House on the Prairie*. By framing the novel in this manner, Wilder suggests that the journey is a vital childhood sphere.

The inversion of the typical paradigm is the first clue to Wilder's validation of childhood space as more fluid than was previously depicted in children's literature. Rather than furnish readers with an argument for the superiority of home, she leaves the judgment for her child reader. The potential ambivalence felt by the reader, who has witnessed the work and sacrifice to build the house on the prairie, is tempered by the sense of adventure and newness that lies before Laura and her family. Corroboration for this fresh perspective may be found in *Pioneer Girl*, where Wilder celebrates the move to Silver Lake, farther west: "for we were on our way again and going in the direction which always brought the happiest changes" (145). Through a reversal of the traditional pattern, Wilder places the journey on equal terms with the destination. She consciously redefines childhood space as more expansive and opens a new world of identity for her readers by empowering them to make their own conclusions.

SPACES OF CHILDHOOD: REALISM OVER ROMANTICISM

The linear pattern provides further clues to the larger themes of the novel. In *Little House on the Prairie*, the linear structure enlarges its childhood space to include the natural world; however, Wilder does not incorporate the romanticized version of idyllic nature portrayed in children's literature of the early twentieth century. Nodelman and Reimer point to many children's books that create a type of pastoral idyll with the innocence of nature imparting a sense of optimism or security (210). Examples include *Anne of Green Gables* (1908) and *The Secret Garden* (1911), in which nature in the safe bounds of the community ennobles children. Nodelman and Reimer theorize that the vision of children as pure and in harmony with nature demonstrates how "the focalization of many texts for children is less through an accurately childlike vision than it is through a form of childlikeness invented by adults for adult purposes" (211). Perhaps the enduring appeal of the *Little House* books is derived from the contradiction of these generalizations.

Wilder does not portray Laura as living an idyllic life: her family is isolated on a prairie where wolves menace them and disease almost overwhelms them. Nor is Laura always cheerful or confidently moral; her world is ambiguous at times. Wilder describes an ordinary family in a realistic environment that experiences the consequences of untamed nature. They face dangers from flood, fire, snow, and wolves, and they risk their health from disease, falling logs, and poisonous gas in a well. Although Wilder does present the beauty of nature in passages that describe "rippling grass" (13) and "pearly clouds ... in the immense blueness overhead" (39), she also describes the howls of wolves that "filled the moonlight and quavered across the vast silence of the prairie" (98). She expands the space of the pastoral idyll by responding to the beauty of nature while at the same time acknowledging the reality of danger. The realism in her writing is further enhanced by Wilder's inclusion of tragedy in her books for children. This realism was unusual in the first decades of the twentieth century, when optimistic conclusions for events were common for children's literature. When her daughter encouraged her to omit Mary's blindness from the novels, Wilder responded in a letter: "A touch of tragedy makes the story truer to life, and showing the way we all took it illustrates the spirit of the times and the frontier" (qtd. in Hill 143). Wilder purposely crafted her narrative to communicate respect for her child readers, who are invited into a larger world that reflects more reality than was typical in children's literature.

For Wilder, security and optimism do not emanate from an idyllic setting but instead grow out of the family relationships, which are stable despite a changing landscape and location. This theme of security within the family travels through *Little House on the Prairie* as a unifying thread. Ma tucking Laura into bed, the dog Jack's watchfulness, and Pa's gun represent safety. The circle that Pa plows around the house to save them from the prairie fire symbolizes the protection of the family. The book ends with a final circle of Ma looking "through the round hole in the wagon cover" (335), watching over Laura as she falls asleep. These images of security in the family circle transcend location and corroborate Bachelard's observation that home is both a physical and psychological space. In this sense Laura is never truly homeless, even on her journeys. Wilder expands childhood space to new frontiers, for unlike traditional protagonists who were not complete until they arrived at home, Laura finds fulfillment in a psychological home that occupies new physical spaces.

In addition to the security of family spaces, Laura transmits a sense of self-reliance despite a continuous barrage of obstacles and disasters. This concept of family self-sufficiency was strategically created by Wilder. In *Prairie Girl*, she narrates how the family moved in the company of other families from their cabin on the prairie, but for the children's novel, she describes them departing alone. Pamela Smith Hill, who curated the publishing of *Pioneer Girl*, posits, "By striking out on their own, the fictional family becomes almost mythic, archetypal characters who embody the frontier experience in the American West" (20). As support for this theory, *Little House in the Big Woods* is placed first in the series to create a western progression among the books, even though the autobiographical account in *Pioneer Girl* reveals that the family returned east to Wisconsin after their first settlement on the prairie. This manipulation of the larger narrative expands childhood space to the frontier, which continues to move farther away from the original home. *Little House on the Prairie* is a microcosm of the larger series; it reflects Wilder's innovation of challenging the prevailing convention in children's literature of idyllic childhoods located in fixed homes and romanticized nature. By extension the family's self-sufficiency has personal implications for the child reader: on the last page of the novel, the "wide, starlit sky" (335), with its boundlessness and reassuring light, becomes a symbol of a new definition of childhood independence in both space and identity.

OPENING UP NARRATIVE SPACE: THE CHILD'S VIEWPOINT

Wilder not only extends physical space for her readers but also redefines the childhood sphere to include internal space, reflected by the child's viewpoint. During the early twentieth century, the majority of books published for children were adventures with a strong emphasis on action and scene. As a result, the genre of children's literature tended to focus on external events rather than internal viewpoint. Some of the most popular books published from 1900 to 1930 were *The Wonderful Wizard of Oz* (L. Frank Baum, 1900), *Five Children and It* (E. Nesbit 1902), *Peter Pan in Kensington Gardens* (J. M. Barrie, 1906), *Anne of Green Gables* (L. M. Montgomery, 1908), *The Secret Garden* (Frances Hodgson Burnett, 1911), *The Adventures of Danny Meadow Mouse* (Thornton Burgess, 1915), *Doctor Doolittle* (Hugh Lofting, 1920), *The Boxcar Children* (Gertrude Chandler Warner, 1924) and *Hitty, Her First Hundred*

Years (Rachel Field, 1929). The writing style mimicked adult literature of the late nineteenth century with the use of the omniscient third-person narrator to describe the action of the plot. The adult perspective often came through the creation of a mature narrator (as with Field's *Hitty*) or the viewpoint of adult characters (as with books by Montgomery and Burnett). These action-oriented stories had popular appeal, seemingly supporting Nodelman and Reimer's assertion that "[children's] main focus is always on the events of the plot" (203). Traditional children's literature of the early twentieth century demonstrated this phenomenon with adult narrators using action to drive the story. Wilder, on the other hand, opens a new space in children's literature by narrating her story through the observations and reactions of her child protagonist. She develops a close third-person perspective that opens children's identity to the inner person. Wilder's narration through Laura's eyes is intimate and individualized in the context of a person similar in age to the reader. Laura's reactions are also present-oriented and immediate, and her impressions engender empathy. Moreover, her responses move the child readers into Laura's interior space; as a result, Wilder's choice of perspective strengthens the value of the child's viewpoint.

Wilder's unique use of the child perspective can be demonstrated by placing several samples of children's literature from the first three decades of the twentieth century beside one another. Each of these excerpts comes from the same page number in the respective book, and the random nature of their selection supports the observations on Wilder's fresh approach to childhood space and identity. In contrast to these other novels, Wilder firmly places the viewpoint from a single child protagonist, as in this excerpt:

> Laura couldn't wait to see the inside of the house. As soon as the tall hole was cut, she ran inside. Everything was striped there. Stripes of sunshine came through the cracks in the west wall, and stripes of shadow came down from the poles overhead. (Wilder 64)

Only the details that can be perceived by Laura are recorded, and they are filtered through her unique brand of perception. In contrast, other novels often consider the children as a group, as in this excerpt from Nesbit's *Five Children and It*:

> The thing that troubled them most was the fear that the old gentleman's guinea might have disappeared at sunset with all the rest, so they went down to the village next day to apologize for not meeting him in Rochester, and to *see*. They found him very friendly. (Nesbit 64)

The aggregation of a group perspective distances the readers so that they do not identify with one character closely. Also, this approach suggests that children are a group, rather than individuals.

Perhaps more importantly, the tone of Wilder's narration identifies closely with a child's point of view at a time when many narrators seemed to speak with an adult voice, as in this excerpt from *Hitty, Her First Hundred Years*:

> There was, indeed, no one but our little party to hear him except some highly colored birds and a number of small brown animals with long tails who ran, chattering, over the branches above us. These, I later learned, were called "monkeys," and I was to see far more of them before my days on the Island were over. (Field 64)

This mature narrator feels the need to explain the unusual animal, and she ranges backward and forward in time, giving the perspective of one who is telling a story from her distant past. Wilder, in contrast, firmly places Laura in the space of the present, imparting immediacy to her impressions such as the "stripes of sunshine" (64) coming through the cracks.

Wilder's choice of a close third-person perspective furnishes the reader with a view of events from Laura's eyes. This viewpoint differs from the detachment of an outside observer, which was a common convention in earlier children's literature. In this excerpt from *Anne of Green Gables*, the narrator seems to be watching Anne rather than experiencing emotions through Anne's perception:

> But Anne continued to face Mrs. Rachel undauntedly, head up, eyes blazing, hands clenched, passionate indignation exhaling from her like an atmosphere.
>
> "How dare you say such things about me?" she repeated vehemently. "How would you like to have such things said about you? How would you like to be told that you are fat and clumsy and probably hadn't a spark of imagination in you?" (Montgomery 64)

While Montgomery provides dialogue and exterior details of Anne's posture, eyes and hands as a means of establishing her responses, Wilder adopts the close third-person to record inner sensations and impressions. As an example, Wilder narrates Laura's experience of hearing a distant gathering of Indigenous peoples with sentences like "It made Laura's heart beat fast," (266) and "It was a wild, fierce sound, but it didn't seem angry" (265). Laura's physical sensations and interpretations communicate her responses to the event. Montgomery's approach in *Anne of Green Gables*, however, was the norm for this period. Indeed, most children's novels of the early twentieth century employed an omniscient narrator who changed viewpoints, as in this passage from *The Secret Garden*:

> In the evening they had all sat round the fire, and Martha and her mother had sewed patches on torn clothes and mended stockings and Martha had told them about the little girl who had come from India and who had been waited on all her life. (Burnett 64)

In this passage, Burnett provides a scene that the child protagonist, Mary Lennox, could not have witnessed, and she conveys judgment on Mary through the viewpoint of another character. This aspect of judgment further separates the reader from the child protagonist by removing a sense of empathy.

Though many of these authors draw sympathetic sketches of child protagonists, none of them maintains a close third-person narration from a single child's viewpoint. Nesbit, for example, focuses more on the children's adventures and the unexpected results than on the inner thoughts of one child. Montgomery crafts Anne's story through several perspectives, many of them adult viewpoints, and primarily reveals the child protagonist's thoughts through conversation rather than inner reflections. Even Field, who employs the first-person viewpoint of the doll Hitty, gives the doll a detachment typical of an adult narrator telling a story many years after the event. Wilder, in contrast, tells her story through conversations, descriptions, actions, and thoughts filtered through the eyes of the child Laura, building the consistency of the larger text through this single perspective. This strategy invites the child reader to enter Laura's space and experience a new identity. It validates the child viewpoint and empowers the child readers to perceive for themselves.

The impact of the close third-person perspective can be observed in the narrative of the night Laura sees the wolf pack. Wilder enables her readers to access the narrative sphere through concrete details perceived through the senses of the child protagonist. The visual description is carefully worded to inspire a child's inner eye: "The moonlight made little glitters in the edges of the shaggy fur, all around the big wolf" (96–97). In addition to visual details, Wilder employs Laura's sense of hearing to describe the scene—"Laura could hear their [the wolves'] breathing" (97), and "Pet and Patty were squealing and running inside the barn. Their hoofs pounded the ground and crashed against the walls" (97). The sense of touch is incorporated as well: "Pa stood firm against her back and kept his arm tight around her middle" (96). Even internal sensations are shared: "Laura was too scared to make a sound. The cold was not in her backbone only, it was all through her" (95). The descriptions are minimal but vivid and personal, and they evoke the setting in an almost tangible way. This intensity of sensory details translates well into children's fiction, in which a child reader can identify with Laura and become part of the action—a significant example of Wilder's creating a space for the reader to enter the story. While earlier children's novels placed the child reader as an outside observer, Wilder pulls her reader into the scene through a close third-person perspective that filters concrete details.

ESTABLISHING INTIMATE SPACES: WILDER'S USE OF INTERIORITY AND STRATEGIC DICTION

The space between child readers and the narrative is further diminished by Wilder's use of what Louise Mowder identifies as "an elementary form of free indirect discourse" (15), which by the nineteenth century was common in adult fiction, such as novels by Jane Austen and Henry James, but almost unknown in children's literature. Free indirect discourse is used to create an intimate connection with the reader. James Wood in *How Fiction Works* asserts that it differs from indirect speech through the omission of "authorial flagging" (7). Wilder often omits authorial flagging, as in this example: "It seemed a long time before the cornbread and the sizzling beef steaks were done" (171). The opinion emanates from Laura, but Wilder crafts the narration to flow seamlessly into her thoughts without the addition of "Laura thought." Free indirect discourse is most powerful when hardly noticeable, and often a single word reveals that the narration is the character's thoughts. In this sentence from *Little House on the Prairie*, the addition of "lonely" communicates that this is Laura's interpretation of the nature of the songs: "Laura lay awake, listening to the lonely songs wandering in the night" (165). The practice of sharing the child's viewpoint with other children is one of Wilder's most significant contributions to the changing perception of childhood space and identity. It is more profound because Wilder speaks across generations and across geography, opening a new world of experience to her child readers.

To create this intimate perspective, Wilder employs a child's diction for her narrator. In many late-nineteenth century and early twentieth-century novels for children, the narrator is an older person, who speaks down to the reader, using words like "little." The word "little" is embedded throughout Wilder's oeuvre and even used in several titles; however, it does not communicate a sense of patronizing diction. Instead, Wilder firmly creates the perspective of a child through context, vocabulary, wording, and phrasing. The craft required to establish the child's diction is evident in Wilder's process. Before writing the children's novels, Wilder wrote the adult narrative *Pioneer Girl*. Although it was not published for an adult market during her lifetime, the manuscript became the seed material for her children's books, and passages from the original document can be compared to their counterparts in the *Little House* series to understand Wilder's craftsmanship. As an example, the *Pioneer Girl* manuscript describes the scene of a prairie fire: "One day the smoke seemed thicker" (14). When Wilder describes the same scene in *Little House on the Prairie*, she writes: "Suddenly the sunshine was gone" (276). Wilder employs simple phrasing to record impressions from Laura's point of view, and then she proceeds to describe her inner feelings: "Laura wanted to do something, but inside her head was a roaring and whirling like the fire" (280). The description uses metaphorical language that makes sense to a child. This approach transforms the episode into a more powerful story than a simple recounting of the fire would accomplish. The immediacy of the sunshine disappearing and the intimacy of her physical reactions heighten the reader's vicarious experience. In addition to crafting diction that maintains a strong child's viewpoint, Wilder developed specialized vocabulary. For example, she employs "Ma" and "Pa" for the parents' names. Wilder's first editor at Alfred Knopf was concerned that it was "a little colloquial" (qtd. in Hill 26), which demonstrates the innovation Wilder was introducing for children's literature. Publishers and their editors were accustomed to a more formal narrator who spoke from an adult viewpoint. Despite editorial criticism, Wilder retained the titles of "Ma" and "Pa" in her quest for an authentic voice. By the time the manuscript found a home at Harper and Brothers, the editors did not try to change it. Wilder had created a fresh voice that brings children into the intimate narrative space.

Wilder's innovations involve the child readers in the space of the novel rather than leaving them outside as observers of an adult interpretation of events. Wolfgang Iser has documented this phenomenon of the inside observer in adult fiction (275), but it is significant that Wilder introduced this process for her child readers in the 1930s. One example of the technique is the change Wilder made in describing the wagon cover. In the original *Pioneer Girl* manuscript, Wilder describes the "nice tight cover to keep out the wind and the rain," but in the children's novel the description becomes a separate episode:

> "I'll tie down the wagon-cover," Pa said. He climbed down from the seat, unrolled the canvas sides and tied them firmly to the wagon

box. Then he pulled the rope at the back, so that the canvas puckered together in the middle, leaving only a tiny round hole, too small to see through. (20)

Rather than explaining that the cover is good and tight, Wilder allows the reader to observe how it was made. This approach satisfies the curiosity of the readers and respects their ability to judge for themselves the qualities of the wagon cover. The last phrase that describes "a tiny round hole, too small to see through" (20) places the child reader inside the wagon. Wilder implies that children have the right to experience and evaluate what they read. She ushers them into a space that respects children's perceptions. Bachelard writes that "imagination augments the values of reality" (3). In this sense the interpretation of space as physical places with ascribed meaning validates the child reader's experience of space through association with a child protagonist.

Wilder further strengthens the child reader's experience of the narrative space by employing subtext for unspoken emotions and thoughts. This technique stimulates readers to supply their own emotions. In the scene of the dangerous creek crossing, Wilder narrates: "Then Pa's voice frightened Laura. It said, 'Take them, Caroline!'" (21). Laura does not understand what is happening at first, and her actions and sensations create the tension: "She felt cold and sick. Her eyes were shut tight, but she could still see the terrible water and Pa's brown beard drowning in it" (23). When they are safely across, Ma only says, "Oh, Charles!" (23). The actual details of how Pa crossed the swollen creek are minimal, creating a phenomenon that Wolfgang Iser terms a narrative gap (283). This narrative gap encourages readers to provide their own details and tensions. Wilder not only empowers her child readers to identify with Laura but opens a space for the reader to construct the narrative through their emotional responses. This approach is a paradigm shift from children's literature of the early twentieth century, in which the adult narrator is prone to telling the child reader how to react and feel. Wilder expands the boundaries of childhood space by sharing intimate spaces with her readers.

AESTHETICISM AND MORAL AMBIGUITY: COMPLICATING THE SPACES OF CHILDHOOD

Wilder's high opinion of her readership is evident in her introducing them to the power of language and the beauty of the world. She creates vivid images, which Charles Frey describes as a type of "prose-poem" (126) that conveys the emotional responses of her protagonist. Though the diction might be more elevated than one might expect of a child narrator, the close third-person perspective allows more heightened emotional expression when the narrator moves into Laura's consciousness. Often Wilder crafts a prose-poem directly following a more prosaic passage that situates the viewpoint as coming from the child Laura. For example, at the beginning of *Little House on the Prairie*, the family is traveling, and Wilder narrates with a child's diction: "They had come in the covered wagon all the long way from the Big Woods" (13), but she follows it with a more sophisticated passage that captures the essence of the experience from Laura's aesthetic viewpoint: "[They] saw nothing but the rippling grass and the enormous sky. In a perfect circle the sky curved down to the level land" (13). Though the vocabulary remains at a child's reading level, the word picture of the sky curving down to the level land is more advanced and poetic.

In the chapter "Prairie Day," this pattern is followed again. First comes the prosaic sentence: "Then they sat on the clean grass and ate pancakes and bacon and molasses from the tin plates in their laps" (39). This short snapshot grounds the scene, but the next paragraph transitions to the prose-poem expressing Laura's emotional response:

> All around them shadows were moving over the waving grasses, while the sun rose. Meadow larks were springing straight up from the billows of grass into the high, clear sky, singing as they went. Small pearly clouds drifted in the immense blueness overhead. (39)

The imagery is poetic, and the passage possesses a lilting quality from the multitude of present participles strung together: moving, waving, springing, and singing. The viewpoint remains with Laura, but the diction is more complex in the service of communicating her emotional response to her surroundings. In this way Wilder complicates the spaces of childhood by interweaving elevated aesthetics. Although in reality an adult narrator constructed these passages, they are firmly grounded in Laura's voice and bring the readers closer to her emotions. Through Laura's aesthetic sensibilities, Wilder implies that childhood space is not limited to the bounds of mundane experience or identity as a young person. The respect for her child reader reflects a growing perception of children and their capacity to respond to beauty.

The close third-person perspective enlarges the childhood sphere in another unexpected manner—through the moral ambivalence revealed within the protagonist's viewpoint. The result is a movement away from a didactic approach and toward the child reader as an independent evaluator. Nodelman and Reimer consider that "the main emphasis in children's literature is the didactic effort to educate children into sharing an adult view of the world, and, also, of what it means to be a child" (200). Their definition of "didactic" includes the connotation that the purpose of teaching is to transmit a moral value. Indeed, children's literature of the early twentieth century had a strong moral purpose. E. Nesbit's five children learn the folly of their wishes, while Dorothy in *The Wizard of Oz* learns that there is no place like home. Anne of Green Gables learns not to be heedless, and Mary Lennox learns the blessing of caring for someone other than herself. As Maria Nikolajeva writes: "The principal difference between research on children's literature and general literary criticism—and this factor is reflected in the way the history of literature is written—is that children's literature has from the very beginning been related to pedagogics" (3). Wilder, on the other hand, moves into new territory, imparting a more realistic ambivalence in many of the scenes experienced by her protagonist. Often she describes Laura's inner feelings but does not apply them didactically. As an example, during the journey west Wilder narrates one of Laura's struggles:

> "I want to camp, now! I'm so tired," Laura said.
> Then Ma said, "Laura." That was all, but it meant that Laura must not complain. So she did not complain any more out loud, but she was still naughty, inside. She sat and thought complaints to herself. (15)

Though Laura is reproved in this passage, Wilder does not bring about events to punish Laura or teach her a lesson, which was a common approach for children's novels of the time. Mowder describes Laura's actions as transgressive, claiming: "They verify that the only way a woman can speak is by recalling the desires of herself-as-child, desires which are always represented as themselves silenced" (15). On the other hand, Claudia Mills interprets Laura's independent spirit as a symbol, because "the individual's moral growth from obedience to autonomy parallels the American polity's growth from subjection to democracy" (128). Although both views hold some merit, they miss the significance of Wilder's use of ambiguity in her narration. This ambiguity allows readers to ponder and deduce their own values. In addition, this approach heightens the inner tension for the protagonist rather than serving a didactic purpose. The struggle creates empathy from children who often share Laura's impatience. Frank Kermode, in his study of literary classics, concludes, "It seems that on a just view of the matter, the books we call classics possess intrinsic qualities that endure, but possess also an openness to accommodation which keeps them alive under endlessly varying dispositions" (44). Wilder manifests this latter quality in the way she strongly aligns with Laura's perspective and leaves events open to interpretation for both experienced and inexperienced readers. She creates a space that accommodates each child's unique identity and power to evaluate.

Wilder intentionally developed this identification with the child viewpoint and the ambivalence that resulted from it. In the original *Pioneer Girl*, for example, the story of the girls stringing beads for the new baby ends with "So we had a baby sister to watch and laugh at" (14). This narrative shows only the positive response to the baby, and it is typical of the colonization of childhood that Nodelman and Reimer describe as the attempt by adults to model how children should think (97). In *Little House on the Prairie*, on the other hand, Wilder uses the same story to reveal Laura's inner struggle. When Mary gives her beads to the baby, Laura reacts: "Her chest felt all hot inside, and she wished with all her might that Mary wouldn't always be such a good little girl" (179). The emotional honesty evokes the readers' empathy, and the episode leaves Laura unconvinced of the need to share.

Wilder's authentic representation of childhood tensions reinforces her commitment to the child viewpoint. A final example of Wilder's complicating the narrative with moral ambiguity is the description of Laura's intense longing for a papoose. She asks Ma for one in chapter 5 and is scolded for her request, but by the chapter entitled "The Indians Ride Away," Laura sobs over a baby that she sees. "'Its eyes are so black,' Laura sobbed. She could not say what she meant" (309). Hill identifies this passage as an example of children's "emotional honesty that sometimes offends and frightens adults" (18–19). Its inclusion in the narrative recreates a genuine child for the reader to empathize with and perhaps relate to on a deeper level. This passage also complicates the moral ambiguity of the treatment of Indigenous people in the late nineteenth century. Frances W. Kaye considers such passages in Wilder's work as "red flags for ... diversity, multiculturalism, and human rights" (123). On the other hand, Wilder's fidelity to cultural norms of the time further imparts authenticity to her narrative and empowers the child reader to address the complex issue of the treatment of Indigenous Americans. In *Little House on the Prairie*, the Ingalls family settles on Osage land and interacts with the Indigenous people in a variety of ways. As Wilder intensifies the growing tension with the Osage, which she will dramatize in the three chapters of the climax, she narrates how the neighbors suggest that "perhaps the Indians had started that fire on purpose to burn out the white settlers" (283). Pa does not agree with the neighbors, and he declares his respect for the Osage chief, who intervenes to bring peace. Despite conflicting opinions, Wilder only records Laura's observations and does not vilify or glorify the Osage people. By today's standards, even the use of the word

"Indian" could be inappropriate; however, by situating the viewpoint as that of a child of the late nineteenth century, Wilder transmits a cultural artifact that allows modern readers to learn about a historical period and draw their own conclusions. Wilder complicates this space of childhood and thereby enlarges the reader's sphere to include different cultures and time periods through Laura's experience.

The focus on the child protagonist, rather than events, makes a statement about the significance of children and how they are individual agents of change, rather than a group being acted on by adults. In *Little House on the Prairie*, Wilder filters scenes through Laura's eyes so that her responses become integral to the plot. This focus validates the idea that children are people with their own values and judgments. Wilder's use of subtext, ambiguity, and transparent emotional responses demonstrates that she trusted her readers to think for themselves. Moreover, her use of poetic diction assumes that children have appreciation for aesthetics in imagery and language, and her writing elevates children as they combine their imaginations with the text to create their own understanding of beauty. As child readers are invited into the story without the buffer of an adult narrator, they identify with the impressions and emotional responses of the protagonist in a type of time-travel. The reader seems to be experiencing the events alongside Laura as Wilder narrates with a solid placement of the story in the "present" without flashbacks or narrative evaluations as to the significance of an event in the future. Her focus on the present can be understood in the final words of *Little House in the Big Woods*:

> She was glad that the cozy house, and Pa and Ma and the firelight and the music, were now. They could not be forgotten, she thought, because now is now. It can never be a long time ago. (238)

Though Nodelman correctly observes that children's books are written by adults for children (203), Wilder maintains a closeness to her child protagonist in contradiction to the conventions of children's literature in the early twentieth century. She communicates that each child is an individual person capable of constructing meaning within the narrative space.

Closely related to the impact of a close third-person perspective, Wilder's innovation of the linear pattern for plot builds on new ideas about children. The linear narrative schema suggests that the journey is as valid a goal as home, and this distinction allows readers to make their own conclusions about independence and security. It has been suggested that "it [the prairie], on the other hand, presents Laura with that side of life which exists in opposition to the values symbolized by the many little houses" (Woolf 168). These oppositions exist in tension throughout *Little House on the Prairie* and the rest of the series, so that the reader must evaluate the issues in their own context. Moreover, the linear pattern results in realism that eschews the tradition of idyllic versions of childhood in children's novels. In the decades that followed, this new approach to children's literature would become another convention for the genre. Deanna Zitterkopf has documented dozens of children's pioneer novels that have been published since the success of the *Little House* series (172); however, the impact of Wilder's oeuvre extends beyond the popularity of pioneer novels.

Wilder's innovations in structure and perspective furthered the dialogic process by promoting new ideas about childhood space. The linear structure extended the boundaries beyond the conventional space of home and introduced readers to a more realistic experience of the world. Wilder further opened the sphere of interiority for her child readers by crafting a close third-person perspective. By drawing her child readers into the experience of the story, she validates their impressions and evaluations. The result is a shift away from spaces shaped by adult conceptions of childhood and toward those that grant freedom to each child to create unique perceptions. The novelist Jill Patton Walsh, writing about children's literature in the second half of the twentieth century, declares that "a good trajectory is the optimum, the most emotionally loaded flight path across the subject to the projected end" (188), but in the first half of the century this concept was still new. Wilder transforms a simple plot about a pioneer family traveling west into a narrative of one child's impressions and emotional responses, inviting child readers to identify with the protagonist and extend their own boundaries, both inward and outward.

Works Cited

Bachelard, Gaston, and Maria Jolas. *The Poetics of Space*. Beacon Press, 1994.
Burnett, Frances Hodgson. *The Secret Garden*. J. B. Lippincott, 1962.
Field, Rachel. *Hitty: Her First Hundred Years*. Macmillan, 1957.
Frey, Charles. "Laura and Pa: Family and Landscape in *Little House on the Prairie*." *Children's Literature Association Quarterly*, vol. 12, no. 3, 1987, pp. 125–28.
Hill, Pamela Smith, editor. *Pioneer Girl: The Annotated Autobiography*. South Dakota Historical Society Press, 2014.
Iser, Wolfgang. *The Implied Reader*. Johns Hopkins UP, 1974.
Kaye, Frances W. "Little Squatter on the Osage Diminished Reserve: Reading Laura Ingalls Wilder's Kansas Indians." *Great Plains Quarterly*, vol. 20, no. 2, 2000, pp. 123–40.
Kermode, Frank. *The Classic*. Harvard University Press, 1983.

Mills, Claudia. "From Obedience to Autonomy: Moral Growth in the Little House Books." *Children's Literature*, vol. 24, 1996, pp. 127–40.

Montgomery, L. M. *Anne of Green Gables*. Grosset & Dunlap, 1970.

Mowder, Louise. "Domestication of Desire: Gender, Language, and Landscape in the Little House Books." *Children's Literature Association Quarterly*, vol. 317, no. 1, 1992, pp. 15–19.

Nesbit, E. *Five Children and It*. Random House, 1948.

Nikolajeva, Maria. *Children's Literature Comes of Age: Toward a New Aesthetic*. Routledge, 2015.

Nodelman, Perry. *The Hidden Adult: Defining Children's Literature*. Johns Hopkins UP, 2008.

Nodelman, Perry, and Mavis Reimer. *The Pleasures of Children's Literature*. Longman, 1992.

Walsh, Jill Paton. "The Lords of Time." *The Quarterly Journal of the Library of Congress*, vol. 36, no. 2, 1979, pp. 96–102.

Wilder, Laura Ingalls. *Little House in the Big Woods*. Harper & Row, 1971.

Wilder, Laura Ingalls. *Little House on the Prairie*. Harper & Row, 1971.

Wilder, Laura Ingalls. *Pioneer Girl: The Annotated Autobiography*. South Dakota Historical Society Press, 2014.

Woolf, Virginia. "Plenary Paper: The Magic Circle of Laura Ingalls Wilder." *Children's Literature Association Quarterly*, vol. 9, no. 4, 1984, pp. 168–70.

Wood, James. *How Fiction Works*. Farrar, Straus and Giroux, 2008.

Zitterkopf, Deanna. "Prairies and Privations: The Impact of Place in Great Plains Homestead Fiction for Children." *Children's Literature Association Quarterly*, vol. 9, no. 4, 1984, pp. 171–98.

Section Three

Transformative Acts
Creating Resistant Spaces in Institutionalized Places

Chapter Seven

PROUD TO BE A RUGBY BOY?

The Shifting Relation between School Space and Student Bodies in *Tom Brown's Schooldays* and *The Loom of Youth*

ANAH-JAYNE SAMUELSON

School stories are a subgenre within children's and young adult (YA) literature in which the school environment is not merely one of several settings: it functions as the main and pivotal site of action. The Golden Age of the school-story genre took place in Britain from the middle of the nineteenth century to the middle of the twentieth century. The stories were primarily set in British public schools,[1] which were characterized as exclusive institutions that socialized Britain's elite children and youth into adults obedient and loyal to the crown and empire. Elisabeth Rose Gruner argues that the school, within school stories, acts as a site of "homogenization and social control" (218). The school often symbolizes and embodies dominant societal ideals and expectations, functioning as a miniature world that offers protagonists the opportunity to experiment with social structures. Characters are consistently stripped of their individual identities and are molded by their school experience into responsible future adult citizens, or, as Jack Zipes puts it, prepped "systematically to fit into institutions, teams, clubs, companies, associations, and corporations to succeed according to standards set by these hegemonic groups" (19–20).

The popularity of public-school stories is linked to the rise of public schools themselves in Britain. Nineteenth-century Britain was an age of economic and imperialist expansion, and to meet this growth the education of young people "demanded new virtues such as ambition and initiative, discipline and team spirit, readiness to take up responsibility, and a talent for leadership" (Petzold 17). Rebecca Knuth states that the British process of nationalization was accelerated in the nineteenth century, and "national ideas were embedded in stories that helped unify the population into a nation" (6), in which "ideological Englishness enshrined obedience, racial pride, and heroism for its own sake. Duty to country and empire was a sacred obligation" (11). If duty to country was sacred, the public-school space was the temple that instilled the sense of the sacred in characters and readers. Public schools, once regarded as "moribund and marginal institutions of ill repute," began to be considered the ideal space to instill desirable imperialist virtues into children and youth, and public schools transformed into "highly prestigious and efficient production plants for the nation's elite" (Petzold 17). The "chivalric ethos" of public-school students informed a "new code of colonial conduct" that distinguished and elevated the British from the people they ruled over (Barczewski 220). Children who did not attend public schools absorbed the public-school ethos through the stories (Knuth 47), and this established a shared (and largely imagined) British history that embodied values intended to direct readers "in such a way that the status quo was reinforced and a plentiful supply of youths would serve England and stand ready to defend the empire" (Knuth 52).

This chapter considers the relation of school space and student bodies as represented in public-school stories and explores a shift in how the schoolboy is depicted as inhabiting the school space. First, through a macro-to-micro focus on the disciplinary structures in Thomas Hughes's *Tom Brown's Schooldays* (1857), I argue that the disciplinary organization of the school space endorses the development of schoolboy docility, obedience, and loyalty. These disciplinary structures not only work upon the fictionalized bodies of students but also aim to influence the identity formation of readers through the transfusion of the public-school ethos. Secondly, I interrogate a moment in which the public-school story supplied room to voice dissent against the development of unyielding obedience and loyalty in Britain's youth in Alec Waugh's *The Loom of Youth* (1917). Waugh's representation of the disciplinary organization of the public-school space remains the same as *Tom Brown*'s, but his protagonist moves through, and relates to, the school space in a way that resists the development of blind obedience and loyalty and instead recommends to implied readers the expansion of schoolboy identity to include critical thinking and resistance.

THE NET OF DISCIPLINE AND EVERYDAY MEANS OF RESISTANCE

The school-story ethos first consolidated by Thomas Hughes in *Tom Brown's Schooldays* is largely constructed through the representation of school space.

The literary representation of public-school space infuses a code of conduct through the structure and organization of space that encourages the formation of a personal identity that embodies "Englishness." Michel Foucault argues in *Discipline and Punish* (1975) that bodies are made docile by space—specifically architecture. Many of Foucault's architectural examples are school spaces, which makes his study especially useful in the consideration of school-space representations in school stories. Foucault considers systems of discipline that aim to order and structure space toward the construction of useful, subjected, and productive bodies. The body is a political field in which "power relations" strive to have hold of the body, and so they "invest it, mark it, train it, torture it, force it to carry out tasks, to perform ceremonies, to emit signs" (25). The school space is an essential space where power relations work upon and train youth-student-bodies to be productive and submissive during their adult endeavors. The future of a society is largely determined and sustained in the hegemonic training of student-bodies in school spaces.

Foucault argues that specific forms of architecture, such as school spaces, develop with the intention to:

> transform individuals: to act on those it shelters, to provide a hold on their conduct, to carry the effects of power right to them, to make it possible to know them, to alter them. Stones can make people docile and knowable. (172)

Foucault claims bodies can be made docile by architecture through various disciplinary tactics that structure space, such as the distribution of bodies in enclosed space through the organization and partition of bodies and continual surveillance and examination that always "compares, differentiates, hierarchizes, homogenizes, [and] excludes" bodies (182–83). Following Foucault's assertions of how space acts upon bodies, in the case of school spaces such as in *Tom Brown* and *Loom of Youth* student-bodies are seemingly inescapably marked and molded by their hegemony's values through the disciplinary organization of their school space.

Henri Lefebvre's pivotal text *The Production of Space* (1974) considers cultural hegemony (what Foucault calls power relations) as essential in the apprehension of space's production. Lefebvre argues that hegemony is exercised over society as a whole: over ideals and institutions. It is inconceivable to Lefebvre that the exercise of hegemony would touch all of society but leave "space untouched" (11). Hegemony is understood in the context of Lefebvre's work as the dominance of one ideological, political, social, and economic vision over all oppositional views (Coleman 60). If "capitalism" is understood as dominant, space will be produced under this hegemony's systems of production and will "embody its values as the cultural dominant, resulting in 'hegemonic-space'" (Coleman 60). Spaces have spatial codes put in place by the hegemonies that construct spaces that restrict bodies' activities within spaces: "space 'decides' what activity may occur ... [and] space commands bodies, prescribing or proscribing gestures, routes and distances to be covered" (Lefebvre 143). The apprehension of spatial codes is not an inherently transparent process, for spaces are not produced by the ruling systems to be easily comprehended by bodies living in the space. Lefebvre insists space is "designed to conceal" (Lefebvre 147) its power over the body and is a covert carrier and communicator of dominant ideological values to those inhabiting the space (Coleman 61). Public-school stories, such as Hughes's, participate in the concealment of space's power over student-bodies by endorsing particular schoolboy activities and gestures that restrict and train youths' bodies both inside school spaces and without.

The disciplinary structures Foucault describes position bodies as passively accepting their being made docile by space, but Lefebvre argues that bodies need not live passively within hegemonically produced spaces. Lefebvre argues that the production of space is not limited to the creators of space (the city planners, architects, bureaucrats, government administrators, and so forth), but is also produced in the everyday practices of the "inhabitants" and "users," or in the case of this chapter, students. For bodies to inhabit a space "is to appropriate something. Not in the sense of possessing it, but as making it an oeuvre, making it one's own, marking it, modeling it, shaping it" (Lefebvre qtd. in Stanek 87). Even in the "midst of constraints" of ruling powers' attempts to control the actions and movements of bodies, to inhabit space "is to be in a conflict—often acute—between the constraining powers and the forces of appropriation" (Lefebvre qtd. in Stanek 42). For Lefebvre, appropriation involves the varied practices of individuals or collectives in space that "modify, reshape, adapt, adjust, or alter space on various scales" (Stanek 88). Small or large appropriation, the inhabits of space make "meaningful choices" (Stanek 90) in how they occupy space, whether that be to be made docile or to resist this demand. Hughes and Waugh endorse different methods of space appropriation to their readers. Following from Lefebvre's arguments, both Hughes's characters in their submissions to being made docile and Waugh's protagonist who resists docility make meaningful choices in how they occupy their school spaces. The difference between the texts and their endorsed schoolboy behaviors lies in their varied balances between the constraining powers of the ruling hegemony and the forces of appropriation of space by the inhabitants/users.

Michel de Certeau's *The Practice of Everyday Life* (1984) explores the everyday practices of individuals and entire societies that function as rebellions, resistances, and subversions to disciplinary space. De Certeau engages directly with Foucault's theories regarding space and agrees that "the grid of 'discipline' is everywhere" (xiv) but that rather than bodies in space being "passive and guided by established rules" (xi), there are means of resisting and manipulating "the mechanisms of discipline and [individuals may] conform to them only in order to evade them" (xiv). Contrary to Foucault, de Certeau argues that there are "innumerable practices by which means users reappropriate the space organized by techniques of sociocultural production" (xiv); his study illuminates methods of "dispersed, tactical, and makeshift creativity of groups of individuals already caught in the nets of 'discipline'" (xiv–xv). Much like Lefebvre, de Certeau contends that, through reappropriation and manipulation of space, individuals and groups can resist the grid of discipline, and when "pushed to the limits, these procedures and ruses ... compose the network of an antidiscipline" (xv). De Certeau's arguments reveal that space, while structured to support the dominance of those in power, has the potential to be manipulated and transformed by those who are dominated through ordinary and everyday practices such as reading (as will be explored in Waugh's work) or walking through cities. *The Loom of Youth* demonstrates the ability of an individual to manipulate mechanisms of discipline to evade being made docile by school space and to occupy space in a way that runs counter to its intentions.

As the remainder of this chapter will explore, Tom Brown and his peers uniformly accept the grid of discipline and encourage readers to do the same, which establishes obedience and loyalty as fundamental to the schoolboy identity. Later subversive texts, like Waugh's, endorse actively living in school spaces by making meaningful choices that resist and subvert the grid of discipline and introduce a rebellious and critically thinking schoolboy. The school space, its disciplinary organization, and pedagogical intentions remain the same from Hughes to Waugh, but it is how the student/schoolboy inhabits the space that shifts.

TOM BROWN AND EARLY PUBLIC-SCHOOL STORIES

Hughes's *Tom Brown's Schooldays* is not the first children's novel to take place in a school, as Sarah Fielding's *The Governess* (1749) is the first piece of children's literature to be set entirely in a school; however, *Tom Brown* is hailed by many as the originator of the school-story *genre* (Honey; Quigly; Musgrave; Richards; Nelson), as several well-known and repeated school-story conventions have their basis in Hughes's novel. The prefect system, fagging,[2] cribs,[3] athleticism, midnight feasts, and the awe-inspiring headmaster/mistress are all repeated conventions first made popular by Hughes. Robert Kirkpatrick argues that *Tom Brown* "consolidate[d] the foundations of the public-school story and . . . popularize[d] the genre as a whole, by virtue of its extensive and almost universal favourable critical reception" (2). Hughes wrote the novel to prepare his son for his impending departure to Rugby School in Warwickshire, England. Drawing heavily from his own education at Rugby, Hughes's representation of Rugby is idealized and nostalgic. *Tom Brown* set the standard for public-school stories as most followed the formulaic blueprint established by Hughes and his representation of the school space.

Living in the 1830s, Tom Brown is an ordinary boy, though a member of the gentry class. *Tom Brown* does not begin at Rugby School, but rather, like the stories that followed, starts with an account of Tom's early childhood, to establish his social situation and raw character. Tom is "a robust and combative urchin" (Hughes 22), and his wild nature is indicated by his playing with the village children and household servants (Hughes 24–43, 58–60). In early childhood sections protagonists are represented as unknowledgeable, lacking moral and spiritual depth, and not yet embodying the chivalric "British" virtues of selflessness, bravery, and leadership. Witnessing protagonists' behavior prior to their public-school socialization provides readers a baseline against which to measure characters' development that is facilitated by the public school.

On the eve of Tom's departure, his father, Squire Brown, ponders why he is sending his son to Rugby. He reasons it is not for the academics—"I don't care a straw for Greek particles" (78)—but for the moral education the school promises to provide that Tom needs to "turn out a brave, helpful, truth-telling Englishman, and a gentleman, and a Christian" (78). Nationhood is emphasized, and the characteristics of bravery, loyalty, obedience, and Christianity are fused with Squire Brown's conception of Englishness. These characteristics, which Squire Brown believes Rugby will instill in his son, are imagined as preparing Tom for his future adult position as a member of Britain's gentry, which will in turn uphold the Brown's traditional familial governing position within Britain. Andrew Sanders describes public schools as "miniature Englands" that function as microcosms of British politics, and where "future patterns of justice and social order could be based" (ix). In the case of Squire Brown, it is suggested the public school's allure is its being a microcosm that will offer a concentrated version of English virtues and values that will be transferred to his son.

The Rugby microcosm is intensified in its physical isolation from the macrocosm of Britain. Rugby is described by Tom's carriage driver as a "werry out-o'-the-way-place . . . off the main road" (Hughes 80–81), and subsequent school stories follow suit in their schools' enclosures. The repeated isolation is significant, as Foucault notes that processes concerned with the discipline of bodies (the intention of the socialization process of public schools) advances "from the distribution of individuals in space" (Foucault 141). A space that is "closed in upon itself" removes outside influences and creates a "protected place of disciplinary monotony" (Foucault 141). The isolated and enclosed school space creates an environment for students to immerse themselves into a microcosm of a "miniature England" that offers controlled and constrained experiences that will constitute their moral education.

The school space in nineteenth- and early twentieth-century school stories takes on mythical qualities as a transformative space of British antiquity that transcends temporal change. The school space in *Tom Brown*, and in the plethora of stories that follow, is a transitional space in which boys are transformed into British men, which constructs the space as a site of identity transformation. Just as Foucault argues that architecture can transform individuals by acting "on those it shelters, to provide a hold on their conduct, to carry the effects of power right to them, to make it possible to know them, to alter them" (172), public schools are represented as capable of altering those they shelter into obedient men of empire.

When characters first arrive at school, they show great interest in the physical architecture of the space, and long, detailed descriptions of the schools are provided by narrators. David Steege argues these descriptions put an "emphasis on the specialness of these places to the entering student, a sense of wonderful novelty and possibility" (145). Hilary Clare and Sue Sims track the sentiment of "specialness" associated with public schools as continuing into the early twentieth century, when the experience of attending a public school was "at its most desirable, even glamourous . . . seen as a privilege" (7). The desirable glamour of attending public schools was reflected in the buildings themselves in that many were housed in medieval castles and grand manors. The lengthy and adoring descriptions seek to characterize the public schools as elite spaces of antiquity that are desirable in their glamorous materiality and as bolstering students' self-worth in their inhabiting this privileged space.

The first physical description of Rugby is laden with emotion that is intent on inspiring the admiration and loyalty of Tom and readers. Hughes describes Tom's first impression of the school thusly:

> Tom's *heart beat quick* as he passed the great school field or close, with its noble elms, in which several games at football were going on, and tried to take in at once the long line of grey buildings, beginning with the chapel, and ending with the School-house, the residence of the head-master, where the great flag was lazily waving from the highest round tower. And he began already to be *proud* of being a Rugby boy. (89, emphasis added)

It is significant that Tom has not yet interacted with anyone at the school, but that it is the school space *itself* that produces an affective response of pride. The "noble elms," demonstration of sportsmanship, the school buildings bookended by the chapel (spiritual growth) and the head's residence (moral guidance) all embody the purported values and virtues of the public school, and the narrator's description emphasizes the spaces' material specialness. Students, like Tom, are themselves made "special" in being members of the exclusive space and feel pride simply in their inclusion. Entering as strangers, new students in their affections of pride and awe inspired by first seeing the school space are immediately drawn into the collective in their devotion to and love for the space aligning and uniting individuals within the collective student body.

The transformation from schoolboys to men of empire is not conducted through academics (as Squire Brown pointed out), but through the disciplinary organization of the school space. The early childhood sections of public-school stories present students as raw materials, and the public-school space as capable of making student bodies docile, or "subjected, used, transformed and improved" (Foucault 136). Foucault posits that disciplining bodies proceeds from how they are distributed within a space. Enclosure involves a space being "closed in upon itself" (141) and was a popular form of distribution that proved useful in army barracks, factories, and schools.

The enclosed school space contains bodies from the outside world and maximizes production through "neutralizing inconveniences" (142) that derive from interruptions and distractions from peers or sources outside the enclosure. However, Foucault argues that simply enclosing bodies within a space does not produce "subjected and practised . . . 'docile' bodies" (138), but that it is through further organization of the enclosed space through partitioning that provides each individual his "own place; and each place its individual" (143). When individuals have their own place within the enclosure:

> Presences and absences [are established], to know where and how to locate individuals, to set up useful communications, to interrupt others, to be able at each moment to supervise the conduct of each individual, to assess it, to judge it, to calculate its qualities or merits. It was a producer, therefore, aimed at knowing, mastering and using. Discipline organizes an analytical space. (143)

Those observing the partitioned individuals (prefects, teachers, headmaster, and so forth) measure and judge individuals against the whole, and an individual student becomes "defined by the place [he] occupies in a series, and by the gap that separates [him] from others" (145). Enclosure and partitions create the possibility for individual bodies to be measured against other individuals and the whole. Because of these measurements, individuals are further organized and distributed in the school space based on their relationality to others. Distributing bodies based on the rank and privileges earned from their performances in partitioned spaces "guarantee[s] the obedience of individuals" (147), manufacturing the desire in students to be found valuable in the eyes of the observers/teachers.

The partitioned spaces are "mixed spaces," because they are both physical and symbolic spaces (Foucault 148). Partitions are architectural and material because they govern the "disposition of buildings, rooms, furniture," and "ideal" because they project over the social makeup of student bodies by characterizing, assessing, and hierarchizing (148). The public-school "house system" is one such mixed space that distributes and disciplines student bodies through partitioning. Public schools are divided into three to ten houses, depending on the size of the school, with as few as fifty students in each house. Students sleep, study, and spend leisure time in their allotted house. The schoolhouses sometimes have a building separate from the academic and administrative buildings, or they inhabit a section within a singular school building. Students are assigned their house upon arrival or acceptance to the public school and remain a member of a house for the duration of their education. Houses are further partitioned by students' sharing sleeping quarters and studies with two to three other house members. Students are not allowed in one another's sleeping quarters, and the privilege of visiting another's study is often reserved for upper-year students further along in their moral education. The house system's partitions are material in their location in a specific space within the enclosure of the school, and they are symbolic/ideal in limiting and controlling how bodies move in the space, influencing the relationships formed between students.

The prefect and fagging systems further order and distribute bodies by naturalized arbitrary ranks. The systems have the veneer of awarding students greater responsibility for their observed performances in the partitioned house spaces. In actuality the systems make individuals more observable to adults. Typically, one to two students held the position of prefect within each schoolhouse and were awarded the title during their senior years by demonstrating superior moral growth; in less opaque terms, prefects best follow the rules and regulations of the school space in their junior years. Rev. John Woolley, headmaster of King Edward VI School in Hereford in 1844, was one such practitioner of the prefect system and described the system as follows:

> Members of the Highest Form in the School shall be invested under the name of Prefects with certain powers, immunities and privileges, which may enable them effectually to co-operate with their Masters, in the maintenance of necessary discipline, and in promoting a spirit of strict integrity, gentlemanly feeling, and Christian principles among their companions generally. (qtd. in Honey 44)

The special privileges of the prefects (which could include private chambers and studies, and the authority to discipline members of their houses) are propagated as providing elite individuals more agency within the school space and create a rhetoric of rewarding submission to public-school values with greater authority and autonomy. In practice, prefects' agency is constrained in that their role is to uphold the rules and regulations determined by the adult teachers and administrators. The "authority" given to prefects functions as another mechanism to control and direct students' energy and attention. Prefects function as agents of the headmaster, enabling the head of the school to seem unobtrusive in his constant surveillance.

While the prefects are a select few working as agents of the head in observing and disciplining other students, the fagging system is more inclusive in that all senior students monitor and directly discipline an assigned junior student. Lower-year "fags" act as a personal assistant to their senior supervisor by performing menial tasks such as cleaning the senior's bedroom and study, maintaining the fireplace, providing daily tea, mailing letters, and running errands in neighboring villages and towns. The fagging system ensures younger students are kept busy (and thus out of trouble) in their service and are under constant observation. If any deviances are witnessed, which could include not being where they should be in the school space, neglecting their fagging duties, performing poorly in class or on the playing fields, or demonstrating any ungentlemanly behaviors (drinking, smoking, swearing), seniors have the right and obligation to discipline their fag, which most often takes the form of a stern lecture or corporal punishment. The rules and expectations of the headmaster and teachers are enforced by the senior students in the discipline of their fags, ensuring the conduct of every student is observed, judged, and corrected without direct interference from adult authorities.

The extent to which students accept this disciplinary organization, to the point that they will actively defend it when threatened, is showcased in Tom's fag strike. The recently graduated prefects and seniors of Tom's house had handled the discipline of juniors "rough, but strong and just," and set "a higher standard" (166) that seemed to promise a bright future for the schoolhouse in regard to discipline. The new prefects and monitors that replace the recent graduates threaten to throw the school into "darkness and chaos" (166). The new sixth form is composed of young students whose "cleverness had carried them up to the top of the school while in the strength of body and character, they were not yet fit for a share in the governments" (166–67), and older boys of the "wrong sort," who had not "caught the meaning of their position and work, and felt none of its responsibilities" (167). The entire sixth form are not morally strong enough to handle and maintain their positions of power properly, which results in the fifth-form students, who are "a sporting and drinking set . . . usurping power" by fagging "the little boys as if they were præpostors, and to bully and oppress any who showed signs of resistance" (167). The junior school students are roughly abused as a result of the misuse of power, for "the fags were without their lawful masters and protects, and ridden over . . . by a set of boys whom they were not bound to obey, and whose only right over them stood in their bodily powers" (167). The disciplinary structures that order and govern the space are perverted because of the sixth form's lack of moral fortitude and the fifth form's usurpation of power. The fifth-formers in their usurpation of power challenge the disciplinary structures and resist being made loyal, obedient, and docile to and by these structures, and are depicted as villains for doing so.

After describing the perverted power structure that has taken hold of Rugby, the narrator speaks directly to readers to warn them of the "wide influence" they have "for good or evil on the society you live in" (167). The narrator preaches to readers on what kinds of behavior benefit a society, foreshadowing Tom's fag strike as honorable:

> Quit yourselves like men. . . . Speak up, and strike out if necessary for whatsoever is true, and manly, and lovely, and of good report. . . . Do

your duty and help others to do theirs, and you may leave the tone of feeling in the school higher than you found it. (167–68)

It is significant that the narrator breaks the fourth wall at this particular moment, and Hughes takes care to define Tom's strike as just because it will uphold the disciplinary organization of the school, because it is "true," "manly" and "of good report," not because Tom is too arrogant or lazy to serve or be subservient to others. Tom leads a "righteous . . . strike against unlawful fagging" (194) by proclaiming he will fag only for the sixth-form students, to whom he has a "lawful" obligation, and refuses to fag for the fifth form, who have no rights to his service. The proclamation marks Tom for violence at the hands of the fifth-formers, but his strike eventually restores the disciplinary structures of the school space by redistributing disciplinary actions from the fifth to the sixth form. Tom makes a meaningful choice in fagging for only the "rightful" sixth form. It is a choice that defends and endorses the disciplinary structures and organization of the school that aims to mold students into obedient, loyal, and docile subjects.

Junior students are monitored by their senior supervisor and their house prefect but are also given a taste of "liberty" through their being partitioned in studies. Students are assigned to a space so as to easily track their movements and are made to feel empowered in their confinement. At Rugby, two to three students share a study. Upon his arrival Tom receives a school tour from his friend, Harry East. The two boys quickly move through the school while readers receive detailed accounts from the narrator describing the "great gates" (91), and schoolhouse hall's "great room" with "two great tables" (92) able to seat the entire student-body. While the narrator emphasizes the prestige of the space through the repeated proclamations of its greatness, Tom's personal reverence is reserved for the "Rugby boy's citadel" (92): the study. Tom is taken by surprise by Harry's study and is "astonished and delighted with the *palace* in question" (93, emphasis added). The narrator attributes Tom's "interest" in the space with the knowledge that he is "to become the joint owner or a similar home, the first place he could call his own" (94). Never having a space that was "his," Tom is excited to have a space partitioned off from the rest of school to call his own, in that it ostensibly provides him more liberty and responsibility than ever previously experienced. Students are empowered with a sense of responsibility and maturity through the *gift* of their own space.

However, there are "bars and a grating to the window" of Harry's study, which is explained by the narrator as a "necessary" precaution "to prevent the exit of small boys after locking-up, and the entrance of contraband articles" (93). The barred windows serve as symbols of the constrained freedom the space affords, as the space is ultimately a partition meant to contain student bodies and is governed by adult-created rules and regulations. There are limitations as to who can enter a study, ensuring that students remain in their assigned portioned spaces. Students are allowed in their own studies only during scheduled hours, and the regular check-ins from prefects and seniors for whom the younger boys fag maintain regular surveillance of students' behavior. The studies function as a disciplinary method of partitioning schoolboy bodies to control and monitor movement and behavior. The studies disciplinary function is not easily comprehended due to the narrator's focus on Tom's emotional response of being "astonished," "delighted," and "charmed" (93–94) by the space, rather than suspicious of the bars locking him in. Indeed, Tom offers no reaction to the barred window, only that "Tom thought" the study, barred window and all, is "uncommonly *comfortable* to look at" (93–94, emphasis added).

Just as the space of the study impresses charm and comfort upon Tom, the emotionality of the description attempts to have readers be similarly affected by the space. The description of Harry East's study establishes what the acceptable social and cultural embodied emotional response is to this space, and the promoted emotional reaction of "delight" hides the disciplinary and manipulative functions behind the rules that structure the space. Fictional characters and readers are socialized through the emotionality of the study's description to not see the markers of discipline and control evident in the barred window, but rather to be content, even "astonished," that they can be in the space.

Student bodies are disciplined and transformed into obedient and loyal citizens through their distribution in enclosed school space using tactics that highly organize the space and ensure that every individual is observable. Discipline through the organization of the enclosed school space by partitions and rank "creates complex spaces that are at once architectural, functional, and hierarchical" (Foucault 148), encouraging the obedience of individuals in order to be successful in the space. The careful organization of the space presents an illusion of agency that lulls students into participation when all the while their energies and ambitions are directed by the agendas and interests of society's governing power structures. In the case of Hughes's characters, they participate in being made docile by becoming obedient and loyal to the space to ensure their continued membership in the exclusive space that bolsters their individual worth.

THE SCHOOL SPACE QUESTIONED

Golden Age boys' public-school stories, as exemplified in *Tom Brown*, venerated imperialist ideologies through their representation of a disciplinary school space that instilled traits of obedience and loyalty in student characters. The Golden Age texts largely do not question hegemonic power structures, and characters are molded by the disciplinary structures of the space into submissive and devout British citizens ready and eager to serve the crown. While the publication of public-school stories slowly declined during the early-to-mid twentieth century, those that were published continued to represent the same type of disciplinary school space present in their Victorian predecessors. The First World War (28 July 1914 to 11 November 1918) provided the ultimate justification for the disciplinary structures of the schools, as it was the ideal market for the products of the public school, and those to which the ethos was transmitted through reading, to demonstrate their loyalty and obedience. The consequences of such obedience and loyalty were made evident in the Great War in the substantial loss of an entire generation.

The First World War was a young man's war. To determine the appeal of serving to young Britons, many critics point to the "potent mythos that figured war as romantic: a time for youthful heroism, male comradeship, and an opportunity to display widely admired characteristics" (Reynolds 256). Some point directly to children's literature, most specifically school stories, as being one source that proliferated the mythical ethos that arguably drew many to enlist. Peter Parker argues that the extreme popularity of the public-school story during the late nineteenth and early twentieth centuries led to the "ideals and codes of the schools reaching a far wider audience than the privileged minority who were educated in them" (18). In light of their popularity, Parker reasons it is "scarcely surprising that when war was declared, volunteers from all levels of society queued at the recruiting stations," for these young men had been instilled with the ethos of the public-schoolboy and were "encouraged to follow in the footsteps of storybook heroes" (18). Kate Agnew and Geoff Fox likewise contend that "stories set in fictional or actual schools . . . also contributed to a confident stance towards any possibility of war" (6), and that "from epic encounters on the playing fields of Eton or Greyfriars, it was a natural progression to exchange cricket flannels or footer kit for army or naval uniform" (6). The patriotism instilled in actual schools and transmitted through the stories about them may have had a part in emboldening the many youth who rushed to prove their worth in the trenches.

As the casualty lists grew, many could not remain uncritical of the systems that had drawn so many young men to the war, and a different school story emerged. Isabel Quigly notes that everything the public schools had been teaching "seemed to come into its own, and their products, almost an entire generation, were killed" (239). Jeffrey Richards claims that some held the public-school system responsible for the Great War, due to the schools' ideologies of "tyranny of the bloods" in which "games took precedence over learning (in particular history) and the ruling elite emerged ignorant, complacent, insular and backward-looking" (232). While these criticisms did emerge, they were met with extreme opposition and did not spur any immediate or lasting revolutions in the actual public-school system. Parker argues that England's need during the war for reassurance that "young men laying down their lives" were doing so "gladly for a just cause, that the old public-school traditions of chivalry, self-sacrifice, fair-play and selfless patriotism were being maintained on the field of battle" (27) outweighed the desire to critically examine the school space and its disciplinary practices for much of the general public.

Though criticisms of public schools were censored in and by society, for some authors the public-school story opened space to voice criticism. Alec Waugh's *The Loom of Youth* (1917) is one such example of the public-school story being utilized to voice criticism and is a rare example of a youth-written public-school story. Waugh engages in the same genre that venerated and fed the public-school ethos and depicts the same highly organized partitioned space as Hughes's Rugby. Waugh deconstructs the school space through the public-school story to examine the disciplinary tactics he felt were responsible for the moral decline of society and the tremendous loss of human life in the First World War, namely, the tyranny of athletics over academics. The assumed automatic pride of being a public-schoolboy is troubled by Waugh's account, and he endorses more active and critical schoolboy engagement in the public-school space.

Waugh wrote *Loom* at age seventeen in the two months between his leaving Sherborne Public School and his army deployment. Waugh admits the novel is autobiographical, and in *Loom*'s 1954 edition preface the author explains that he was in a "nostalgic" and "rebellious" mood when writing the novel ("Preface" 10). In 1915 Waugh was at the top of Sherborne: a house captain, prefect, top batsman of the elevens, and winner of the English verse prize. At the height of schoolboy achievement, Waugh was accused of a sexual relationship with another student. The headmaster strongly suggested Waugh's father remove Waugh from the school to avoid the shame of expulsion. Several housemasters felt this was not an appropriate sentence and organized a boycott to have Waugh expelled. However, two masters stood by Waugh, and he was able to finish out the term with their support. He avoided expulsion, but Waugh still felt he had been "prematurely ejected from paradise," and as he waited to join the army, he was "consumed with longing for Sherborne and resentful that his time there had been curtailed" (Richards 230).

Though Waugh admits he "intensely" ("Preface" 10) enjoyed his time at public school, he was in "constant conflict with authority," due to their "inability or refusal to recognize the true nature of school life" ("Preface" 10). Waugh was frustrated by the myth of the schoolboy, which he "in no sense had incarnated" ("Preface" 10), and he was regularly irritated by what he believed to be unreal expectations for himself and his peers. Waugh contends that prior to World War I, "Britain's imperial destiny was never questioned, and the Public School system as a bulwark of Empire was held sacrosanct," and never had the "inevitable emotional consequences of a monastic herding together" ("Preface" 12) of children and adolescents in public schools been questioned. Waugh attributes much of the corruption and impurity that festered in the school space as a result of the "monastic herding," or the enclosure of the school space. The isolated microcosm of public schools was heralded in *Tom Brown* as the key method of students' moral education and character formation, but Waugh argues that an immoral education is truly fostered in the enclosure.

The novel follows protagonist Gordon Caruthers through his four years at the fictional Fernhurst public school, and Gordon's existential crisis regarding the values and characteristics Fernhurst has entrenched in him. Gordon, like Tom Brown when first seeing Rugby, is initially "so *proud* of Fernhurst, with its grey cloisters and dreaming Abbey" (*Loom* 84, emphasis added), but after reading Arnold Lunn's school story *The Harrovians* (1914), Gordon comes to believe his school's emphasis on games and the suppression of critical thinking are largely responsible for the great loss of life in the war and for the deterioration of Britain's moral state. During his fourth year, Gordon finds himself at the top of the schoolboy power hierarchy, but he is the last of his generation in the school (all older boys have enlisted), and his privileges feel empty and meaningless. Hearing the names of his esteemed peers on the casualty lists, and continually told by his teachers, "If you aren't good at games you'll be useless in the trenches" (*Loom* 163), Gordon comes to question the value of his public-school education. Gordon finds himself trapped in the tyranny of the norm in which he is valued only as a cog in a bigger, national, soldier-producing machine. He questions whether his peers, in excelling at games, were simply preparing for dying in the trenches. Rather than remain trapped in the net of discipline, Gordon begins to model active living and everyday resistance to the school space through reading and critical thought.

When entering Fernhurst, Gordon is described as "innocent" (*Loom* 26, 30, 39) and is slowly corrupted by the school environment. The corruption of "innocent" Gordon is indicated in the decline of his academic pursuits. As a naive new student, Gordon is horrified to hear his peers speak so openly of cheating on lessons and exams, but he comes to see cribs as a necessity in order to allocate more time to athletics. He studies in the first semester without the use of cribs and wins the Term's Prize with "pure, unalloyed joy" (23), but the monastic herding of the students creates a mob mentality, and behaviors that Gordon previously condemned are normalized and quickly incorporated into his own behavior through witnessing the widespread accepted practice of cheating as he begins using cribs in his second semester (26). There are few consequences for students' cheating, as Fernhurst creates an environment in which cribs are approved in valuing athletic performance far above academics. This is evident in that Gordon's winning academic prizes provides him no power, influence, or even admiration from peers, but his strength on the playing fields endears him to the community and moves him up the hierarchical social ladder. The use of cribs is not portrayed as an obviously corrupt behavior that underscores the innocence of others who valiantly refuse (such as Arthur in *Tom Brown*, who on his sickbed makes Tom vow to stop cribbing to honor Arthur's memory, should he die), but is presented as a common and accepted practice of the majority.

The moral degradation that comes from a focus on athletics is best made evident (though disturbingly) when a sexual relationship between students is discovered by the headmaster. Most likely a cathartic chapter for Waugh, the narrator subtly references a sexual relationship between students as proof of the moral deficit Fernhurst's education provokes. During Gordon's first year, his friend Jeffries is abruptly expelled when the headmaster "found out all about me and Fitzroy" (29). That Jeffries and Fitzroy had a sexual relationship is strongly implied in Jeffries and his peers' omissions and inability to directly name what the two are accused of doing. For example, Gordon says, "I never thought there was really anything in *that*" (29, emphasis added), and Mansell is unable to verbalize the accusation: "You have to go just because—Oh, it's damn unfair" (29). Gordon's subtle language and Mansell's omission strongly imply a sexual relationship between Jeffries and Fitzroy. As with cribs, Waugh casts this "corrupt behavior" not as evidence of an individual's sin, but as the fault of the school. Hearing of his expulsion, Jeffries's peers clear him of any blame, and he most clearly recuses himself of his actions in the emotional exclamation:

> Who made me what I am but Fernhurst? Two years ago I came here as innocent as [Gordon] Caruthers there; never knew anything.

Fernhurst taught me everything; Fernhurst made me worship games, and think that they alone matter, and everything else could go to the deuce. I heard men say about bloods whose lives were an open scandal, "Oh, it's all right, they can play football." (30)

While this episode is disturbing in suggesting homosexuality is a situational behavior and a sign of moral degradation, it is nonetheless significant in Jeffries's blame of Fernhurst's emphasis on athletics (a focus on the surface) as being responsible for his degradation of moral character. According to Jeffries, he entered Fernhurst an innocent, and it is the disciplinary structures of the school space that created a devotion to sports above everything that is detrimental to his character formation. Jeffries argues it is the space of the school, not the individual, who is at fault for moral decay.

For Gordon, it is the everyday and common practice of reading (both poetry and Arnold Lunn's *The Harrovians*) that defamiliarizes Fernhurst, enabling his comprehension of the disciplinary structures and his quiet manipulation of them through active living. The first shift occurs when Gordon's roommate reads aloud Charles Swinburne's *Atalanta in Calydon* (1865), and Gordon is confronted with "beauty" that he had not known existed (81). Fernhurst offers a "classical" education that cannot compete with the "beauty" of Shelley, Keats, Byron, Tennyson, Swinburne, and Rossetti, whom Gordon starts to obsessively read. In conjunction with the lessons of poetry, reading Lunn's public-school story *The Harrovians* ignites Gordon's existential crisis in outlining the empty lessons the moral pedagogy of public-schools supplies.

De Certeau cites reading as an everyday practice that produces without capitalizing, and that poaches and appropriates spaces in which "a different world (the reader's) slips into the author's place" (xxi). Gordon slips into Lunn's space of Harrow as presented in *The Harrovians*, and through the act of reading he functions like a renter who "transforms another person's property into a space borrowed," and makes "comparable changes in an apartment they furnish with their acts and memories" (xxi). Readers do not take "the position of the author" (169), but Gordon's personal memories make his experience of reading *The Harrovians* completely his own. In slipping into Lunn's space of Harrow, Gordon furnishes the space with his own experience of public school at Fernhurst. Gordon "combines . . . fragments and creates something un-known in the space organized by their capacity for allowing an indefinite plurality of meanings" (de Certeau 169). Facilitated in the act of reading, Gordon compares the place of the novel to that in which he physically resides and considers Fernhurst with a new lens.

De Certeau argues that stories about space "tell us what one can do in it and make out of it" (122). Lunn's novel extends Gordon's expectations and conceptions of what can be done in the school space. The ways Gordon comprehends *The Harrovians* provides him a new roadmap of what can and should be done in a public-school space and inspires him to consider the means of operating in the space differently to challenge the current pedagogical objectives of Fernhurst. The reading even changes how Gordon views the physical space of Fernhurst; seeing the school steeped in the shadows of twilight Gordon comes to the realization that

> Fernhurst, which should have been a home of dreams and of ideas, had, by the inefficiency of a vacillating system, become immersed in petty intrigues, and was filled with a generation that was being taught to blind itself to the higher issues. (85)

What had once made him proud and instilled a sense of the sublime, the buildings themselves embody and signify to Gordon that the "dreams and ideas" of students have been dimmed and diminished by the structures of the space.

Inspired by his reading, Gordon inhabits Fernhurst in ways that run counter to its disciplinary aims. In his senior years, Gordon chooses to major in history because it has been taught at Fernhurst "the same from time immemorial" (137). It is the easiest subject to master due to prior students having left behind detailed cribs to Master Finnemore's assignments and exams, which he does not alter from year to year. A history major is a meaningful choice on Gordon's part, for it opens up time to read contemporary poetry and prose. Finding the offered academic education at Fernhurst lackluster, Gordon takes an active role in the direction and aims of his own education in spending hours reading poetry and prose, which the narrator praises as "incidentally doing himself far more good than he would have done by binding himself down to the classical regime, which trained boys to imitate, and not to strike out on their own" (138). Gordon lives actively at Fernhurst through pursuing knowledge outside the offered curriculum that stimulates his critical thought, which as the narrator points out, paints Gordon as an outlier in the space rather than the desired obedient and loyal follower.

Hughes's and Waugh's representations of the disciplinary organizational structures of British public schools are uniform, and both intended to develop children into obedient and loyal schoolboys who would graduate to be defenders and soldiers of the empire. What differs is how Tom and Gordon choose to inhabit the public-school space. Tom largely accepts the net of discipline's influence over his identity formation, and in the case of his fag strike, he even acts as the defender of these disciplinary structures when they are threatened. Tom's compliance and defense function as meaningful choices on his part to submit to the character and moral formation intended by the school space, a submission often repeated throughout the public-school genre. Waugh's use of the public-school story to voice criticism of the public schools encourages his readers to live actively within their school spaces rather than accept without question the net of discipline and the docility, obedience, and loyalty they seek to instill. A different set of meaningful choices is showcased in *Loom* that recasts the schoolboy as resistant to the intended character and moral formation promised by a public-school education. Waugh demonstrates the ordinary and everyday methods of resistance to, and appropriation of, the school space that are usable by the schoolboy, which make it possible to live more actively in the spaces they inhabit. Waugh reimagines the obedient and loyal public-schoolboy as a covertly rebellious, resistant, and critically thinking student.

Notes

1. Not to be confused with American and Canadian public schools that are state funded, British public schools are independent from the state and called "public" because they are open to anyone who can pay the tuition fees.

2. A system in which lower-year boys do menial tasks for the upper-year boys, such as providing tea and snacks, cleaning out their studies, doing laundry, and so forth. The fagging system offers an education in managing subordinates, a very important skill for Britain's future imperial men.

3. Cribs are a translation or annotation of a text, and "cribbing" is the verb for using the translations. Often conflict arises from a crib being found, an innocent student being accused of using it, and eventually the guilty party stepping forward with a humbled heart, ready to accept his punishment.

Works Cited

Agnew, Kate, and Geoff Fox. *Children at War: From the First World War to the Gulf.* Continuum, 2001.

Barczewski, Stephanie. *Myth and National Identity in Nineteenth-Century Britain: The Legends of King Arthur and Robin Hood.* Oxford UP, 2000.

Clare, Hillary, and Sue Sims. *The Encyclopaedia of Girls' School Stories.* Ashgate, 2000.

Coleman, Nathaniel. *Lefebvre for Architects.* Taylor & Francis, 2014. *ProQuest*, ebookcentral-proquest-com.ezproxy.lib.ucalgary.ca/lib/ucalgary-ebooks/reader .action?docID=1883856&ppg=72.

de Certeau, Michel. The Practice of Everyday Life. Translated by Steven F. Randall, U of California P, 1988.
Foucault, Michel. Discipline and Punish: The Birth of the Prison. 1975. Translated by Alan Sheridan, Vintage, 1995.
Gruner, Elisabeth Rose. "Teach the Children: Education and Knowledge in Recent Children's Fantasy." Children's Literature, vol. 37, 2009, pp. 216–35. Project Muse, doi.org/10.1353/chl.0.0815.
Honey, J. R. De S. Tom Brown's Universe: The Development of the Public School in the 19th Century. Millington, 1977.
Hughes, Thomas. Tom Brown's School Days. 1857. Edited by Andrew Sanders, Oxford UP, 1999.
Kirkpatrick, Robert J. The Encyclopaedia of Boys' School Stories. Ashgate, 2000.
Knuth, Rebecca. Children's Literature and British Identity: Imagining a People and a Nation. Scarecrow Press, 2012.
Lefebvre, Henri. The Production of Space. Translated by Donald Nicholson-Smith, Blackwell, 1991.
Lunn, Arnold. The Harrovians: A Tale of Public School Life. 1914. Viewforth Press, 2010.
Musgrave, P. W. From Brown to Bunter: The Life and Death of the School Story. Routledge and Kegan Paul, 1985.
Nelson, Claudia. "The Angel in the School." Boys Will Be Girls: The Feminine Ethic and British Children's Fiction, 1857–1917. Rutgers UP, 1991.
Parker, Peter. The Old Lie: The Great War and the Public-School Ethos. Constable, 1987.
Petzold, Dieter. "Breaking in the Colt: Socialization in Nineteenth-Century School Stories." Children's Literature Association Quarterly, vol. 15, no. 1, Spring 1990, pp. 17–21. Project Muse, muse.jhu.edu/journals/chq/summary/v015/15.1.petzold.
Quigly, Isabel. The Heirs of Tom Brown: The English School Story. Oxford UP, 1984.
Reynolds, Kimberly. "Words about War for Boys: Representations of Soldiers and Conflict in Writing for Children before World War I." Children's Literature Association Quarterly, vol. 34, no. 3, Fall 2009, pp. 255–71. Project Muse, muse.jhu.edu/article/315219.
Richards, Jeffrey. Happiest Days: The Public Schools in English Fiction. Manchester UP, 1988.
Sanders, Andrew. "Introduction." Tom Brown's Schooldays. Oxford UP, 1989, pp. vii–xxv.
Stanek, Łukasz. Henri Lefebvre on Space: Architecture, Urban Research, and the Production of Theory. U of Minnesota P, 2011. ProQuest, ebookcentral-proquest-com.ezproxy.lib.ucalgary.ca/lib/ucalgary-ebooks/reader.action?docID=765500&ppg=8#.
Steege, David K. "Harry Potter, Tom Brown, and the British School Story: Lost in Transit?" The Ivory Tower and Harry Potter: Perspectives on a Literary Phenomenon, edited by Lana A. Whited, U of Missouri P, 2002, pp. 140–58.
Waugh, Alec. The Loom of Youth. 1917. Pantianos Classics, n.d.
Waugh, Alec. "Preface." The Loom of Youth. 1917. Methuen, 1954. Project Gutenberg, gutenberg.org/files/18863/18863-h/18863-h.htm.
Zipes, Jack. Sticks and Stones: The Troublesome Success of Children's Literature from Slovenly Peter to Harry Potter. Routledge, 2001.

Chapter Eight

"AN ELABORATE COVER"

Staging Identities at School and Abroad in Robin Stevens's Murder Mysteries

REBECCA MILLS AND ANDREW McINNES

In *Jolly Foul Play*, the fourth book in Robin Stevens's 1930s-set *Murder Most Unladylike* mystery series, fourteen-year-old detectives Daisy Wells and Hazel Wong solve their fourth murder and recover a missing student. Acknowledging their success, Inspector Priestley combines condescension, congratulation, and normative command: "You've been very successful detectives. I'm sorry I ever doubted you, but now it's time for you to be schoolgirls again. Think of it as an elaborate cover" (337). Daisy and Hazel's investigation has disrupted the boundaries between adult and child realms, which the inspector seeks to rebuild while allowing space for ambiguity. The ironic suggestion "Think of it as an elaborate cover" recognizes the girls' challenge to established norms. In Stevens's series both the "cover" of schoolgirl and the identity of detective are mapped onto the conventional spaces of English boarding-school stories and detective fiction, enhancing the transgressive potential of this duality: the school and the playing field become crime scenes, while murders at a country house and on the Orient Express are solved by schoolgirls rather than expert private detectives. Hazel and Daisy's role and position as schoolgirls is a disguise that conceals their real life and identity as amateur detectives, obscures their development from childhood to adolescence, and contains their shift from learning about death and passion via books to unmediated experience and witnessing of crime, trauma, and adult desires and motivations.

English Golden Age (1918–1939)[1] detective fiction and interwar boarding-school stories delineate spaces where individual, communal, and national identities and relationships are reflected in tensions between transgression and conformity. The detective often reassuringly affirms collective values and morals, while the boarding school is held to be an institution designed to erode differences and encourage conformity to national, group, and class mores. Stevens's pairing of Hazel Wong, from Hong Kong (a British colony in the 1930s), and the Honourable Daisy Wells, whose background is firmly in the English upper classes, allows Stevens to exploit and negotiate spaces and notions of home, school, and travel—and by extension England and the "Orient"—and show how the identities of her adolescent heroines are formed and performed in these spaces. Stevens frames negotiations of identity and rites of passage within the generic conventions of English school and adventure stories, with explicit intertextual and implicit spatial reference to Sir Arthur Conan Doyle, Agatha Christie, and Dorothy L. Sayers, combining the geographies of classic genre fiction for both children and adults—Deepdean boarding school in *Murder Most Unladylike* (2014) and *Jolly Foul Play* (2016), an isolated aristocratic country manor in *Arsenic for Tea* (2015), and the Orient Express in *First Class Murder* (2015).[2] To this self-conscious dual generic signposting, however, Stevens introduces disruptive elements, thereby avoiding a simplistic nostalgic evocation of Angela Brazil and Agatha Christie.[3]

Our reading of Stevens's novels therefore is informed by the sense that both genres have until recently been critically perceived as formulaic; in each a crisis threatens a community but is ultimately resolved by detective work or peer pressure as applicable. By taking an approach that looks beyond detective fiction and school stories as formulaic fiction, we argue not only that Stevens foregrounds the original narratives' subtextual concerns with national, racial, and sexual Others intruding into traditional English places, but that space is crucial to framing and figuring these anxieties and tensions. Both English boarding-school stories and interwar detective fiction have been accused by critics of insularity, conservatism, and reliance on stock characterization and narrative formula,[4] but Stevens's knowing and critical approach to the tradition offers us a questioning lens on the tropes of each genre, and thereby the exclusionary and thus containing structures and spaces of English society and tradition. Stevens's challenging perspective is embodied and inscribed by first-person narrator Hazel. Not only does her narrative agency disrupt the outsider/insider dynamic that shapes communities and narratives in both boarding school and detective fiction, but as an outsider and newcomer familiar with interwar England and boarding schools only through fiction, she focalizes Stevens's twenty-first-century sensibility.

Disrupting the expectations set by the paratexts of twee titles, pastel colors, and cover art of cute girlish silhouettes, Stevens's *Murder Most Unladylike* series explores shifting and performed individual, communal, and national identity, examining 1930s English society and its fictions. This period and setting are underscored by racist, classist, sexist, and homophobic prejudices. Stevens celebrates the children (and some adults) who, if unable to transcend the situation, can create a space for resistance and critique. Maria Cecire et al.'s discussion of "spaces of power and places of play" (1) in children's literature is useful here. Drawing on Yi-Fu Tuan's formulation of space as empty, and place as space made meaningful through experience, Cecire et al. articulate the shifting and contested terrain between adults and children in spatial terms:

> A recurring characteristic of canonical children's literature in English is the designation of special spaces of childhood into which only children may pass.... Childhood itself is often seen as a world apart, with its own logic and landmarks that distinguish it from adult reality. (1)

Here these scholars refer to fantasy worlds such as Narnia, Neverland, and Wonderland, but this internal logic is evident in the schoolgirl rituals and practices of the interwar boarding school spaces. These customs include "sending to Coventry," or excluding a girl from conversation, strict hierarchies, midnight feasts, and a stern prohibition against snooping and talebearing. Although adults nominally control the space, they are usually distant providers of punishment and reward, or objects of passion and suspicion, rather than equal and intimate antagonists. We suggest that Stevens's introduction of crime and its social and emotional consequences into these realms of childhood disrupts this idea of "a world apart" as Hazel and Daisy take on adult roles *within* an "adult reality," endorsed by the inspector. Cecire et al. suggest, "From Alice's ability to grow and shrink at will to the Pevensie children's undisputed rule as monarchs of Narnia, fiction for children often depicts new spaces of child-dominated power" (3), but they continue:

> In other words, children's literature that reflects the disadvantaged position of children relative to adults (and other larger beings) often models ways of navigating this landscape of power. Such instances privilege the child's purported capacity for superior imagination and creativity, making marked-off spaces of power into simultaneous places of play.
>
> In this way play may become a means of immediate resistance or an opportunity to practice scenarios for later life, suggesting the blurred line between playing and reality. Spatiality, again, seems crucial to navigating these apparent poles. (3)

Crime in Stevens's novels offers a means of transforming spaces of play into places of power for Hazel and Daisy. As we discuss later, part of Hazel and Daisy's methodology is reconstructing the crime; in *Arsenic for Tea*, they use dolls in a doll's house to plot the sequence of events, as the children transcend their own position in the margins of adult life, not only taking center stage but directing the action behind the scenes—asserting their authority over space, and thereby their own identity.

MAPPING TRADITIONAL SPACES: INVESTIGATING THE SCHOOL

Christie, Sayers, and Conan Doyle are not the only precursors invoked in the crime-solving aspects of the novels. Stevens also builds on a tradition of children's fiction dating from the Victorian era that involves children (temporarily) pushing the boundaries of childhood—which are often represented spatially, as Cecire et al. argue—and finding peril or mystery, which they escape or resolve using their initiative and reasoning powers. English boarding-school stories for girls frequently included mild mysteries alongside hockey games, pranks, and form rivalries; for instance, Angela Brazil's boarding-school oeuvre, as Mary Cadogan and Patricia Craig observe, is riddled with puzzles of missing wills, long-lost relations, and mysterious strangers that must be solved (111–25). Routledge summarizes that "elements of mystery, crime, and detection have long been important features of stories enjoyed by young readers [including fairy tales and animal fables]" but notes the beginning of *Hardy Boys* series in 1927 as "the landmark moment in the emergence of detective fiction for children" ("Young Readers" 322). Christopher Routledge notes that detective fiction opens a space for

> the child detective operating in between the discourses of adulthood and childhood. The child detective, in this system, is the point of engagement between the two, and, crucially, is able to interrogate them both [as well] as combine elements from both discourses in their detection. ("Perfect Crime" 73)

Additionally, from 1930 the *Nancy Drew* series offered specifically female detection, presenting the girl sleuth "invoking and recuperating [feminine intuition] that quality of women that had been around for centuries" (Fisher 6). Nancy's instincts offer solutions where policemen's skills do not; as Amy

Boesky writes, her detection is "finding clues where others see nothing, locating suspicious persons with her uncanny (and unerring) "intuition," identifying criminals through such superficial symptoms as bad posture, unusual accents, or poor vocabulary" (189). Nancy's instincts, therefore, reinforce the distinction between those who belong and those who are out of place within her community, the all-American (white) middle-class town of River Heights. By contrast, both Hazel and Daisy, in their own ways, are inherently out of place, as we discuss later; their own belonging and conformity are performative, which affords them insight into other performed identities—queer girls conforming to heteronormativity, foreigners adopting Englishness, and criminals acting as upstanding members of the community.

In interwar children's fiction, foreignness is often in opposition to British values, even as "inside" and "outside" a community are sharply differentiated, particularly during the wars. Schoolgirls in Brazil's novels patriotically support the home front to the point of xenophobia, for instance, but even in peacetime the school story frequently centers on taming a rebellious spirit, or Anglicizing a foreign one, into a productive and assimilated member of the community. Architecturally as well as figuratively, traditional boarding-school spaces are enclosed. Brazil's school gardens often have old stone walls, and in Elinor Brent-Dyer's *Jo of the Chalet School* ([1926] 1949), a wooden fence is built around the school grounds: "the shed, and the cricket-ground and tennis-courts were safely enclosed within a six-foot barrier, which not only shut the school out from curious eyes, but also cut off interesting sights from inattentive pupils—a rather necessary thing" (230). Within these walls, British values of "service," "honour," "self-restraint," and "bravery" (Knuth 112–13) are reinforced, while moral and physical threats are expelled. Even the Austrian and German girls at the Chalet School, located in the Austrian Tyrol for the first years of the *Chalet School* series, read English school stories, absorbing their notions of "playing the game" along with pranks and social hierarchy. Hazel's expectations of English school life and social identity are similarly based on books. Sally Mitchell notes the endurance of the

> set of clichés central to Meade and the girls' formula; . . . the spoiled rich girl accustomed to having her own way; the "Wild Irish Girl" (or American, or Spanish, or Tasmanian) who has to be broken in to an English school—and manages to teach the English girls something about emotions and frankness while she's at it; the child who is overburdened by working for a scholarship because she will have to support herself. (58)

Stevens's novels respond subversively and ambivalently to these clichés of identity, partly because of her contemporary sensibility, but partly because of the insertion of the detective genre into the school story. The "overburdened" young people in *Arsenic for Tea* and *Jolly Foul Play* turn out to be murderers. Daisy certainly fits the "spoiled rich girl" persona, but this is a performance. The "wild" foreigner should be Hazel, but she is the focalizing narrator of the novel, and she and Daisy facilitate each other's deceptive performances.

Danger from outside may breach the walls in Enid Blyton's and Brent-Dyer's fiction, but it is not permitted to break up the school or traumatize the pupils. While Judith Humphrey comments that Brazil took "the boarding school, a place of safety and closure, always ideals of female destiny, and made it into a site of adventure, experience and opportunity" (qtd. in Knuth 112), the boarding school at this period, we suggest, remains a safe space due to the closure and resolution at the end of these adventures. This sense of closure and safety is frequent in mysteries for children and adults as well. Blyton's Famous Five foil crooks and find treasure during holidays, returning to everyday life afterward, and the Five Find-Outers, as Cadogan and Craig point out, "imitate a detective-story pattern, with 'clues,' a list of suspects, the step-by-step elimination of all but the culprit" (346). This is the clue-puzzle formula of Golden Age detective fiction, designed to offer intellectual exercise and satisfactory resolution, and create a securely contained space for both the child character and the implied child reader. Heather Worthington remarks:

> In classic realist children's fiction such as Enid Blyton's *Malory Towers* school stories . . . the child may misbehave or indulge in petty crimes such as "borrowing" another child's property, but real crime and violence remain in the adult realm . . . sombre subjects are balanced by "they all lived happily ever after," an ending upon which children's literature insists. (97)

Stevens enters more complex territory in her work, resisting this formulaic trajectory and closure. Although murderers are caught in Stevens's series, and Hazel and Daisy's triumph is ratified by adult approval, there are traces of trauma caused by contact with bloodshed and dark passion across the series, as Stevens refuses to fully endorse the idea of a "happy ending" and its concomitant secure and contained spaces. In *Murder Most Unladylike* the danger is already within the walls; in *First Class Murder*, Daisy and Hazel are still disturbed by the murder in Daisy's home and revelations about Daisy's parents in the preceding *Arsenic for Tea*.

The emphasis on formulaic narrative structure, accusations of "two-dimensional characterisation" (Knight 91), and "euphemising death, passion and politics" (Knight 83) in scholarship of Golden Age detective fiction, we suggest, parallels criticism of school stories. John Scaggs notes "air-brushed depictions of violent death in Golden Age fiction" (45) and claims that especially "Christie's inter-war fiction is characterised by its absence of violence, and its curiously sanitised and bloodless corpses" (45). Along similar lines, Cadogan and Craig suggest that Brazil's First World War fiction is "glamorizing," "vapidly patriotic," with "war, in the main, an abstraction" (120–21), despite plots featuring correspondence with soldiers and catching German spies. The "bloodlessness" of the Golden Age has been challenged in recent scholarship, as we go on to discuss, but what is interesting about Stevens's work is that making murder bloodless would offer an easy way of making her books palatable for a young audience, as well as invoking the "cosy crime" perception of the Golden Age. However, the first body of the series is bloody:

> My patting made Miss Bell's head loll away from me. Her glasses slid down off her nose and I saw that what I had thought was only a shadow behind her head was actually a dark stain the size of my handkerchief. . . . I put out my finger and touched the stain, and my finger came away covered in blood. (*Murder Most Unladylike* [hereafter, *MMU*] 16)

Hazel is thirteen here; two novels later, Hazel remembers: "I found a body once, almost a year ago. There was not much blood at all, and no screaming; only someone lying very still in the half-dark—but it is in my mind as the worst horror there could be. It still makes my skin crawl" (*First Class Murder* [hereafter, *FCM*] 135–36). Hazel seems to have repressed the bloodiness of the original scene, where she feels sick and cannot wait to scrub it off—but the trauma and visceral memory linger, breaking the containing formulas of both the Golden Age and the school story, and disrupting the notion that childhood can be contained within a safe space. Gill Plain argues against a limiting critical focus on the reassurance and structure of the clue-puzzle formula, examining uncertainty rather than fixity in narratives of containment, and asking "Do we pay attention to what we expect of crime fiction (repetition, resolution, containment), or to what we actually find: namely, the individual piece of writing, representing variation and resistance to the containment encoded in the formulaic message?" (14). Hazel's position in the margins at school but central to detective investigations, subordinate to

Daisy but empowered to chronicle their narratives, suggests variation, while the lingering trauma of her experience of crime resists containment.

Plain suggests, "Although the detective has appeared to be the lynchpin of the formula, providing certainty and stability at the centre of the narrative, closer inspection reveals an ambiguous and uncertain figure" (3). Daisy's certainty in her own powers of investigation and performance is shaken by events in her family, when crime is too close to home, while Stevens undermines the very concepts of a secure identity and a stable locus where it can be formed. Knuth observes that in British interwar books aimed at children, "Cultural strangeness is tied up with quest and danger; cognitive disturbance is part of the experience. Home, in contrast, is a place where one can relax and feel secure and comfortable in one's own identity" (17). This distinction applies here, as the boarding school becomes a site of "quest and danger" for Hazel and Daisy, and identity—and the concept of home—is revealed to be slippery and shifting. Hazel's narration doubly underscores "cultural strangeness," as her schoolmates find her exotic and foreign, even as she observes the strangeness of the "real" cruelty of the English climate and her companions, as opposed to the "jolly school story" (*MMU* 62) she expected. Hazel's out-of-placeness informs her recognition that behind Daisy's sporty and cheerful facade and impeccable breeding, "the inside of her is not jolly-good-show at all" (*MMU* 4).

Stevens's awareness of identity performance shaped by the demands of a specific place—and a specific genre—also resonates with recent critical perceptions of the Golden Age. Alison Light argues that Christie's work displays more anxiety than airbrushing, particularly the concern that "troubles her whodunits which compulsively reiterate the same question, one which has the character of both fascination and fear: is this person what they seem?" resulting in "a sense of a safe, known world thrown out of kilter" (88). This duality and this lability are recurring themes in Stevens's series—the safety and comfort of "home" are undermined for Daisy and Hazel but also for nostalgic readers familiar with the tradition. In *Murder Most Unladylike*, headmistress Miss Griffin murders Miss Bell, and possibly her own illegitimate daughter as well. Beneath the "neat swooped-back grey hair and immaculate Harris tweed" (37), then, lies a woman capable of transgressive sexual passion, filicide, and murdering a colleague and two schoolgirls: "Miss Griffin was following us.... The most awful expression came over her face, a *pounce* like a cat on two mice, and she began to stride purposefully towards us" (288). Hazel and Daisy perform conventional identities as schoolgirls, while their real selves are detectives—in a grim refraction, Miss Griffin's real identity is a murderer disguised by her performance as an authoritative headmistress.

The secure space of the school/home is predicated on the maintenance of these performances; the disguise itself can be read as a safe space disrupted when these disguises are breached.

SUBVERSIVE SPACES IN FAMILIAR PLACES: INTERTEXTUALITY AND THE SCENE OF THE CRIME

The breaches in the wall of the boarding school, the "world apart" of the child, and the secure disguise of the schoolchild and schoolteacher increase throughout the series. In *Arsenic for Tea* a schoolboy commits murder at Daisy's own home; in *First Class Murder* a schoolboy is also a detective, and in *Jolly Foul Play* crime returns to Deepdean, this time with schoolgirl murderers and victim. This continuity of violence, and the evolution of the detective identity and skill set that Hazel and Daisy's memories of these events enable, contrasts with the *Nancy Drew* series, for instance, which offers no evidence that frequent peril and contact with crime affect Nancy's psyche or emotional landscape, and with Blyton's bloodless crimes of blackmail and robbery—indeed, Nancy Drew and Blyton's detective clubs remain frozen at their original age. Fisher remarks that Nancy's "sleuthing also depends on freedom from school," which Nancy has never attended (7). Similarly, for Blyton's mystery solvers, adventure and detection are contained within the school holidays—a time and space apart from real life and, often, adults.[5]

For Hazel and Daisy, however, school and crime scene, school and holiday, and home and school, bleed into each other—a lack of temporal and spatial compartmentalization that parallels the porousness of the borders between each experience of crime and the rest of Hazel's and Daisy's lives, as well as enhancing the uncertainty of these spaces. At Fallingford Manor, Hazel is treated as an exotic outsider by Daisy's family, her insecurity heightened by the murder and its aftermath:

> I missed my Hong Kong home, where everything was hot and light and safe. I missed Deepdean. . . . For a moment I thought I could almost smell it, chalk and not-clean socks and cold water. It washed over my memory of home, which was only very faint now, like my mother's perfume on my clothes. I wasn't sure which place I wanted more. (*Arsenic for Tea* [hereafter, *AFT*] 240)

"Safe" is a crucial word here—at this point, both Deepdean and Daisy's home have been invaded by violence. But this unfixed notion of home, enhanced by the fluidity and erasure of the phrase "washed over," is also a key to the shifting spatial categories that reflect the unfixed and layered identities of the novels. English expatriates in the colonies would send their children "home" to England for school, even though this "home" might be alien and unrecognizable to them, or only familiar through books, as Ysenda Maxstone Graham discusses.[6] Stevens here challenges this idea of England, and boarding school, as a traditional locus of security, subversively undercutting social stability not only by presenting headmistresses and schoolchildren as suspects and murderers but by situating safety in the (popularly perceived to be) dangerous "Orient."

As well as subtexts of national and ethnic out-of-placeness, Stevens foregrounds the social environment and class dynamics of English Ur-texts of detection. The clue-puzzle functions best in a spatially "sequestered" (Knight 77) setting that is also "socially enclosed" (Knight 78)—limited to an upper-middle-class/aristocratic milieu. Stevens explicitly draws on this strategy in *Arsenic for Tea*, as Daisy's father is Lord Hastings, and the manor becomes isolated by a rising flood. Ernest Mandel remarks:

> While the criminalization of the lower classes is a special feature of the more trivial Anglo-Saxon detective novels, it is not unusual to find middle-class, and even wealthy, murderers in the classic crime stories of the twenties and thirties (Agatha Christie's novels for example). The key point is not the class origin of the murderer, but his presentation as a social misfit, a "bounder" who violates the norms of the ruling class and must be punished for that very reason. (45)

The novel's Mr. Curtis is a textbook "bounder." Hazel narrates: "He came into the hall, slouching fashionably, and I saw his face was good-looking, his dark hair very smooth and his smile toothpaste-wide. He did not look at all the sort of man who might belong in the front hall of Fallingford House" (17). Mr. Curtis is having an affair with his host's wife, Daisy's mother, and is casing the joint for valuable art and jewelry. He is also the murder victim, fulfilling Mandel's formula. But his murderer is also a misfit, the poor scholarship boy Stephen, a friend of Daisy's brother, whom Hazel befriends. The bounder and the poor boy are therefore eliminated, as Stephen is arrested—the only outsider left at Fallingford Manor, rather chillingly, is Hazel.

Although she employs locations, tropes, and period detail and language from the interwar period, Stevens's contemporary outlook fits into the "more complex and darker fiction" for children of the 1960s onward, which "necessarily incorporated delinquency and violence and sometimes crime in response to sometimes troubled realities of young adulthood" (Worthington 101). The teenaged murderers in *Arsenic for Tea* and *Jolly Foul Play* certainly illustrate the fact that young adults face pressures and feel resentments and obsessions to the same extent as adults. Adulthood and childhood therefore coexist uneasily in the spaces of Stevens's novels, as do "spaces of power" and "places of play," to recall Cicere et al. The idea of the schoolgirl disguise is signified via reading choices: Hazel reads Ransome's wholesome sailing adventure *Swallows and Amazons* while eavesdropping on a passionate and suspicious encounter between two staff members at Deepdean as "camouflage" (*MMU* 135). We are clued in to Daisy's identity performance when she reads Christie's *Peril at End House* (1932), which hinges on a performance of surface innocence and charm by an aristocratic young blonde woman—like Daisy—who is devious and fragmented underneath (*MMU* 6). Routledge argues, "The child-adult detective's efforts to uncover and capture the adult-child criminal point still more decisively towards a tendency to expose, punish and finally remove childhood and childish behaviour from society at large" ("Perfect Crime" 65), but we find this unconvincing in relation to Stevens's series, because her murderers include adults and children, her adult murderers are authority figures supposed to care for children, and finally because she carefully shows how "childhood" is already part of a performance for Daisy and Hazel. While teenagers are driven to murder behind the facade of youthful innocence, Daisy and Hazel's assumed naivete—and schoolgirlishness—conceals a fierce intellect as well as an adult sense of responsibility for restoring order.

Golden Age detective fiction is therefore important in Stevens's articulation and delineation of Daisy's and Hazel's identities and narrative structures, but it also shapes and inflects Stevens's spaces.[7] Christie's *Murder on the Orient Express* is explicitly invoked in *First Class Murder*, for instance, and offers Daisy and Hazel a clue to investigating and mapping the premeditation of the murderer. The intrusion of crime into the children's story, and the destabilizing recognition of the insecurity of its space and the disguises of its inhabitants that follows, not only subverts the Brazil/Blyton tradition but echoes the subversive use of the boarding-school "space of play" in Josephine Tey's *Miss Pym Disposes* (1946) and Christie's *Cat among the Pigeons* (1959), which Stevens cites as inspirations, and in which sports and games equipment become deadly. Similarly to these authors, Stevens challenges the "jolly hockey-sticks" nostalgia associated with boarding school by exploring passionate but warped relationships, ambitions, and desires, volatile emotions heightened in the claustrophobia of the contained boarding school community. There is little room for privacy or secrecy within the shared spaces of the boarding school, and behind its walls and fences, life is dominated by strict routines. Ju Gosling analyses adolescence and sexuality in Brent-Dyer's work, noting, "The message . . . is that adolescent girls are affected by the natural environment and need fresh air and exercise to keep their sexual energy under control" (15). Tey, Christie, and Stevens share an awareness that the building up of resentment as well as desire—among staff or pupils—leads to outbursts that cannot be entirely sublimated in game-play, and sports fields and games equipment become deadly.

Stevens's novels decode subtexts of queer identities and relationships encoded in the oeuvres of Brazil and Blyton.[8] The negotiation of these themes is focalized via Hazel, however, offering the perspective of an adolescent uneasily situated within the community, instead of the more usual adult outsider's point of view. Schoolgirls' queer identities are presented sympathetically and included in Hazel and Daisy's challenge to convention across the series. Stevens distinguishes between a younger schoolgirl's "pash" on a senior or popular girl, and a physically intimate relationship between equals. Daisy has several followers in lower forms who give her "awfully soppy cards" (*MMU* 191) and bring her information; this exemplifies what Martha Vicinus describes as a common dynamic in which "the new student could worship an all-knowing older girl, who, in turn, received her first taste of power" (606). "Pashes" in Stevens's series are primarily a source of comedy, a rite of passage taken for granted, but a physically intimate lesbian relationship between prefects in *Jolly Foul Play* is presented in a more serious, tolerant, and open-minded way. Daisy vocally defends the schoolgirl lovers from malicious gossip in a rare deviation from her conventional cover. Indeed, it is gently suggested that Daisy sympathizes with the pair in part because of her own queer identity, coming out to Hazel in *Death in the Spotlight* (2018) and falling in love with Egyptian classmate Amina in the final installment of the series.

Hazel's narrative inscribes resistance to tradition and ritualized oppressions and hierarchies within the community. Stevens's insertion of the tropes of adult Golden Age detective fiction, therefore, with its death and passion, into traditional children's literature, means a breaking free of the containing spaces of both genres; change and growth are possible for Daisy and Hazel, even if their environments seek to contain them. Violence and danger are revealed to reside within the exclusionary walls of boarding school and country manor, undermining their safety and stability but also allowing "places of play" to be transformed into "spaces of power" for Daisy and Hazel. Tey's and Christie's detective figures are adults solving crimes among young women and their teachers, but Daisy and Hazel demonstrate that it is possible to develop their own agendas and take control over their environments, resisting adult notions of normativity.

WATSON AND HOLMES: RESISTING GENDERED SPACES

Daisy reads adult novels and stories, living vicariously through adult detectives, and thereby skips narratives of girlhood identity formation common in boarding-school stories, sidestepping the containing spaces of the dormitory and nursery in a way she finds satisfactory; she trespasses into "out of bounds" places, repurposes them for her own use, and ignores rules as she sees fit. In doing so she resists adult supervision and limitation:

> "I don't like the thought of the two of you roaming about carrying on your Young Miss Marple routine while [the murderous headmistress is] still a free woman."
> "Miss Marple!" hissed Daisy under her breath. "Holmes and Watson, *if* you please." (*MMU* 281)

The inspector's use of "roaming" emphasizes the contained and restricted exploration expected of teenaged girls. Ironically, Daisy does use Miss Marple's detection methods of surveillance and presenting a feminine angelic facade; she employs a network of younger girls as informants that echoes Miss Marple's use of servant gossip.[9] Daisy combines these tactics with Holmes's physical dynamism and unscrupulousness in getting results, however—she rejects the schoolgirl honor code against eavesdropping and snooping. Daisy associates freedom and logic with masculinity; by articulating herself and Hazel as fully-formed adult detectives, and male detectives at that, Daisy assumes the right to know, roam, and manipulate her environment as she sees fit.

The Holmes/Watson dynamic is echoed in Hazel's writing-up of the Detective Society's adventures, but the power structure that it evokes is complex, especially as Daisy is a member of the English aristocracy, and Hazel is not only foreign but from a British colony. By describing herself and Hazel as Holmes and Watson, then, Daisy attempts to break through the containing limits of their gender, but in doing so she effaces Hazel's Chinese identity, subsuming it under the umbrella of classic English detective fiction, and continuing her determined subordination of Hazel into the sidekick role.[10] Hazel agrees to this hierarchy: "This is probably fair. After all, I am much too short to be a heroine of this story, and who ever heard of a Chinese Watson?"

(*MMU* 3). "Probably" here suggests, however, that Hazel has not quite internalized the narrative of empire; indeed, Hazel takes a more active and critical role in Detective Society investigations than the hero-worshipping Watson does. Stevens is careful to stress that her investigative skills equal Daisy's, even if they are directed toward empathy more than intellect. Hazel's narration affords her a subversive voice that resists the pressure to conform to the boarding-school Englishness: "Usually, once they know me, English people simply pretend that I am not Oriental, and I simply do not remind them about it. But sometimes they slip . . . which can be quite difficult for me to politely ignore" (*MMU* 43–44). The narration therefore helps to counter her subaltern role by inscribing her discomfort with both narratives of exoticization and assimilation upon the space of English authority.

Hazel's narration and critical comments are unusual for the sidekick in the girl detective genre, as well as unheard-of for a foreign girl in traditional English boarding-school fiction. Comparing the *Nancy Drew* series with Janet Evanovich's Stephanie Plum novels, Julie D. O'Reilly argues that Nancy's and Stephanie's sidekicks normalize their heroines through their aberrant physical appearances, narrative impropriety, mitigation of danger, and comic relief, and by receiving them into the company of women (62, 66, 67, 68). By making their extraordinary heroines seem acceptable in comparison, Nancy's and Stephanie's sidekicks "serve both resistant and conservative functions," because they are both marginal figures and sites of resistance to normative discourse (70–71). Although Hazel resembles these earlier sidekicks in her concern for Daisy's safety and her position as a foreign foil for Daisy's Englishness, she differs throughout the series from her precursors in her self-conscious recognition of difference and in the equal weight Stevens gives to her sleuthing abilities compared with Daisy. Further, instead of normalizing each other in accordance with these generic demands, their difference remains a key source of productive tension throughout the series.

Hazel and Daisy's encounters are initially antagonistic. *Murder Most Unladylike* is chronologically nonlinear; the narrative of the murder and the course of the investigation is interspersed with flashbacks to Hazel's arrival in England, her culture shock at Deepdean, and her interaction with Daisy, stressing themes of otherness and performance. On her first day, Hazel encounters Daisy on the school's hockey field, where she is doubly out of place, being unathletic and conspicuously foreign. The cold, disoriented Hazel, with "lumpy legs sticking out underneath [her] itchy grey games skirt and games knickers" (*MMU* 61) is contrasted with Daisy as an aggressive embodiment of Englishness:

> Her hair was falling out of its plaits chaotically and her eyes were extremely blue, and although the rest of England was not exactly turning out as I had expected, here, at least, was one English ideal—my golden-haired friend come to life; a person absolutely made from the England of my books and paintings. (65)

Daisy's golden hair and pink skin are quintessentially Angela Brazilian; the descriptors "a fair complexion," "flaxen hair," and "blue eyes" are sprinkled throughout her novels.[11] However, Daisy exhibits a lack of sportsmanship that Brazil's heroines would strongly condemn, as she attacks Hazel under the guise of the game and deliberately knocks her over on the hockey field in a show of mastery and racial superiority. This subtly undercuts the discourse of "playing the game" that appears in schoolgirl fiction, as well as Daisy as an "English ideal." Hazel's rueful conclusion to the chapter inscribes her disillusionment with both: "When I think back to that moment, I realize how silly I was" (65).

After a series of cruel pranks, which also violate fictional codes of fair play, Hazel realizes that Daisy pretends to be an average schoolgirl, embracing the image if not the ideals: Daisy "was exactly in the middle of our form, neither a swot nor a dunce. Her English essays were utterly dull, her French hopped tenses like anything, and she mixed up the Hapsburgs and the Huns" (114). The "exactly" is telling: in a literal-minded fashion, Daisy works hard to be precisely average, disguising her intelligence behind girlish charm to pass as normal and absorb information about students and staff, "not to blackmail them or do anything awful like that, that's not Daisy at all—but just to know things. Daisy always has to *know* things" (116–17). In these flashbacks, Stevens not only layers two investigations—the murder and Hazel's deduction of Daisy's real self—but also emphasizes that Daisy's personality is split between a deliberate representation of ideal English girlhood—beautiful, sporty, but not too smart—and a cannier spy, a "different Daisy underneath" (117) for whom knowledge is power, a way of breaking out of the containing space of the classroom.

Hazel's marginal position at the school gives her space to exercise her own perceptiveness: she sees through Daisy's performance and mimics it to fit in, herself: "I could behave like a don't-care girl on the outside, but inside I could still be me" (*MMU* 205). She scuffs her new shoes, mistreats her books, and muddies her bag and hands on the way to lessons the next day, and in lessons she mirrors Daisy's performance by making mistakes: "In my French composition I told Mamzelle that I had brown eyes and a long black horse" (207), playing on a common confusion of *cheveux* and *chevaux*. In response, Hazel's classmates begin to accept her and ignore her difference, as she begins to be assimilated. Daisy remains unconvinced, however, and confronts Hazel: "You've cut this shoelace.... And all the scratches on your shoes are new as well. Before this week I'd never seen you with a button out of place. I was beginning to think they hadn't heard of dirt in the East. What are you playing at?" (209). Daisy's interrogation combines her Sherlockian skills with her ingrained sense of command, stressing Hazel's otherness with her reference to the East. Hazel retaliates that she is "fitting in.... Just like you do!" (209); her observation of the English girl's real intelligence delights Daisy, and she helps Hazel to perfect her own disguise. The two girls emerge from this confrontation as best friends, but not quite equals—Daisy carefully maintains her own position as head of the detective society, but this is perhaps related more to her fierce confidence in her own abilities than to her Orientalism. Both girls, then, self-consciously perform a conventional schoolgirl identity, including slovenly dressing and posture and a deliberate (and playful) lack of knowledge, to disguise or ameliorate their divergence from the norm, even before their "elaborate cover" as detectives disguised as schoolgirls over the course of the series.

REMAPPING CHILDHOOD SPACES AND RETRACING A MURDERER'S STEPS

Each *Murder Most Unladylike* novel includes a map that aids the reader in tracing the progress of the investigation, and regularly updated lists of suspects and motives within the narrative. These diegetic devices echo Christie and Sayers and highlight the disruption of the boarding-school narrative. *Where*, then, is as important as "how" and "why" in figuring out "whodunit." Worthington observes that the popularity of the clue-puzzle, which coincided with a surge in intellectually satisfying games such as the crossword puzzle, and its logical and attainable solutions

> can be mapped onto society; by capturing the amoral and abnormal member of society, the detective restores the proper order of things. The texts also represent, respond to and offer a comforting illusion of the containment of contemporary social anxieties. (120)

Again we return to "containment"; this idea of transforming violence and fear into a puzzle recurs throughout Stevens's series. Hazel remarks: "I felt the same old detective excitement rising up in me. Daisy was getting to me, turning real things into puzzles to be solved—but then I wondered whether it wasn't better to think of Mr Curtis as a puzzle than a real person who had been murdered" (*AFT* 147–48). The puzzle here is a coping strategy for Hazel, even as it is a method of intellectual engagement for Daisy; both are distinct and mature responses to an adult situation. Stevens knowingly undercuts the implied appeal to order and hope of restoration, however, not only by allowing for the possibility of lingering psychological trauma for Hazel and Daisy but also by having Daisy read Sayers's *Whose Body?* hidden within the covers of *Paradise Lost*, just before Hazel stumbles upon the body of Miss Bell in *Murder Most Unladylike*. Paradise is already lost; there can be no recovery of either Hazel's innocence or the "comforting illusion of containment" of the boarding school.

Daisy and Hazel's methodology of restoration involves reconstructing the crime scene. The chaotic state following the murder is imaginatively and physically mapped in order to contain and regularize the chaos of conflicting witness and suspect narratives and emotions into a single orderly sequence of events, a logic of space and time. In *Jolly Foul Play*, this reconstruction becomes an uncanny meditation on space and identity, as the murder victim and suspects constitute a clique of older prefects who darkly reflect the personalities of the expanded Detective Society. Head girl and secret blackmailer Elizabeth is murdered by one of her prefects during a fireworks display. In the reenactment, Daisy plays the role of Elizabeth as murder victim, underlining a series of unpleasant parallels between the power-hungry and deceitful Elizabeth and Daisy's desire to know everything about the secret lives of everyone. Hazel, along with new assistant members of the Detective Society Lavinia, "Beanie," and Kitty, perform the roles of the prefect-suspects—even as the line between Daisy and Elizabeth is blurred, so their lesser role in the Detective Society mirrors the anxious subordinate prefects under Elizabeth's control. Lavinia, who longs for full rather than assistant status, takes a turn as one of the suspects, playing up the theatricality of the re-creation. Hazel observes her actions:

> Lavinia went walking up to Daisy, moving slowly and carefully (she had been thirty seconds now), then raised her right arm and made a hitting motion towards Daisy's head. Daisy turned and raised an eyebrow at her, and Lavinia grinned. (280)

Lavinia's performance triggers a series of epiphanies for the Detective Society whilst playfully hinting at Lavinia's desire to challenge Daisy for leadership. Her actions mean that they can eliminate a suspect, but they also mean that the murder must have been premeditated, with the murderer leaving both the real murder weapon (a hockey stick) and the assumed instrument of accidental death (a rake) on the scene before the fireworks display. Hazel notes:

> I felt, as I always do when we begin a re-creation, that we were stepping back in time, back to the night of the murder. I think I have a little too much imagination for re-creations. I feel it, I don't just see it—I feel the horror of what happened, and what the murderer felt—and can almost begin to imagine why they did what they did. (*Jolly Foul Play* 274–75)

By imaginatively occupying the mental and emotional space of the murderer, induced by occupying her physical space, Hazel risks losing her own identity. Her comments here underscore crucial themes in the novel and the series. By re-creating the scene of the crime, the Detective Society uncannily embodies the identities of murder victim and murderer, blurring the boundaries between detective and murderer: Hazel's empathy aligns her, horrifically, with the murderer's psyche. Hazel's empathetic response is contrasted, here as elsewhere, with Daisy's more intellectual vision—Daisy merely sees, whereas Hazel feels. Stevens is careful to value Hazel's emotional responses as much as Daisy's rationality. This scene demonstrates Stevens's complex representation of space, time, and identity in her children's detective fiction: the Detective Society performatively inhabits the role of victim and suspects in order to ghost the temporal and spatial movements of the murderer.

This reconstruction also involves remapping space on a wider level; spaces inhabited by schoolgirls are recharted as detectives. Deepdean boarding school, Fallingford Manor, and the Orient Express are sites designed to be isolated and containing, with fixed roles, hierarchies, and routines for children and adults—routines that attempt to ensure that children remain children rather than taking on adult roles. At Fallingford the need to solve the murder transforms Lavinia, Kitty, and Beanie into assistant members of the Detective Society—but they, with Daisy and Hazel, are expected to spend their time in the nursery, in the schoolroom with a governess, and playing outdoors, interacting with adults only at designated times. The Orient Express case follows the same pattern—Hazel and Daisy are limited to their cabin, mealtimes and intervals with Hazel's strict father in his cabin, and supervised tourist trips. At Deepdean, surveillance and schedules are also ingrained, but on an institutional rather than domestic basis. Mavis Reimer suggests that early school stories can be studied "in the context of the disciplinary society which Michel Foucault argues is forming in the seventeenth and eighteenth centuries," which is designed to produce a "subject who takes responsibility for constraining himself, who participates in his own subjection" as a result of "panoptic surveillance," or "as a state of 'conscious and permanent visibility' in which one is sure one might be seen at any time" (211). At Deepdean the girls have an ordered schedule of sleep, lessons, music practice, and sports and recreation, with designated spaces and times. Hazel writes, "One of the first things you learn at Deepdean is that bells are sacred. Our lives are parcelled up into the spaces between one and the next, and to ignore the summons is simply criminal" (*MMU* 23)—foreshadowing later events and roles in "criminal" here!

This "parcelling" is ensured through surveillance, which takes on particularly sinister Foucauldian overtones in *Jolly Foul Play*: "We were under siege, and the worst thing was that none of the mistresses or Matron noticed.... It felt as though we were rabbits waiting for the fox to pounce. Elizabeth and her five prefects patrolled the school, and their viciousness spread down, until we were all at each other's throats" (12–13). Here schoolgirls themselves become complicit in creating subjects existing in a state of "conscious and permanent visibility"—Stevens's military and hunting imagery emphasizes the breakdown of the order decreed and maintained by adults, and the creation of an alternative world within a world, led by a dictatorship. The theme of visibility is augmented by the proliferation of anonymous fragments of paper that reveal private information about pupils; head girl Elizabeth collected secrets and revealed them for her own ends. This practice of observation is mirrored in the watchword of Hazel and Daisy's Detective Society: *Constant Vigilance*—indeed, in this novel, the five prefects are foils for the Detective Society, with the dictatorial Elizabeth a dark double for Daisy: "In Daisy's mind she is quite different to Elizabeth, and all the things she asks us to do are sensible and good, but is that entirely true?" (50). This tension is not fully resolved in the series—a further resistance to closure.

Despite these temporally and spatially prescribed lives, Hazel and Daisy trespass across these boundaries and circumvent the containing supervision of teachers, prefects, and parents, both as part of their remapping process as detectives, and as acts of normal schoolgirl rebellion. Before Brazil's and Blyton's high-spirited twentieth-century schoolgirls, Charlotte Brontë's Belgian school in *Villette* is defined by a dynamic of habitual surveillance by staff and regular deception and breaking out of bounds by pupils; Louisa M. Alcott in *An Old-Fashioned Girl* and *Little Men* recounts midnight feasts and holiday infractions in boarding schools. Mitchell suggests that these escapist and rebellious practices coalesced into tropes in the late nineteenth century in the novels of L. T. Meade, who also instituted the "secret society or clique" as a regular element in the school-story formula (57). At Deepdean, Daisy and Hazel find opportunities to rebel within the "spaces between" the bells, and private places for communication at prohibited hours: the Detective Society meets in an airing cupboard, their dormitory holds a midnight feast, girls whisper to each other in bed, and, most drastically, Daisy and Hazel induce vomiting with ipecac, thereby gaining time in the sanatorium away from the bells and surveillance and the chance to search the premises at night looking for clues.

The architecture of the school enables this sneaking around—between the areas designed for leisure, health, and education lie abandoned tunnels and rooms with "brickwork, broken bits of cobweb and steps going down into darkness" (*MMU* 168). Even everyday spaces can be remapped from the wholesome to the queer, emphasizing the lability of the site—as Daisy points out, the prefects use the airing cupboard for illicit "canoodling." As David Rudd observes of Blyton's adventure novels, "a discourse which constructs children as knowing their place, as being marginalized, simultaneously gives them the latitude to exploit these margins, to eavesdrop and peek through keyholes—in short, to inhabit the interstices of the homely fabric" (86). In Fallingford's public-facing spaces, children should be seen and not heard, but secret passages and little-used corridors enable the evasion of adult observation. After the murder Daisy leads Hazel down the dark servants' staircase: "I imagined us vanishing down them and never coming out—but that was a silly, shrimp-like fear, of course. I took a deep breath and followed Daisy carefully down twenty steps. . . . 'Halfway down,' she breathed" (*AFT* 112). This hidden halfway position, and the overcoming of childish fear, reflects Hazel's liminality between childhood and adulthood—she is aware that the flirtation between Daisy's mother and the visiting (murder victim) Mr. Curtis is "the sort of nasty grown-up thing that I do not understand . . . or understand, but wish I didn't" (*AFT* 19). Similarly, the nursery is remapped into a place for adult detective work, as an old doll's house and dolls are used to reconstruct the crime. Daisy and Hazel and their friends may not be quite ready to put away childish things, but they are ready to use them for adult purposes. The borders between childhood and adulthood in these spaces are therefore flexible and porous; Daisy and Hazel perform the role of schoolgirls in public and embody detectives in private.

CONCLUSION: RITES OF PASSAGE

The spaces of Stevens's novels reflect the rites of passage that the girls are going through as they confront shifting forms of home and security, and develop their ideas of both. These uncertainties are heightened by the slippery generic position and function of the novels, as the reassuring geographies and interior spaces of the boarding-school novel are inscribed with the formulas and anxieties of detective fiction. And yet these formulas and anxieties offer escape and empowering self-definition for Daisy and Hazel. Hazel writes of life beyond the confines of Deepdean:

> I am so used to being at Deepdean now—and everyone there is so used to me—that I can sometimes forget that I'm different. But as soon as I leave school I remember all over again. . . . I know it is the way things are, but I wish I was not the only one of *me*—and I wish that the me I am did not seem like the wrong sort of *me* to be. (*AFT* 8)

It is only when they are detecting that Hazel and Daisy escape the confines of class, ethnicity, and childhood, as well as the constant surveillance of these identities; after the murder on the Orient Express, for instance, Hazel realizes: "I think [my father] was in shock as well. You see, he loves his world to be controlled, and a murder quite ruined that. He looked somehow smaller as he leaned against the wall, and with amazement I realized that for once, I was the expert and he was only an onlooker" (*FCM* 101). In *Jolly Foul Play*, after the murder, Hazel becomes the observer rather than the observed: "When I am on a case I suddenly become utterly noticing, as though I am even more in my skin than usual" (38); and when detecting, Daisy is free to allow "her secret side, clever and fiercely interested in everything," to emerge (*AFT* 10). Detection thereby becomes an emotional and intellectual space of freedom and agency. To be a detective, for Hazel and Daisy, is to be *right* in and with the world.

Notes

1. See, for example, Martin Edwards's *The Golden Age of Murder: The Mystery of Writers Who Invented the Modern Detective Story* (2015).

2. The series was concluded with *Death Sets Sail* (2019), in which Daisy and Hazel are in their late teens.

3. Stevens lists Brazil, Blyton, Christie, and Josephine Tey among her influences (*The Guardian*, 2014).

4. See, for example, Colin Watson's *Snobbery with Violence* (1971), Julian Symons's *Bloody Murder—From the Detective Story to the Crime Novel: A History* (1972), and *You're a Brick, Angela! The Girls' Story from 1839–1975* (1976) by Mary Cadogan and Patricia Craig.

5. For more on Blyton and the holiday adventure, see David Rudd's chapter "Digging up the Family Plot: Secrets, Mystery, and the Blytonesque" in *Mystery in Children's Literature from the Rational to the Supernatural* (2001).

6. For more on real English boarding schools, see *Terms & Conditions: Life in Girls' Boarding Schools, 1939–1979* (2017) by Ysenda Maxstone Graham.

7. The country house is a staple location in Golden Age (ca. 1918–1939) detective fiction, appearing in Christie's *A Mysterious Affair at Styles* (1920), A. A. Milne's *The Red House Mystery* (1922), and J. Jefferson Farjeon's *Thirteen Guests* (1936), but it also appears in school stories, for example, Brazil's *The Mystery of the Moated Grange* (1942).

8. See, for example, Florence Tamagne's chapter "An Inversion of Values: The Cult of Homosexuality," in *A History of Homosexuality in Europe: Berlin, London, Paris, 1919–1939, Volume I & II* (2006), in which she notes that while Brazil may not have been aware of the "sexual implications" in her novels, "for the reader, the atmosphere of the schools seems heavily charged with eroticism and sentimentality" (123), and Martha Vicinus's "Distance and Desire: English Boarding school Friendships" (1984).

9. For more on Miss Marple as a feminine detective, see Merja Makinen's *Agatha Christie: Investigating Femininity* (2006).

10. This colonial aspect is particularly problematic, as Conan Doyle's Dr. Watson was in the British Army in India and fought in the Second Anglo-Afghan War.

11. See, for example, *A Patriotic Schoolgirl* (1918) and *For the School Colours* (1918).

Works Cited

Alcott, Louisa M. *Little Men*. 1879. London: Puffin, 2015.
Alcott, Louisa M. *An Old-Fashioned Girl*. 1869. London: Puffin, 1991.
Blyton, Enid. *Famous Five Series*. London: Hodder and Stoughton, 1942–1963.
Blyton, Enid. *Five Find-Outers Series*. London: Methuen, 1943–1961.
Blyton, Enid. *Malory Towers Series*. London: Methuen, 1946–1951.
Boesky, Amy. "Solving the Crime of Modernity: Nancy Drew in 1930." *Studies in the Novel*, 42.1 (2010): 185–201. Project MUSE, doi:10.1353/sdn.2010.0004.
Brazil, Angela. *For the School Colours*. 1918. Project Gutenberg, https://www.gutenberg.org/ebooks/35972. Accessed 24 January 2017.
Brazil, Angela. *The Mystery of the Moated Grange*. 1942. Blackie, 1960.
Brazil, Angela. *A Patriotic Schoolgirl*. 1918. Project Gutenberg, www.gutenberg.org/ebooks/25145. Accessed 24 January 2017.
Brent-Dyer, Elinor M. *Jo of the Chalet School*. 1926. London: W. R. Chambers Ltd., 1949.
Brontë, Charlotte. *Villette*. 1853. London: Penguin, 2012.
Cadogan, Mary, and Patricia Craig. *You're a Brick, Angela: A New Look at Girls' Fiction, 1839–1975*. London: Victor Gollancz, 1976.
Cecire, Maria Sachiko, Hannah Field, Malini Roy, and Claudia Nelson. "Introduction: Spaces of Power, Places of Play." Ed. Cecire et al. *Space and Place in Children's Literature, 1789 to the Present*. Surrey: Ashgate, 2015. 1–20.

Christie, Agatha. *Cat among the Pigeons*. 1959. London: HarperCollins, 2014.
Christie, Agatha. *Murder on the Orient Express*. 1934. London: HarperCollins, 2001.
Christie, Agatha. *Peril at End House*. 1932. London: HarperCollins, 2001.
Edwards, Martin. *The Golden Age of Murder: The Mystery of Writers Who Invented the Modern Detective Story*. London: HarperCollins, 2015.
Fisher, Leona W. "Introduction: The Girl Sleuth." *The Girl Sleuth*, special issue of *Clues: A Journal of Detection* 27.1 (2009): 5–10.
Gosling, Ju. *Virtual Worlds of Girls*, 1998. www.ju90.co.uk/start.htm. Accessed 27 July 2018.
Graham, Ysenda Maxtone. *Terms & Conditions: Life in Girls' Boarding Schools, 1939–1979*. London: Abacus, 2017.
Humphrey, Judith. *The English Girls' Story: Subversion and Challenge in a Traditional, Conservative Literary Genre*. Bethesda, MD: Academica Press, 2009.
Keene, Carolyn (pseud.). *Nancy Drew Mystery Stories*. Various publishers, 1930–2003.
Knight, Stephen. "The Golden Age." *Cambridge Companion to Crime Fiction*. Ed. Martin Priestman. Cambridge: Cambridge UP, 2003. 77–94.
Knuth, Rebecca. *Children's Literature and British Identity: Imagining a People and a Nation*. Scarecrow Press, 2012.
Light, Alison. *Forever England: Femininity, Literature and Conservatism between the Wars*. London: Routledge, 1991.
Makinen, Merja. *Agatha Christie: Investigating Femininity*. New York: Palgrave Macmillan, 2006.
Mandel, Ernest. *Delightful Murder: A Social History of the Crime Story*. London: Pluto, 1984.
Mitchell, Sally. "Children's Reading and the Culture of Girlhood: The Case of L. T. Meade." *Victorian Popular Culture*, special issue of *Browning Institute Studies* 17 (1989): 53–63.
O'Reilly, Julie D. "The Legacy of George and Bess: Sidekicks as Normalizing Agents for the Girl Sleuth." *The Girl Sleuth*, special issue of *Clues: A Journal of Detection* 27.1 (2009): 61–73.
Plain, Gill. *Twentieth-Century Crime Fiction: Gender, Sexuality and the Body*. Edinburgh: Edinburgh UP, 2001.
Reimer, Mavis. "Traditions of the School Story." Ed. M. O. Grenby and Andrea Immel. *Cambridge Companion to Children's Literature*. Cambridge: Cambridge UP, 2009. 209–25.
Routledge, Christopher. "Children's Detective Fiction and the 'Perfect Crime' of Adulthood." Ed. Adrienne E. Gavin and Christopher Routledge. *Mystery in Children's Literature: From the Rational to the Supernatural*. Basingstoke: Palgrave Macmillan, 2001. 64–81.
Routledge, Christopher. "Crime and Detective Literature for Young Readers." Ed. Charles J. Rzepka and Lee Horsley. *A Companion to Crime Fiction*. Oxford: Blackwell-Wiley, 2010. 321–32.
Rudd, David. "Digging up the Family Plot: Secrets, Mystery, and the Blytonesque." *Mystery in Children's Literature: From the Rational to the Supernatural*. Ed. Adrienne E. Gavin and Christopher Routledge. Basingstoke: Palgrave Macmillan, 2001. pp. 82–99.
Sayers, Dorothy L. *Whose Body?* 1923. London: New English Library, 2003.
Scaggs, John. *Crime Fiction*. London: Routledge, 2005.

Stevens, Robin. *Arsenic for Tea*. London: Puffin, 2014.
Stevens, Robin. *First Class Murder*. London: Puffin, 2015.
Stevens, Robin. *Jolly Foul Play*. London: Puffin, 2016.
Stevens, Robin. *Murder Most Unladylike*. London: Puffin, 2014.
Stevens, Robin. "Robin Stevens' Top 10 Boarding School Stories." *The Guardian*, 29 May 2014, www.theguardian.com/childrens-books-site/2014/may/29/robin-stevens-top-10-boarding-school-stories. Accessed 26 July 2018.
Symons, Julian. *Bloody Murder—From the Detective Story to the Crime Novel: A History*. London: Faber and Faber, 1972.
Tey, Josephine. *Miss Pym Disposes*. 1946. London: Arrow Books, 2011.
Tamagne, Florence. *A History of Homosexuality in Europe: Berlin, London, Paris, 1919–1939, Volume I & II*. New York: Algora Publishing, 2006.
Tuan, Yi-Fu. *Space and Place: The Perspective of Experience*. U of Minnesota P, 2001.
Vallone, Lynne. "Ideas of Difference in Children's Literature." Ed. M. O. Grenby and Andrea Immel. *Cambridge Companion to Children's Literature*. Cambridge: Cambridge UP, 2009. 174–91.
Vicinus, Martha. "Distance and Desire: English Boarding School Friendships." *The Lesbian Issue*, special issue of *Signs* 9.4 (1984): 600–622.
Watson, Colin. *Snobbery with Violence: Crime Stories and Their Audience*. London: Eyre and Spottiswoode, 1971.
Worthington, Heather. *Key Concepts in Crime Fiction*. Basingstoke: Palgrave Macmillan, 2011.

Chapter Nine

SPACE, IDENTITY, AND VOICE

Angie Thomas's *The Hate U Give*

WENDY ROUNTREE

> And to every kid in Georgetown and in all "the Gardens" of the world: your voices matter, your dreams matter, your lives matter. Be roses that grow in the concrete.
>
> —ANGIE THOMAS, ACKNOWLEDGMENTS FROM *THE HATE U GIVE*

INTRODUCTION: BLURRING THE LINE BETWEEN FICTIONAL SPACES AND REAL-WORLD PLACES

The epigraph above illustrates Angie Thomas's motives for writing her 2017 young adult novel, *The Hate U Give*. She is primarily writing for, and about, young African Americans who are living in urban neighborhoods throughout the country, whose voices are often silenced, and who are attempting to transform their communities to ritual grounds that better fit their needs. Through her protagonist, sixteen-year-old Starr Carter, Thomas offers a contemporary portrayal of African American youth who have in recent years been increasingly terrorized and victimized in familiar spaces such as their family homes, neighborhoods, and schools. Ideally, these spaces should be "safe spaces" where young people can feel emotionally and psychologically safe. However, with the rise of police brutality, school shootings, and the persistent problem of gangs and drugs, many young Americans, especially African Americans, are subjected to gun violence and the consequential trauma that follows. In this milieu some youth can be "roses that grow in the concrete" and overcome the obstacles that they face as they grow up in the "ghetto," yet many others succumb to the existing vices for various reasons.

The difference in outcomes can, in part, be attributed to the absence or presence of ritual spaces—spaces with the potential to empower and protect.

In this essay I use Robert Stepto's ritual ground concept as my theoretical framework, as well as W. E. B. Du Bois's double consciousness concept to analyze the novel. Starr simultaneously finds comfort and kinship/friendship/companionship within two particular ritual grounds in the book—Garden Heights, her urban neighborhood and Williamson Prep, the private, predominantly white school she attends—*and* experiences psychological anxiety in both because she feels she cannot reveal her true self in either. In "Locating Identity: Sense of Place, and Belonging," Hurriyet Babacan posits, "Space and place constructions are integrally connected to our sense of being—history, geography, monuments, cities and communities. These relationships are not simple and can involve tension among various identities in the spatial contexts" (114). Starr's internal struggles within these spaces challenge the young protagonist to claim both spaces as her own, while growing emotionally, socially, and psychologically through the process, which leads her to finding her personal and political voice.

RACE AND THE EXPERIENCE OF SPACE: ESTABLISHING A THEORETICAL FRAMEWORK

First, I must establish the theoretical framework that I will be using to analyze Thomas's novel. In *From behind the Veil* (1977, 1991), Stepto defines "ritual grounds" as "those specifically Afro-American spatial configurations within the structural topography that are, in varying ways, elaborate responses to social structure *in this world*. They serve as a spatial expression of the tensions and contradictions besetting any reactionary social structure, aggressive or latent, subsumed by dominant social structure" (69). For African Americans, their communities/homes can be "ritual grounds," "black spaces" where they are generally separated from surrounding "white spaces." The borders of the "ritual ground" are seen not only as boundaries but barriers between "black and white spaces," which suggest an illustration of protection from white oppression. In other words, ritual grounds for African Americans are imperfect spaces and places that create emotional and psychological support but at times can exhibit negative attributes. According to Babacan:

> Ethnicity often relies on the notion of common origin which is often linked with both geography and history (real or imagined). Geographic

icons possess symbolic attributes and become significant in attachment and evoke emotions, sentiments and longing to be in a particular location. Notions of territory are also linked up with concepts of place. Place is a complex phenomenon and implies people's connections to locales. Places enable association between lived experiences, personal stories, myths, images, memories which present legacies that carry meaning to individuals and communities. (113)

Babacan goes on to state, "*Places* are defined by locale whose form, function and meaning are contained within the boundaries of physical continuity while *spaces* are more abstract and have the properties of securing anchor to stabilise identities, personal rootedness, provide local knowledge and give permission for social interaction" (114). Some of the classical "places" in African American culture, literature, and film are the kitchen, the porch, the church, the barbershop, the beauty salon, and the 'hood. However, for African Americans, whole regions such as "the South" and "the North" historically have held "abstract spatial" psychological connections to abject societal oppression and utopian-style freedom, respectively. Significantly, many African Americans' views on these regions have reversed in recent years due to the desire to escape the ghettos of "the North" and return to "the South." In *The Hate U Give*, Starr's primary ritual grounds are places—her childhood neighborhood, Garden Heights—and specific structures in Garden Heights—her family home—and the predominantly white school she attends, Williamson Preparatory School.

W. E. B. Du Bois's concept of double consciousness is useful to further examine Starr's experiences navigating through Garden Heights and Williamson. Eboni Njoku states, "Sixteen-year-old Starr Carter lives a life many African American teenagers can relate to: a life of double consciousness, caught between her rough, predominantly black neighborhood and the 'proper,' predominantly white prep school she attends" (1). Du Bois coins "double consciousness" in his seminal book *The Souls of Black Folk* (1903), as a term to describe the African American experience of living in the United States. Du Bois explains, "This sense of always looking at one's self through the eyes of others, of measuring one's soul by the tape of a world that looks on in amused contempt and pity. One ever feels his twoness,—an American, a Negro; two souls, two thoughts, two unreconciled strivings; two warring ideals in one dark body, whose dogged strength alone keeps it from being torn asunder" (3). The definition accurately describes Starr's emotional and psychological state in both places. Many African Americans who traverse between black and white spaces face double consciousness and its consequences. African Americans can opt to ignore acknowledgment of double consciousness, can directly address double consciousness, or can succumb to double consciousness. Oftentimes, how an African American (or African American character) responds to double consciousness is linked to socioeconomic background, psychological grounding, and motivations.

Starr's parents, Maverick and Lisa, move Starr, her older brother Seven, and her younger brother Sekani to Williamson Prep after Starr's friend Natalie is shot and killed during a drive-by shooting. They want the children to be able to learn in a safer environment; however, their decision still causes emotional strife for the children, Starr and Sekani in particular. Because the children no longer go to school in Garden Heights, some of the peer relationships have weakened; as a result, their Garden Heights peers often challenge their "racial" authenticity. For example, Starr observes that Sekani does not fit in with his Garden Heights peers well: "In Garden Heights, kids play in the streets. Sekani presses his face against my window and watches them. He won't play with them though. Last time he played with some neighborhood kids, they called him 'white boy' 'cause he goes to Williamson" (Thomas 88). Starr can recognize and empathize with Sekani's plight because she is undergoing similar emotions and situations. For instance, when Kenya, Seven's sister (Seven and Kenya share the same mother), says Starr does not want to go to a Garden Heights party because she thinks she is better than everyone, Starr yields and goes to the party even though she does not want to go: "Kenya begged me to come to this party for weeks. I knew I'd be as uncomfortable as hell, but every time I told Kenya no she said I act like I'm 'too good for a Garden party.' I got tired of hearing that shit and decided to prove her wrong" (Thomas 11). Starr knows that even her parents would not want her to attend the party. Gang and gun violence, some of the vices her parents have wanted her to avoid and why they sent her to Williamson, would undoubtedly be present, yet the desire to not be seen as a "sellout" pushes her to make the decision to attend the party. Starr's identity and peer/"racial" allegiance to her self-identified "racial" group are habitually contested by her Garden Heights peers. As a result Starr is continuously experiencing double consciousness.

Simultaneously, when Starr attends Williamson Prep, she fears revealing her "true" self because she does not want to be perceived as "ghetto" or lesser-than by her non–African American counterparts and boyfriend. For example, when she is interviewed by two police officers after Khalil's death, she puts on the same type of mask that she uses at Williamson Prep. Starr recognizes, "My voice is changing already. It always happens around 'other' people, whether I'm at Williamson or not. I don't talk like me or sound like me. I choose every word carefully and make sure I pronounce them well. I can never, ever let anyone think I'm ghetto" (Thomas 95). The emotional and psychological pressures that Starr encounters throughout the novel may derive from diverse scenarios and people, but they all ultimately lead to Starr suffering negative consequences from double consciousness. For Starr, both Garden Heights and Williamson Prep hold positive and negative experiences, and yet all of these experiences enable her to develop into a more socially aware young adult.

CONTEMPORARY CULTURE AS THEORETICAL FRAMEWORK

During the twentieth century and into the twenty-first century, African American youth have often expressed their concerns about continuing inequity and race-based vulnerability through a combination of stratagems. Protest songs from Billie Holiday's "Strange Fruit" (1939), Nina Simone's "Blacklash Blues" (1967), and Marvin Gaye's "What's Going On" (1971) tackled such realities as lynching, segregation, police brutality, and war. More-contemporary musical artists use the rap music genre as a vehicle to expose economic, social, and political injustice. For example, Grandmaster Flash and the Furious Five's "The Message" (1982), Public Enemy's "Fight the Power" (1988), N.W.A.'s "Fuck the Police" (1988), and Ice-T's "Cop Killer" (1992) in the 1980s and 1990s to J. Cole's "Immortal" (2016) and Kendrick Lamar's and The Weeknd's "Pray for Me" (2018), all speak to urban strife that uniquely, and negatively, affects the lives of young African Americans.

Young people continue to employ protest marches and sit-ins; however, with the advent of social media, youth have utilized this technology to disseminate information and to mobilize citizens on a large scale. Black Lives Matter is the most influential and recent illustration. In the epigraph that begins this essay, Thomas repeats the word "matter," which is a clear reference to BLM. Frank Leon Roberts explains, "By using the tools of social media, BLM was the first U.S. social movement in history to successfully use the internet as a mass mobilization device" (4). In 2013 BLM began in response to the George Zimmerman not-guilty verdict in the Trayvon Martin death trial. Three African American women—Patrisse Khan-Cullors, Alicia Garza, and Opal Tometi—led the charge through social media to protest the verdict and to express the need for the acknowledgment that Black people, especially young Black men, were falling victim to aggressive and often lethal police enforcement. Roberts posits, "Black Lives Matters has always been more of a human rights movement rather than a civil rights movement. BLM's focus has been less about changing specific laws and more about fighting for a fundamental reordering of society wherein Black lives are free from systematic dehumanization. Still, the movement's measurable impact on the political and legal landscape is undeniable" (Roberts 2). In other words, the movement's success is undeniably attributed to social media and to newly "woke" young people who use it. Participants seek to transform the societal mind-set in the United States that enables members of the dominant culture to see and treat African Americans as second-class citizens—or less; the hope is that, by doing so, the economic, social, and political policies that adversely affect African Americans will also be transformed. This is a noble yet arduous mission, indeed—one that Thomas wants young people to embrace. At the end of the novel, after speaking at a protest march, Starr reflects on her participation and the future: "Yet I think it'll change one day. How? I don't know. When? I definitely don't know. Why? Because there will always be someone ready to fight. Maybe it's my turn" (Thomas 443). Here, Starr expresses the ambiguity about when more substantial social and political change will happen, but she also expresses hope for the future and seems to believe she should be a part of movement that brings about that change. In addition, she goes further and speaks to the participation of others: "Others are fighting too, even in the Garden, where sometimes it feels like there's not a lot worth fighting for. People are realizing and shouting and marching and demanding. They're not forgetting. I think that's the most important part" (Thomas 443–44). Through Starr, Thomas expresses the realistic difficulties in bringing about substantial social and political change while encouraging young people to join and continue the struggle for it.

A key cultural influence for Thomas's work is Tupac Shakur, who proves to be inspirational for her protagonist and many of her friends. The iconic figure allows Thomas to tap into a pop culture that builds on a history of political protest: some of his most politically conscious songs were "Brenda's Got a Baby" (1991), "Keep Ya Head Up" (1993), and "Dear Mama" (1995); and his mother, Afeni Shakur, was a member of the Black Panther Party. In direct connection to the Black Panther Party, Maverick, Starr's father, follows the party's Ten-Point Program and has his children memorize and follow it as well. The Ten-Point Program includes the following:

1) We want freedom. We want power to determine the destiny of our Black community,
2) We want full employment for our people,
3) We want an end to the robbery by the capitalists of our Black community,

4) We want decent housing fit for the shelter of human beings,
5) We want education for our people that exposes the true nature of American society. We want education that teaches us our true history and our role in the present-day society,
6) We want all Black men to be exempt from military service,
7) We want an immediate end to police brutality and murder of Black people,
8) We want freedom for all Black men held in federal, state, county and city prisons and jails,
9) We want all Black people when brought to trial to be tried in court by a jury of their peer group or people from their Black communities, as defined by the Constitution of the United States, and
10) We want land, bread, housing, education, clothing, justice and peace. ("The Black Panthers' Ten-Point Program")

These tenets are extremely important because they provide some of the novel's characters' arcs and motivations toward Black excellence and acceptance, as in the case of Starr and Maverick, and to a certain extent drive the book's focus on social activism as well.

Thomas directly connects Tupac to her novel through Khalil, one of Starr's childhood Garden Heights friends. Starr is with Khalil when they are stopped by a police officer who shoots and kills Khalil during a traffic stop. Khalil's death triggers the events of the novel and Starr's emotional journey. Thomas takes the novel's title from the tattoo on Shakur's abdomen: THUG LIFE. Moments before he dies at the hands of the officer, Khalil explains the meaning to Starr: "Listen! The Hate U—the letter U—Give Little Infants Fucks Everybody. T-H-U-G L-I-F-E. Meaning what society give us as youth, it bites them in the ass when we wild out. Get it?" (Thomas 17). Thomas certainly "gets it" and is communicating this sentiment to her readers. Anna Diamond states, "Thomas's book derives its title from Tupac Shakur's philosophy of THUG LIFE . . . and it's a motif the novel returns to a few times. The acronym tattooed across Tupac's abdomen could be read as an embrace of a dangerous lifestyle. But, Khalil explains to Starr, just minutes before the cop pulls them over, it's really an indictment of systemic inequality and hostility" (2). Thomas is obviously commenting on the social, economic, and political institutions that stifle the development of young African Americans, constrain them in lower socioeconomic and sociopolitical power positions, and kill or incarcerate them in the prison industrial complex, which silences their voices. Anna Diamond states:

As a book written for teens, *The Hate U Give* reminds readers of just how often racialized violence is carried out against that age group (Michael Brown was 18 when he was killed; Trayvon Martin was 17; and not-yet-teen Tamir Rice was 12). And it illustrates how young people of color who might speak out to defend their late friends are unfairly criticized, as happened to Rachel Jeantel when she testified against Martin's killer, George Zimmerman. (2)

Starr and her Garden Heights friends are fictional and contemporary portrayals of their real-life counterparts—those who are casualties of the system and those who are left behind to fight against systemic and systematic discrimination and racism.

GARDEN HEIGHTS AS A RITUAL GROUND: THE HIGHS AND LOWS OF HOME

Garden Heights is the prototypical fictional contemporary urban neighborhood. Here, African American youth are exposed to drugs, gangs, and gun violence and must make difficult life choices for survival in urban neighborhoods. They also experience love from family members and friends as well as emotional support from longtime neighbors; these urban neighborhoods are home despite any shortcomings. Garden Heights is home for Starr: it is where she has grown up, shared experiences, and created memories with family, friends, and neighbors. Within Garden Heights, many locations function as smaller ritual grounds for Starr, such as her family home and Reuben's, the neighborhood soul food restaurant. It is also where she witnesses Khalil's murder by a police officer and the subsequent transformation of the neighborhood into a war zone during protest riots. Yet Starr maintains her love for her neighborhood even when she simultaneously feels conflicted about it and within it. For example, Starr describes Cedar Grove, the main housing project in Garden Heights as the following:

> At Cedar Grove Projects there's graffiti on the walls and broken-down cars in the courtyard. Under the Black Jesus mural at the clinic, grass grows up through the cracks in the sidewalk. Trash litters every curb we pass. Two junkies argue loudly on the corner. There's lots of hoopties, cars that should've been in the junkyard a long time ago. The houses are old, small. (Thomas 379)

Nevertheless, Starr is highly sensitive about how others such as her peers and the media—outsiders—perceive it. While watching a news interview by the father of the officer who killed Khalil with Williamson Prep friends Hailey (white) and Maya (Asian American), Starr says, "I tense as footage of my neighborhood, my home, is shown. It's like they picked the worst parts—the drug addicts romancing the streets, the broken-down Cedar Grove projects, gangbangers flashing signs, bodies on the sidewalks with white sheets over them. What about Mrs. Rooks and her cakes? Or Mr. Lewis and his haircuts? Mr. Reuben? The clinic? My family? Me?" (Thomas 245). Starr is commenting on the humanity of the neighborhood, which is undermined by the images selected to be used during the interview. Starr retains positive associations to her neighborhood. Mrs. Rooks is thought of as a caring neighbor who makes the best red velvet cakes, which everyone in the neighborhood looks forward to during community celebrations. The barbershop run by cranky yet lovable Mr. Lewis is where many young boys have their first haircuts and is located near Maverick's store. The clinic is where Lisa works and assists the members of the community. At one point Starr states, "I can call Garden Heights the ghetto all I want. Nobody else can" (Thomas 139), which is an insider (those who live in the location)/outsider (those who do not live in the location) experience of space. Garden Heights, and locations within Garden Heights, have deep emotional correlations for Starr, and she becomes increasingly protective of her neighborhood as her burgeoning social/political awareness and self-confidence increase throughout the novel.

Mr. Reuben's restaurant also functions as a ritual ground for Starr and Garden Heights residents. Starr notes, "The smoky aroma hits us on the sidewalk, and a blues song pours outside. Inside, the walls are covered with photographs of civil rights leaders, politicians and celebrities who have eaten here, like James Brown and pre-heart-bypass Bill Clinton. There a picture of Dr. King and a much younger Mr. Reuben" (45). It is known throughout the neighborhood that Reuben's is where you go when you want great soul food for lunch or dinner. Starr also observes that Reuben's is the one place in Garden Heights that is frequented by white patrons. Reuben's is the only place in Garden Heights that is integrated and is known nationally. The photos of Black icons and those generally believed allies in the establishment also connect the restaurant with African American history and culture—all positive qualities. Still, Starr notes, "A bulletproof partition separates the customers from the cashier. I fan myself after a few minutes in line. The air conditioner in the window stopped working months ago, and the smoker heats up the whole building" (Thomas 45). Mr. Reuben's partition and nonworking air conditioner illustrate the economic limitations and potential for violence in the area. The positive and negative characteristics that contribute to a ritual ground are evident.

EXPULSION FROM THE GARDEN: THE NEED TO LEAVE HOME

Despite the positive associations of the neighborhood, Maverick and Lisa ultimately move the family to another neighborhood, Brooks Falls, which is closer to Williamson Prep. Although their new neighborhood is not in a gated community like Riverton Hills, where Uncle Carlos (Lisa's brother) lives, the dangers of Garden Heights have been, for the most part, left behind. Starr describes Brook Falls in this way: "It reminds me of Uncle Carlos' neighborhood yet it's different. For one, there's no gate around it, so they're not keeping anyone out or in, but obviously people feel safe. The houses are smaller, more homey looking. And straight up? There are more people who look like us compared to Uncle Carlos's neighborhood" (Thomas 306–7). Maverick has been reluctant to move, because he believes that there should be some successful people who stay as role models and examples for the young people whose families cannot move. Maverick believes that if they move "we just like all the other sellouts who leave and turn their backs on the neighborhood. We can change stuff around here, but instead we run? That's what you wanna teach our kids?" (Thomas 180). His underlying Black Panther Party beliefs are fundamental to his outlook; however, he is aware of the overall dangers in Garden Heights, especially gang activity. For example, when DeVante, another one of Starr's Garden Heights peers, becomes involved with the gang leader King's drug activities, then wants to leave the gang life, Maverick is there to assist. In fact, he and Carlos agree to let DeVante stay with Carlos's family in Riverton Hills.

The relocation takes place before Maverick acquiesces and moves his own family out of Garden Heights. Lisa is livid. During an argument, she says, "And I love how you insist on getting somebody else's child out of Garden Heights, but you want ours to stay in that hellhole!" (Thomas 231). Lisa has been wanting the family to move for years; however, Maverick continuously refuses. He retorts, "You want them in the suburbs with all this fake shit?" (Thomas 231). He believes he and his family will lose the connection to the community if they move from the neighborhood, especially since he has a business there. He does not want to feel like a hypocrite; nonetheless, with increasing pressures surrounding Starr's association with Khalil's death, subsequent neighborhood riots, and new threats from King, Maverick gives in to his wife's wishes. In doing so, he recognizes that it is not hypocritical for him to assist the people of Garden Heights while protecting the best interests of his family: "But I realize real ain't got anything to do with where you live. The realest think I can do is protect my family, and that means leaving Garden Heights" (Thomas 308–9). He goes on to say, "And that living in the suburbs don't make you any less black than living in the hood" (Thomas 309). Maverick and Lisa's struggle and ultimate decision is similar to the one that many African American parents have and continue to face, leaving urban neighborhoods for the suburbs or going "down South" in hopes of higher education and safer environments to raise children. Ironically, these parents experience a reverse type of double consciousness, not wanting to be seen as inauthentically Black by other African Americans, like their children who attend predominantly white schools.

Prior to her family's physical relocation, Starr experiences emotional and psychological wounds that diminish her sense of security in her neighborhood. The specific negative properties of Garden Heights include Starr witnessing two of her close friends—Natasha and Khalil—die by gun violence. The group was called "The Hood Trio," a nickname that denotes deep affection for each other and their home. Natasha was killed during a drive-by shooting, and Starr still suffers from nightmares about the incident. When she witnesses Khalil's death, the nightmares intensify and begin including Khalil. Locations in Garden Heights that once reminded Starr of joyful times with her friends now spark sorrow. For example, when she and her family visit Ms. Rosalie, Khalil's grandmother, after Khalil's murder, Starr recalls: "Going up Ms. Rosalie's walkway floods me with memories. I have scars tattooed on my arms and legs from falls on this concrete. One time I was on my scooter, and Khalil pushed me off 'cause I hadn't given him a turn. When I got up, skin was missing from most of my knee. I never screamed so loud in my life" (Thomas 59). Her memories continue: "We played hopscotch and jumped rope on this walkway too. Khalil never wanted to play at first, talking about how those were girls' games. He always gave in when me and Natasha said the winner got a Freeze Cup—frozen Kool-Aid in a Styrofoam cup—or a pack of 'Nilators,' a.k.a. Now and Laters. Ms. Rosalie was the neighborhood Candy Lady" (Thomas 60). As a result of the tragic events, Ms. Rosalie's house now holds bittersweet memories for Starr.

"RETURN" TO GARDEN HEIGHTS: THE INESCAPABILITY OF HOME

The events that follow Khalil's death force Starr to recognize the double consciousness that accompanies her division of ritual space. Starr feels guilt after Khalil's death. She suffers from a combination of survivor's guilt and guilt that she did not spend more time with Khalil once she began going to school at Williamson Prep. For example, while watching Khalil's Garden Heights classmates at his funeral, Starr thinks, "They give his family the cap and gown Khalil would've worn in a few months and cry as they tell funny stories I'd never heard. Yet I'm the one in the front row on the friends' side. I'm such a fucking phony" (Thomas 128). Starr also is feeling guilty for not speaking up and doing more to clear Khalil's name to show support for Garden Heights as the police and the media paint a picture of Khalil as a drug dealer and of Garden Heights as a bastion of depravity. She is fearful of police and gang retaliation. Starr says, "I've seen it happen over and over again: a black person gets killed just for being black, and all hell breaks loose. I've tweeted RIP hashtags, re-blogged pictures on Tumblr, and signed every petition out there. I always said if I saw it happen to somebody, I would have the loudest voice, making sure the world knew what went down. Now I am that person, and I'm too afraid to speak" (Thomas 35). "Snitching," an urban term for reporting criminals and criminal activity to the police, has serious repercussions in her neighborhood, and she is concerned about the safety of her family members. Njoku states, "Between her neighborhood's 'no-snitching' code and inaccurate media portrayals, Starr must decide whether or not to speak out—and her decision could endanger her life" (Njoku 1). "No snitching" has been a common practice in African American communities, since many African Americans do not have confidence in police protection.

Even so, Kenya "calls out" Starr for her actions, or more specifically, her inaction, claiming she has become emotionally distant from her Garden Heights friends and neighborhood. Kenya says, "Go on TV or something, I don't know. . . . Tell everybody what really happened that night. They're not even giving his side of the story. You're letting them trash-talk him" (Thomas 198). Out of anger and frustration, Kenya also takes this moment to confront Starr. Kenya continues, "You dropped him for them bougie-ass kids, and you know it. You probably would've dropped me if I didn't come around 'cause of my brother" (Thomas 198). Starr denies the accusation, but Kenya will not relent. She says, "Fucked-up part about this? The Khalil I know would've jumped on TV in a hot second and told everybody what happened that night if it meant defending you. And you can't do the same for him" (198). Consequently, Starr is silenced because "it was a verbal slap. The worst kind too, because it's the truth" (198.) Internally, Starr has been grappling with this reality. Starr has indeed been keeping the worlds separate. After her early days at Williamson and after her white friends' parents did not want them visiting her at her house in "the ghetto" (Thomas 36), Starr says, "That's when I realized Williamson is one world and Garden Heights is another, and I have to keep them separate" (Thomas 36). Still, she has not fully acknowledged and realized that this separation has gradually created a certain emotional distance from and shame for Garden Heights. The truth hurts, but this moment with Kenya enables Starr to begin addressing her own attitudes and double consciousness. Even after Starr begins "speaking out," Officer Cruise is not held accountable for his actions, which is unfortunately typical in these real-life cases. Consequently, Garden Heights becomes the site of protest riots and is essentially put under martial law: "My neighborhood is a war zone" (Thomas 139). Once again, Starr ascribes the negativity to herself and her inaction: "All of this is my fault. The riots, gunshots, tear gas, all of it, are ultimately my fault. I forgot to tell the cops that Khalil got out with his hands up. I didn't mention that the officer pointed his gun at me. I didn't say something right, and now that cop's not getting arrested. But while the riots are my fault, the news basically makes it sound like it's Khalil's fault he died" (Thomas 140). With her ritual ground burning and becoming more dangerous than ever, Starr's motivation to take back her voice is mounting.

It is only after she learns the reasons Khalil sold drugs and has a heartfelt discussion with her father that Starr finally gains control of her voice, her narrative, and her political consciousness. After DeVante begins staying with Starr's uncle Carlos, he becomes comfortable enough to tell her the truth about Khalil's situation. DeVante reveals that Khalil didn't want to sell drugs: "Look, his momma stole some shit from King. King wanted her dead. Khalil found out and started selling to pay the debt" (Thomas 237). King and his gang members put a bandana on Khalil's coffin during his funeral to signify that he was a member of his gang, which was inaccurate. The media also portrays Khalil as a gangbanging drug dealer, which dehumanizes the victim in the public eye. The truth, which even Starr did not fully know until this moment, becomes clear: both King and the media appropriate and manipulate Khalil's narrative to suit their own needs. King gains more street credibility, and the media gains a sensational story. To a certain extent, Starr herself has been blaming and judging Khalil for making a detrimental life choice to sell drugs, especially since her father hired him to work in the family store as a legal means to earn money and to stay away from the gangs. Starr knows she must make amends and, during a local news interview, tells the public what actually happened that night, in order to clear Khalil's name. His socioeconomic circumstances and his dedication to his drug-addicted, negligent mother caused Khalil to enter the drug trade. This is in opposition to how the media and police portray him. Starr finally, and publicly, adds her voice to the Khalil narrative.

Starr's discussion with her father is the final straw that enables her to directly address Khalil's death and the unfair treatment of African Americans. Maverick reminds Starr about the lack of access to a proper, quality education and job opportunities for Black youth and how this leads to many young people entering into the gangbanging, drug-dealing lifestyle as a means of survival. He wants her to understand the underlying factors that have also led many of the same people in the neighborhood to now protest and riot. Starr comes to the conclusion that real change must happen and that she must be a part of it. She says to Maverick, "That's why people are speaking out, huh? Because it won't change if we don't say something" (Thomas 171). This is a turning point for Starr: "So *I* can't be silent" (Thomas 171). Starr now has clear motivations and confidence to speak her truth and to defend Khalil's and Garden Heights' names. Thus, Starr's better-informed sense of home functions as a catalyst.

During the television interview, she publicly tells her side of the story, which has been silenced and ignored by the police. She describes Khalil's actual character in personal terms, which gives him back his humanity and "dry-snitches," or indirectly implicates, King's involvement with contributing to the ongoing drug dealing and violence in the community. As she speaks out, Starr remembers that "Ms Ofrah [local activist and Starr's pro bono attorney] once said that this is how I fight, with my voice. So I fight" (Thomas 287). Starr's words recharacterize her neighborhood and undermine King's neighborhood dominance by "snitching." Ultimately, while words are not enough to lead to Officer Cruise's arrest in Khalil's death, they do lead to King's arrest and imprisonment, which brings some improvements to the community. By asserting her point of view, Starr finds her voice and reclaims her personal identity, while embracing Garden Heights once again.

WILLIAMSON PREPARATORY SCHOOL: A CHALLENGING NEW RITUAL GROUND

Concurrent with her attempts to reconcile the effects of Garden Heights, Starr is struggling to regain her identity in her second ritual ground, Williamson Prep. Babacan postulates, "Identities are intricately bound up with the places we move from and to. The articulation of 'identity' and 'place' highlights unpredictability and notices our role as both products and producers, as constructs and constructors of what we are and what we become" (116). Starr's identity journey is complicated and yet also complemented by her experiences at Williamson Prep. As noted earlier, Starr begins suppressing her true identity and distancing herself from Garden Heights while interacting with Williamson Prep peers. Days after Khalil's death, Starr comments on her desire to stay home from school and to watch her favorite television show, *The Fresh Prince of Bel-Air* (1990), with which she identifies:

> I wanna stay home and watch *The Fresh Prince of Bel-Air*, my favorite show ever, hands down. I think I know every episode word for word. Yeah it's hilarious, but it's also like seeing parts of my life on screen. I even relate to the theme song. A couple of gang members who were up to no good made trouble in my neighborhood and killed Natasha. My parents got scared, and although they didn't send me to my aunt and uncle in a rich neighborhood, they sent me to a bougie private school. (Thomas 35)

It is a show that depicts an urban outsider acculturating himself to affluent Bel-Air society, which is similar to Starr's own acculturation process. Like Will, the protagonist of *The Fresh Prince of Bel-Air*, Starr finds friends and a position in school. Starr is a good student and makes the basketball team. Through the basketball team, she meets and befriends Hailey, a white American, and Maya, an Asian American. Starr also begins dating her white boyfriend, Chris. Chris plays on the boys' basketball team, loves rap music, and even creates his own beats. Moreover, they share an affinity for Will Smith's *The Fresh Prince of Bel-Air*: "Chris gets The Fresh Prince, which helps him get me. We once talked about how cool it was that Will remained himself in this new world. I slipped up and said I wished I could be like that at school. Chris said, 'Why can't you, Fresh Princess?'" (Thomas 83). Starr and Chris share an interest in African American culture. She goes on to say, "Ever since, I don't have to decide which Starr I have to be with him. He likes both. Well, the parts I've shown him. Some things I can't reveal, like Natasha. Once you've seen how broken someone is it's like seeing them naked—you can't look at them the same anymore" (83). So, while Starr feels closest to Chris, she still keeps him emotionally at arm's length. Starr is keenly aware of the socioeconomic differences between herself and her Williamson peers, and she consciously separates her Garden Heights life and friends from her Williamson life and peers. Diamond states: "This question of appearance versus reality recurs throughout *The Hate U Give*. Starr, familiar with perceptions of her neighborhood, community, and herself, code-switches to adapt to the environment and others' expectations" (2). Subsequently, Starr does not often have interactions with both sets of friends at the same time. She also has a "Williamson Prep" persona, and a "Garden Heights" persona:

> I just have to be normal Starr at normal Williamson and have a normal day. That means flipping the switch in my brain so I'm Williamson Starr. Williamson Starr doesn't use slang—if a rapper would say it, she doesn't say it, even if her white friends do. Slang makes them cool. Slang makes her "hood." Williamson Starr holds her tongue when people piss her off so nobody will think she's the "angry black girl." Williamson Starr is approachable. No stank-eyes, side-eyes, none of that. Williamson Starr is nonconfrontational. Basically, Williamson Starr doesn't give anyone a reason to call her ghetto. I can't stand myself for doing it, but I do it anyway. (Thomas 71)

Starr's perceptions and decisions create emotional distance between herself and her Williamson Prep peers, even Chris. Additionally, because of her father's pro-Black beliefs, Starr has not introduced him to Chris. She even feels guilty about the relationship and fears it is disrespectful to her Black male family members and friends. Still, Starr admits that "Chris is the kind of normal I really want" when the pressures after Khalil begin and she has pushed Chris away.

It is only after an argument at the prom, which occurs toward the end of the book, that Starr reveals to Chris she is the then-unnamed witness to Khalil's murder and all of the details. She also shares with him how different she feels from him and at Williamson Prep, and they only become closer. In fact, when she, Seven, and DeVante return to rioting in Garden Heights after Officer Cruise is not indicted, Chris insists on joining them. Starr's worlds have collided, and she and Chris are still together. She now knows how deeply Chris cares for her and how willing he is to embrace all facets of her identity. This bolsters Starr's self-confidence.

While Starr symbolically merges spaces with Chris, the experience of spatial division continues, indeed intensifies, in the case of Hailey and other schoolmates. Even before the Khalil incident, Starr began to notice a difference in her relationship with Hailey: "Hailey never texted me during spring break. She barely texts me at all lately. Maybe once a week now, and it used to be every day. Something's changed between us, and neither one of us acknowledges it. We're normal when we're at Williamson, like now. Beyond here though, we're no longer best friends, just . . . I don't know" (Thomas 77). As Starr becomes more frustrated at the unjust treatment of Khalil in the media and in the criminal justice system, her patience toward white privilege is tried. When the kids at Williamson decide to "protest" for Khalil in order to get out of class, Starr is livid. Hailey, and Maya to a lesser degree, doesn't understand why she is upset. A potential space of political activism is distorted into a self-serving gesture; their lack of awareness equals a lack of amelioration of the space.

The oppressive nature of the school space is concretized/symbolized by the fracturing of Starr's personal connections. Their relationship is strained even more when Hailey says to Starr, "Hustle! Pretend the ball is some fried chicken. Bet you'll stay on it then," during a heated pick-up basketball game (Thomas 111), thus racializing/politicizing what pretends to be a neutral space. Maya attempts to bring everyone together at her house to clear the air and to make up; however, the attempt backfires, and Hailey storms out. She simply cannot understand why Starr is so upset with her. Afterward, Starr explains that she never understood why Hailey unfollowed her Tumblr account. Maya says, "All the 'black stuff,' she called it. The petitions. The Black Panther pictures. That post on those four little girls who were killed in that church. The stuff about that Marcus Garvey guy. The one about those Black Panthers who were shot by the government" (Thomas 250). Maya is confirming what Starr thought, if not acknowledged, about Hailey. Maya also reveals that she has experienced Hailey's racist comments herself; she has "joked" about Asian Americans eating domesticated animals like dogs and cats. Maya, who is dating an African American, calls for a "minority alliance" between the two of them. She and Starr both plan to distance themselves from Hailey until she understands the consequences of her racist statements and actions.

Everything comes to a head, however, when Hailey says a disrespectful remark toward Khalil, and Starr slaps her. This leads to an actual physical fight between two. In this instance, Starr is no longer masking as "Williamson Starr." The differences between her relationship with Hailey and Chris is significant. Starr is able to be herself and to talk to Chris. He actually wants to know and to embrace the "real" and complete Starr. Hailey, on the other hand, refuses to do so, and ultimately she rejects the "real" Starr. When Hailey half-heartedly tries to make up through text messaging, Starr already knows this friendship is over. Her experiences in her ritual ground, Williamson Prep, have tested her thoroughly; she can now recognize true relationships and has gained the strength and confidence to let go of the false ones. Starr emerges with regained independence and acceptance of her complete/authentic identity.

CONCLUSION: NOVEL AS RITUAL SPACE

Thomas's novel ends with a protagonist who is uncertain yet hopeful for the future but has found her voice within the ritual spaces she traverses. This sentiment is not unlike her real-life counterparts who have become social-justice warriors. In reaction to circumstances similar to those portrayed in the novel, many young people have chosen to mobilize, protest, and use their voices to argue for legislative changes in the criminal justice system and gun laws. These actions should not be surprising: the young have often been the catalyst for social and political change throughout the world. African American youth are no exception; in fact, they have often been the leaders and the inspiration for other young people throughout the world. For example, African American youth were on the front lines of the civil rights and Black power movements during the mid-twentieth century. They used nonviolent, and at times militant, approaches to make their presence and stances known. Protest marches and sit-ins were popular tactics. Oftentimes megaphones and protest music were used to literally and figuratively amplify their voices. These methods of demonstration were used to condemn housing discrimination, police brutality, racial profiling, all unequal educational access—issues present in urban neighborhoods and rural enclaves.

In the twenty-first century, some social and political advancements have ameliorated African American status in the country; nonetheless, some comparable problems from the past remain and affect the African American community at large. For instance, African American parents still have "the talk" with African American youth, particularly boys and young men, about how to behave when interacting with the police to try to avoid arrest—or worse, death. Traditionally, the youth should keep their hands on the steering wheel of the car, not talk back to the officer, and always be on guard. While such self-preservation strategies are reminiscent of southern segregation-period "black codes" and "racial etiquette," the threat to young African American lives is obviously still a problem that must be addressed and is being addressed in Thomas's novel. Despite the challenges, many of the real-world activists have found their voices as well, insisting on their right to create their own destinies, to determine their own identities, and to improve the world in which they live. This is precisely what Thomas seeks: to empower young people through her literary works. She uses narrative space to enable them to recognize political/ritual spaces in their own backyards.

Works Cited

Babacan, Hurriyet. "Locating Identity: Sense of Place, and Belonging." *International Journal of Diversity in Organisations, Communities and Nations*, vol. 5, no. 5, 2005/2006, pp. 113–24.

"The Black Panthers' 10-Point Program." *Marxist History: USA: Black Panther Party*. https://www.marxists.org/history/usa/workers/black-panthers/1966/10/15.htm.

Blair, Elizabeth. "'The Hate U Give' Star Says the Novel Was like 'Reading My Own Diary.'" NPR, 20 Oct. 2018, https://www.npr.org/2018/10/20/658251028/the-hate-u-give-star-says-the-novel-was-like-reading-my-own-diary.

Diamond, Anna. "*The Hate U Give* Enters the Ranks of Great YA Novels." *The Atlantic*, 28 Mar. 2017, https://www.theatlantic.com/entertainment/archive/2017/03/the-hate-u-give-angie-thomas-review/521079/.

Du Bois, W. E. B. *The Souls of Black Folk*. 1903. Bantam Books, 1989.

Njoku, Eboni. "Review of *The Hate U Give*." *Horn Book*, 7 Mar. 2017, https://www.hbook.com/?detailStory=review-of-the-hate-u-give.

Roberts, Frank Leon. "How Black Lives Matter Changed the Way Americans Fight for Freedom." ACLU, 13 Jul. 2018, https://www.aclu.org/racial-justice/race-and-criminal-justice/how-black-lives-matter-changed-ways-americans-fight, 1–7.

Stepto, Robert. *From behind the Veil: A Study of Afro-American Narrative*. 1979. U of Illinois P, 1991.

Thomas, Angie. *The Hate U Give*. Balzer + Bray/HarperCollins, 2017.

CONCLUSION AS INCLUSION

At first glance, the purpose of a conclusion is to establish boundaries—summation as closure—but that is not the intent of this conclusion. Rather than shutting down a discussion—containment as detainment—the final pages of this book are an invitation to continue the conversation beyond its borders—containment as accommodation. The essays in this volume raise provocative points about the relationship between children's literature and space through close textual analysis. Room for alternative or modified readings certainly exists; as Philip Pullman theorizes, "while parts of the borderland belong to the book, other parts belong only to that particular reader" (216). A single story can open the space for multiple interpretations; the contributors have offered their analyses to both inform and inspire our readers. Do the theoretical frameworks apply to additional works? Do the selected texts trigger other comparisons? It is our hope that the answer is a resounding yes. While confident in our arguments, we do not adhere to the either/or approach to criticism; multifaceted approaches result in a more invigorating critical space.

Binaries are commonplace in theories of space. The labels vary but the oppositional relationship dominates. This paradigm implies rigid divisions, but the categories (and boundaries) are in fact more porous and, to a large extent, interconnected. Seemingly linguistically exclusive, the pairings are mutually dependent—defined, in part, against each other. Adult/child, access/exclusion, control/defenselessness, inside/outside, psychological/physical—such binaries expose the enigmatic nature of space. The categories serve an organizational purpose, but the divisions are artificial and incomplete. There is a real danger of binaries taking on an air of inevitability, of seeming "natural"; this in effect masks the fact that they are tactics of control and containment that inevitably privilege one side. Seeing beyond the binaries is particularly important in relation to children's literature; informed criticism must reexamine children's relationships to/with space.

Why is the subject of children's literature and space significant? On a practical level, as Stuart Aitken observes, we "inhabit the same spaces as children, and, as such, we negotiate a shared experience of places" (29). Negotiation requires comprehension. Recognizing that children can manipulate space to serve their own purposes is crucial in challenging the binary of adult/child space. They are not inherently separate and distinct. Spatial divisions are socially constructed and serve the needs of those with power. Such divisions are not inviolable; as the essays in this volume illustrate, children are more than capable of subverting the spatial hierarchies that seek to contain them. The "permeability" of these borders, Jessica Elbert Decker and Dylan Winchock argue, "opens up possibilities for reimagining our categories and creating new paradigms that recognize difference and resist hierarchical structures of identity" (12). A more equitable "distribution" of space is possible (at least conceptually), but of a more pragmatic concern is the role children play in that redistribution of space.

While the focus in our work is on the fictional child, the essays do raise pointed implications about children's real-world experiences of space. It would be disingenuous for adults to assume that children lack spatial awareness. "Children's daily lives," notes R. Hart, "are complex, unique, and inherently spatial" (quoted in Blades and Spencer, 13). Personal and vicarious experience of their environments makes children's lives complex and unique. Karen Fog Olwig and Eva Gulløv, the editors of *Children's Places: Cross-Cultural Perspectives*, explore "the social and cultural construction of children's place in society" (1). One means of socially and culturally constructing "children's place in society" is the literature aimed at them; spatial experiences in fiction are interconnected with real-world experiences of space. Olwig and Gulløv offer a compelling argument: "The kinds of places that society allows to children will, to a great extent, influence their ability to develop new social and cultural contexts of life that do not just reflect the existing social order of which they are part, but rather carry the potential to modify this order" (3). Opening up actual and imaginative territory for children is empowering; they move beyond mere consumption of, and become producers of, space. Jones deems such space "otherable space" (30). He raises the question of whether "adults' geographies are, or can be, rendered flexible or porous enough for children to form their own geographies within them" (30). The texts under discussion in this volume answer in the affirmative. Child characters, and perhaps by extension, child readers access the "otherable space" Jones identifies. More than mere curiosity, the "question is vital," insists Jones, "because the opportunity to create their own geographies, . . . to spatialize their lives according to their own agendas . . . is vital to their self-expression and their 'development'" (30). Competence and character require an ability to navigate space. Accessing spaces officially denied to them, embracing the potential of liminal spaces, and manipulating spaces to fulfill their own needs and agendas empowers the child characters under discussion in the preceding chapters. Children cannot simply be "placed"; they must be equipped to place themselves.

Works Cited

Aitken, Stuart C. *Putting Children in Their Place*. Washington, DC: Association of American Geographers, 1994.

Blades, Mark, and Christopher Spencer, eds. *Children and Their Environments: Learning, Using and Designing Spaces*. Cambridge: Cambridge UP, 2006.

Cecire, Maria Sachiko, Hannah Field, Kavita Mudan Finn, and Malini Roy. "Introduction: Spaces of Power, Places of Play." Ed. Cecire et al. *Space and Place in Children's Literature, 1789 to the Present*. Surrey: Ashgate, 2015. 1–19.

Decker, Jessica Elbert, and Dylan Winchock. "Introduction: Borderlands and Liminality across Philosophy and Literature." Ed. Decker and Winchock. *Borderlands and Liminal Subjects: Transgressing the Limits in Philosophy and Literature*. New York: Palgrave Macmillan, 2017. 1–18.

Holloway, Sarah L., and Gill Valentine, eds. *Children's Geographies: Playing, Living, Learning*. New York and London: Routledge, 2000.

Jones, Owain. "Melting Geography: Purity, Disorder, Childhood and Space." Ed. Sarah L. Holloway and Gill Valentine. *Children's Geographies: Playing, Living, Learning*. New York and London: Routledge, 2000. 29–47.

Olwig, Karen Fog, and Eva Gulløv. "Towards an Anthropology of Children and Place." Ed. Olwig and Gulløv. *Children's Places: Cross-Cultural Perspectives*. London and New York: Routledge, 2003. 1–19.

Pullman, Philip. "Epilogue: Inside, Outside, Elsewhere." Ed. Maria Sachiko Cecire, Hannah Field, Kavita Mudan Finn, and Malini Roy. *Space and Place in Children's Literature, 1789 to the Present*. Surrey: Ashgate, 2015. 215–39.

ABOUT THE CONTRIBUTORS

Miranda A. Green-Barteet is an associate professor, cross-appointed in the Departments of Gender, Sexuality, and Women's Studies and English and Writing Studies. She is the coeditor of *Female Rebellion in Young Adult Dystopian Fiction* (Ashgate, 2014), *Reconsidering Laura Ingalls Wilder: Little House and Beyond* (UPM, 2019), and *Race in Young Adult Speculative Fiction* (UPM, 2021). She has published articles on Harriet Jacobs, Harriet Wilson, Sarah Pogson, and young adult dystopian fiction. Her work has appeared in *South Central Review*, *Girlhood Studies*, *Canadian Review of American Studies*, and *The Lion and the Unicorn*.

Kathleen Kellett is a doctoral candidate in the Department of Childhood Studies at Rutgers University Camden. She received her MA in Children's Literature and MFA in Writing for Children from Simmons University. Her article "Beyond the Collapse of Meaning: Narratives of Monstrosity in Philip Pullman's His Dark Materials" was published in *University of Toronto Quarterly* in 2018.

Andrew McInnes is Reader in Romanticisms at Edge Hill University. He is currently an Arts and Humanities Research Council Early Career Leadership Fellow on "The Romantic Ridiculous," which aims to take Romantic Studies from the sublime to the ridiculous. The first publication from the project, "Coleridge, the Ridiculous Child, and the Limits of Romanticism," recently appeared in the edited collection *Romanticism and the Cultures of Infancy* (ed. Cian Duffy and Martina Domines Veliki, Palgrave, 2020). He has also published widely on Romantic period women's writing, Gothic fiction, and children's literature.

Joyce McPherson teaches English at the University of Tennessee at Chattanooga. She holds an MFA from Pine Manor College and a PhD from the University of Tennessee at Chattanooga. Her research interests include children's literature and writing pedagogy.

Rebecca Mills is Lecturer in Communication and English at Bournemouth University, UK, where she teaches crime fiction, celebrity culture, and other literature and media units. Recent projects include the essay collection *Agatha Christie Goes to War*, coedited with J. C. Bernthal (Routledge 2019).

Cristina Rivera is a PhD candidate at The Ohio State University in the Department of English. Her dissertation and most recent publications focus on representations of Latinx identities in CYA Literature and Media. She also volunteers for LASER (Latinx Space for Enrichment and Research) mentoring Latinx high school students in Columbus, Ohio.

Wendy Rountree is Full Professor in the Ethnic Studies Program at Northern Arizona University. Her expertise is in twentieth-century American literature, ethnic American literature (emphasis African American literature), and twentieth-century ethnic American drama. She has published scholarly books, journal articles, book chapters, and book reviews, as well as a young adult novel. Her current research interests are African American children's and young adult literature, African American cultural studies, African American popular culture, and African American women's literature.

Danielle Russell is Associate Professor of English at Glendon College (York University). Her previous publications include *Between the Angle and the Curve: Mapping Gender, Race, Space, and Identity in Cather and Morrison* (Routledge, 2006) and chapters on Libba Bray, Willa Cather, Neil Gaiman, Zora Neale Hurston, L. M. Montgomery, Toni Morrison, the Lemony Snicket series, and Alice Walker.

Anah-Jayne Samuelson completed her PhD at York University in 2019 and is currently an English Instructor at Medicine Hat College. Her dissertation examined oppressive school spaces in the school-story genre and methods of student character resistance and rebellion. Work from this dissertation has been published in the *International Research in Children's Literature Journal*. Dr. Samuelson's work is focused on children's and young adult literature, and she is currently researching the intersections of youth activism and children's literature.

Sonya Sawyer Fritz is Associate Professor of English at the University of Central Arkansas, where she researches and teaches courses on children's and YA literature and culture, Victorian literature and culture, and women's and girls' studies, among other topics. She is the coeditor with Sara K. Day of *The Victorian Era in Twenty-First-Century Children's and Adolescent Literature and Culture* (Routledge, 2018); her work has also appeared in *Neo-Victorian Studies*, *Girlhood Studies*, and various essay collections. She is the general editor of *Slant: A Journal of Poetry* and an associate editor of the *Children's Literature Association Quarterly*.

Andrew Trevarrow is a PhD candidate in Literature for Children and Young Adults at The Ohio State University.

Richardine Woodall currently teaches at York University in Toronto, Ontario, Canada. She teaches children's literature courses, which range from a historical study of children's literature to filming children's literature. She has a few research projects in development; one is on Ezra Jack Keats's *The Snowy Day*, and another focuses on Jarrett J. Krosoczka's *Hey, Kiddo*. Her interests in ontology shape her research, in particular, of children's literary characters whose being is a problem.

INDEX

adolescence: as journey, 30, 37, 39, 42, 46, 75, 88, 176; liminality of, 13–14, 19, 30, 33, 43; mobility of, 40, 41, 44; and race, 120, 127; uncontainable, 30, 39, 42, 44, 46
Agnew, Kate, 168
Aitken, Stuart C., 11, 17, 219–20
Alcott, Louisa May: *An Old-Fashioned Girl*, 194; *Little Men*, 194; *Little Women*, 50
Aldama, Frederick, 130
Alston, Ann, 69–70, 75, 92
alternative educational spaces, 49, 56, 57, 58
Anzaldúa, Gloria, 122
Apseloff, M. F., 7
Atkinson, David, 51

Babacan, Hurriyet, 201–2, 213
Bachelard, Gaston, 8–9, 98, 136, 138, 145
Barczewski, Stephanie, 156
Bauman, Zygmunt, 13
Bavidge, Jenny, 17
bedrooms: institutionalization of, 63; as refuge/retreat, 62, 63, 64; as site of personal and social development, 62, 63, 64, 65; as subversive space, 63
Beltran, Mary, 123
Beynon, Hun, 14
Bhabha, Homi, 101
binaries, 19, 36, 219
Bird, Anne-Marie, 31, 36
"black and white spaces," 201, 202
Black Lives Matter (BLM), 204–5
Black Panther Party, Ten Point Program, 205–6

Blades, Mark, 9, 10, 220
boarding schools, 16, 48, 177, 194
body as border: primal, 75, 76; as sacred space, 79; violation of, 75, 76, 78
Boesky, Amy, 179–80
Bolvangar: anti-Eden, 35; exodus from, 41; fortress, 34; prison, 35; as space of enforced innocence, 35; unnatural space of, 34, 38
borders: conceptual and physical, 19, 76, 201; identity formation/preservation of, 31, 201; limitations of, 19, 81, 82, 122; political/power dynamic of, 76, 77; as porous, 126, 195, 219, 220; as spaces of potential, 19, 184, 201; transgression of, 19, 76, 122; unnatural, 38, 39
borderlands: as imaginative territory, 6; permeability of, 19; reading space, 6
boundaries: cultural/natural, 20, 32, 38, 42, 43, 45; division of, 30, 201, 202; navigating, 18, 82, 86, 92, 122, 128, 150; physical and symbolic, 19, 201; porous, 38, 43, 184, 195, 220; as textual constructions, 32; transgressions of, 18, 20, 35–36, 38, 42, 49, 57, 59, 76, 79, 88, 107, 126, 145, 150, 176, 179, 184, 194, 219; unnatural, 39, 42
Bourdieu, Pierre, 30
Brent-Dyer, Elinor, *Jo of the Chalet School*, 180
Brontë, Charlotte: *Jane Eyre*, 50; *Villette*, 194
Bull, Jacob, 60

Cadogan, Mary, 179, 181, 182
Cantrell, Sarah K., 30, 33, 45
Carroll, Jane Suzanne, 14, 18, 73, 79
Carroll, Lewis, *Alice's Adventures in Wonderland*, 12
Caws, Mary Ann, 51
Cecire, Marie Sachiko, 11, 99, 102, 112, 178, 179, 186
censorship: artificial world of, 7; of children's literature, 110, 119
child as detective: empowerment of, 176, 179, 182, 183, 184, 186, 188, 189, 191, 194, 195, 196; liminal space of, 17; pushing boundaries of, 179
childhood as concept: as blank slate, 12; Romantic, 9, 12
childhood space: adult construction of, 8, 14, 136; expansion of, 138, 140, 143, 145, 146, 150; validation of, 137
children's literature: adaptability of, 6; closed space of, 8; complexity of, 4, 5; diversity, potential for, 8, 128, 130; exploration through, 10; negotiation of space, 99, 136; social practice in, 111
Childress, Herb, 17
Christensen, Pia, 71, 84, 85
Christie, Agatha: *Cat among the Pigeons*, 186; *Murder on the Orient Express*, 186
cities: empowerment of, 18, 103, 104, 130; and children, 17, 18; navigation of, 121, 130, 131
Clare, Hilary, 161
Clark, Clifford Edward, 51
classrooms: as communal space, 60; social control in, 50, 63; "unwholesome" social interactions in, 51, 59, 62
clue puzzle formula and detective fiction, 181, 182, 185, 191
Coleman, Nathaniel, 158
colonization: of childhood, 11, 97, 100–101, 105, 148; gentrification of, 122
communities of choice, 80–81, 82, 83, 85, 87–88, 91
community space: defense of, 89, 90–91; under attack, 116

Cornell, Edward H., 9
Craig, Patricia, 179, 181, 182
crime scene reconstruction: boundary blurring in, 193; mapping of, 192–93
cultural spaces: as boundaries, 33; constructed, 31, 126; transgression of, 38, 43

Daniels, Stephen, 14
De Certeau, Michel, 159, 172, 173
Decker, Jessica Elbert, 19, 75, 76, 77, 220
de Conick-Smith, Ning, 17
defense in the doorway: body as, 79; as threat to sacred spaces, 79
Diamond, Anna, 206–7, 214
diversity and children's literature: limitations of, 115, 117, 118, 119, 127, 132, 133, 148; and space for genuine depictions, 8, 115, 116, 119, 124, 128, 130
Dobrin, Sidney I., 11
domestication of childhood, 14
domestic ideology: exclusion, 52; racism, 52; restrictions, 56
double consciousness, 23, 201, 202, 203, 204, 210, 212
Doughty, Terri, 11, 13
Du Bois, W. E. B., 23, 201, 202

Eden: childhood space, 30, 32; containment, 31; limited safety, 30, 33, 44; method of control, 35; paradise, 41, 42; rejection of, 45
empathetic reader-response, 115, 119–20, 127, 128–29, 130
English expatriates, home for: alien, 185; unfixed, 184
English Golden Age detective fiction, 176, 177, 186

fall narratives: comparison to adolescence, 30; punishment, 36; recreations/inversions, 30, 31
family as process: empowerment of, 89, 90, 91; as form of resistance, 89; mothering/fathering, 89; and security, 138

fantastical mobilities, 18
fantastic literature: and barriers to diversity, 117, 119; as space for diversity, 115, 116, 124, 128–29
Farrar, Margaret, 51
Feingold, Ruth, 14
felicitous space, 9
Fischer, Sara, 99, 179, 184
Flynn, Richard, 97, 101
Foreman, Gabrielle P., 52
Foucault, Michel, 157, 158, 159, 162–63, 167, 193–94
Fox, Geoff, 168
Francis, Christine Doyle, 69
Fresh Prince of Bel-Air, The, 214
Frey, Charles, 145
Friedman, Marilyn, 87
frontier, 22, 135–38, 139

gardens: as liminal space, 44; outsider/insider paradigm of, 180; walled security of, 29, 180
Gargano, Elizabeth, 59
Gaye, Marvin, "What's Going On," 204
Gillhouse, Elizabeth, 33, 34
Gillis, John, 3, 4, 8
Giuliani, Vittoria M., 9
Goodenough, Elizabeth, 15–16, 18
Gosling, Ju, 187
Graham, Ysenda Maxstone, 185
Grandmaster Flash and the Furious Five, "The Message," 204
Greenwell, Amanda M., 45
Gruner, Elisabeth Rose, 155
Gulløv, Eva, 8, 16, 220
Gutman, Marta, 16–17

Hall, Stuart, 12
Hardy Boys series, 179
Hart, R., 220
Hayden, Dolores, 15
hegemonic whiteness: challenge to, 124, 127, 132; colonizing consciousness, 120–21; colonizing space, 120, 126
Heywood, Colin, 111

Hill, Pamela Smith, 139, 148
Holiday, Billie, "Strange Fruit," 204
Holloway, Sarah L., 10, 15
home: association with childhood, 69, 71, 98, 135, 136; challenges to, 18, 72, 73, 75, 201; failure/inability to protect, 37, 71; link with family, 69, 72, 83, 84, 138, 139, 199, 207; political quality, 15, 71, 72, 73, 75, 77, 82, 83; as process/experience, 15, 44, 45, 79, 81, 82, 138, 139, 210; as sanctuary/nurturing space, 69, 71, 82, 84, 90, 138, 139, 183, 200, 213, 214; survival strategy, 20, 37, 70, 71, 73, 74, 78, 79, 83, 84, 213
home-journey-home paradigm, 136–37
Honey, J. R. De S., 160
hooks, bell, 15, 82
Horning, Kathleen T., 99
hostile space, 9, 30
"house system": as empowered confinement, 166, 167; enclosure and partition, 162–64, 166–67
Hudson, Ray, 14
Hull, Kenneth A., 9
Humphrey, Judith, 181
Hunt, Peter, 4, 6, 99, 100

identity, performance of, 13, 20, 23, 54, 177, 180, 183, 184, 186, 190, 191, 213, 214–15
implied child reader, 5, 127, 181
Inoue, Asao B., 124–25
intercision: imposed innocence, 34; interrupted development, 34; sexual dimension, 34, 40
interwar boarding-schools: identity formation, 177; identity performance, 177; imposed conformity, 176, 177, 180; insertion of detective genre, 181, 182–83, 184, 196; twenty-first-century adaptation, 177–78
Iser, Wolfgang, 144, 145
islanding of children, 8

Jansson, Tove, 6
Jones, Owain, 17, 19, 220

journey: contrast to home, 22, 135, 136, 137, 138, 149; emotional, 206; freedom to explore, 22, 39, 135, 136; identity, 213; vital childhood sphere, 30, 137
journey-home-new journey paradigm, 135, 137, 149

Kaye, Frances W., 148
Keen, Suzanne, 128, 129
Kelly, Lori Duin, 59
Kermode, Frank, 147
Kessler, Carol Farley, 56
Keyes, Marian Thérèse, 110, 111
Kirkpatrick, Robert, 160
Knight, Stephen, 182, 185
Knuth, Rebecca, 155–56, 180, 181, 183

Lamar, Kendrick, and the Weeknd, "Pray for Me," 204
landscape of childhood, 4
"languaging" as humanizing space, 124
Latina body: erotic politicizing of, 120–21; positive recognition of, 116; as subversive spaces, 121, 131
Lefebvre, Henri, 102, 157–58, 159
Levey, David, 43, 44
liminality, 13, 19, 20, 55, 58, 61, 195
liminal school spaces: developmental, 51, 55, 58, 61, 62, 65; peripheral, 51, 60, 62, 195; relative safety of, 54, 59, 61
liminal space: boundary between public and private, 51; challenge to domestic space, 51, 52, 57; potential of, 37, 51, 62, 66, 221; as refuge, 52, 61, 65; as site of autonomy, 20, 62
Loomba, Ania, 101
Lowry, Lois, 7

magical realism: Puerto Rican origins, 131; transformation of space, 131, 133
Mandel, Ernest, 185
margins: based on race, 53, 55, 82; subversive uses of, 20, 62, 65, 82, 84, 182, 190, 195
Massad, Carolyn Emrick, 17

Matthews, Hugh, 18
McGillicuddy, Áine, 110, 111
Mendible, Myra, 121
Menozzi, Filippo, 75
Mills, Claudia, 147
Mitchell, Sally, 180, 194
Mowder, Louise, 143, 147
Murray, Lesley, 18
Musgrave, P. W., 160
mythical landscapes: critique of, 9; imposed innocence, 8; John Gillis, 3, 4, 8; real-world repercussions, 4

Nancy Drew series, 179, 180, 184, 189
"narrative empathy": bounded strategic, 129; broadcast strategic, 129; strategic, 128, 130
narrative focalization: adult agenda, 138; child's viewpoint, 139, 144, 145, 149; close-third person perspective, 97, 135, 140–43, 146; first-person as agency, 177, 187, 189; free indirect discourse, 143; idiosyncratic voice, 97; interiority, 135, 140; narrated monologue, 122
narrative gap, 145
nature: challenge to pastoral idyll, 135, 137, 138, 139; harmonious, 29; idealized, 9, 10, 135, 138; protective, 10; as space of escape, 4, 10
Nelson, Claudia, 160
New York City, 99, 103, 104
Nikolajeva, Maria, 136, 147
Njoku, Eboni, 202, 211
Nodelman, Perry, 15, 100, 105, 106, 107, 109, 111, 136, 137, 138, 140, 146, 148, 149
nostalgia, 10, 80, 186
nuclear families: alibi, 75; ameliorated, 85, 92; critiqued, 73, 74, 85, 88, 92; idealized, 73, 74, 84
Nuyen, A. T., 101
N.W.A., "Fuck the Police," 204

O'Brien, Margaret, 71, 84, 85
Olwig, Karen Fog, 8, 16, 220
O'Reilly, Julie D., 189

O'Sullivan, Keith, 103
othering of childhood, 11, 12, 23
Overall, Sonia, 18

Parker, Peter, 168, 169
Petzold, Dieter, 155, 156
phase spaces, 30, 33, 36
Phelan, James, 127, 128
Pitts, Reginald H., 52
place in African American culture, 202
Plain, Gill, 182, 183
Plester, Beverly, 9, 10
Prado, Rocio Isabel, 118
prefect and fagging systems, 164–66
producers of space: children, 17, 20, 21, 51, 97, 101, 103, 104, 118; Harriet (fictional character), 97, 98–99, 100, 104, 109, 110
"prose poem," 145, 146
Public Enemy, "Fight the Power," 204
Pullman, Philip, 6, 219

queer identities: masked by heteronormativity, 180; subtext, 28, 187, 195
Quigly, Isabel, 160, 169

race and space, 118, 119, 121, 125, 127, 201, 202
Ray, Sheila, 16
reading: as act of negotiation, 6, 172; as act of resistance, 14, 159, 172, 173, 186, 219; potential effect of, 3, 5, 7, 9, 10, 16, 99, 119, 129, 130, 168, 170
Reimer, Mavis, 15, 69, 70, 100, 136, 137, 138, 140, 146, 148, 193
Reynolds, Kimberley, 5, 7, 168
Richards, Jeffrey, 160, 169, 170
Rissotto, Antonella, 9
ritual ground, 23, 200, 201, 202, 207, 208, 209, 212, 213, 216
Rivera, Maritza Quiñones, 120–21, 123
Roberts, Frank Leon, 204–5
Romantic model of childhood, 9, 12
Rose, Gillian, 11
Routledge, Christopher, 179, 186
Rudd, David, 195

Russell, Mary Harris, 41, 42
Rycroft, Simon, 14

safe spaces, 15, 46, 136, 200
Sanders, Andrew, 160
Sawyer Fritz, Sonya, 104
Scaggs, John, 182
schools: disciplinary structure of, 156, 158, 164–66, 169, 178; as liberating spaces, 48, 49, 60, 187; as liminal/interstitial space, 20, 49, 50, 65; racism in, 53, 188–89, 190, 215–16; as site of containment, 4, 50, 158, 162, 163, 166–67, 186, 187, 216
school settings: enclosed, 180; inadequacy of conventional spaces, 61–62; microcosm, 16, 60, 160, 161, 162; as privileged space, 161, 162; as site of action, 155; unofficial spaces, 16
school space as alternative to domestic sphere, 49, 50, 55, 56, 65
school story: effect of First World War on, 168–69, 170; effect on First World War, 168–69; Golden Age, 155, 168; hegemony, 157–58; informal classroom in, 16, 160, 167; as means of social control, 155; nationalization of, 155–56, 157, 160, 161, 162, 180
Scott, Carole, 39
secret spaces, 15–16, 33
separate spheres of adulthood and childhood: concept of, 11; disruption of, 178, 195
setting: depictions of, 3; heightened significance of, 4, 10, 14, 21
Shakur, Tupac, 205, 206
sheltering spaces, 9, 19, 48, 72
Simone, Nina, "Blacklash Blues," 204
Sims, Sue, 161
Smith, Karen Patricia, 45
social environment and class dynamics, 185
social space, 100, 101, 102, 103, 105, 106, 110, 111, 112, 113
Soja, Edward, 51, 52
space: complexity of, 3, 4, 98, 108, 115; forbidden, 33; and identity, 3, 4, 14, 116,

177–78, 179, 201, 202; mobility in, 4, 21; of play as place of power, 178–79, 186, 187; primordial structure of, 98, 101, 102
space and children: manipulation of, 17, 38, 159, 187–88, 201, 220; "otherable," 17, 220
spaces of suffering/trauma, 36, 41, 181, 200
Spencer, Christopher, 9, 10
Stanek, Lukasz, 158
Steege, David, 161
Stepto, Robert, 23, 201
story telling: as act of resistance, 77, 212, 213; liberating, 40; role of reader in, 128; self-definition, 77
Stott, Jon C., 69
street and children: as challenge to authority, 18, 34, 103, 104; exclusion of, 17, 98; and identity formation, 21, 98, 103, 104, 203; liminal space of, 18, 51; subversion of domestic space of, 18, 21, 98, 103

Tey, Josephine, *Miss Pym Disposes*, 186
Thomas, Angie, *The Hate U Give*, 119
Thomas, Ebony Elizabeth, 117, 118, 119, 120, 125, 127, 132
Thompson, Dawn, 11
Todd, John, *The Daughter at School*, 48
Tuan, Yi-Fu, 8, 178

urban fantasy: amelioration of stereotypes in, 118, 119, 130; as challenge to "white literary space," 118, 130, 133; as space for diversity, 115, 116

urban neighborhoods: exodus from, 210; importance of ritual spaces in, 201; nurturing, 201, 207, 208; police brutality in, 200, 217; violence in, 200, 207, 212, 217

Valentine, Gill, 10, 11, 15, 18
Vicinus, Martha, 187

Waller, Alison, 13
Walsh, Jill Patton, 150
Weber, Max, 125
Weinreich, T., 6
Whitebrook, Maureen, 13
whitewashing, 120, 121, 122
Whyte, Pádraic, 103
wilderness: as adult space, 30, 32, 44; contrast to Eden, 30; escape to, 34; and multiverse, 29; threat of, 34, 35
Winchock, Dylan, 19, 75, 76, 77, 220
Wolstenholme, Elizabeth, 48
Wood, James, 143
Wood, Naomi, 14
world of the dead: containment of, 38, 39; unnaturalness of, 38, 39, 42
Worthington, Heather, 181, 186, 191
Wright, Nazera Sadiq, 52

Youngbear-Tibbets, Holly, 79

Zipes, Jack, 155
Zitterkopf, Deanna, 150

CPSIA information can be obtained
at www.ICGtesting.com
Printed in the USA
BVHW071442011122
650042BV00001B/6